2.7.16

Prodigal Daughter

No matter where you begin, where you end, is what really Counts.

By

Desiree Bowers

Cover Illustration by Desiree Bowers

Thank You Barbara. you are a jewel! :)
Desiree Bowers

The Prodigal Daughter

This book is a work of fiction based on a true story. Names and places have been changed in order to protect the innocent.

The Library of Congress has cataloged *The Prodigal Daughter* edition: Desiree Bowers

Printed In The United States Of America

The Prodigal Daughter

This book is dedicated to all women who are imprisoned by drugs and alcohol; those in a domestic violence relationship; and those who are in search of ever lasting Peace with our Savior. To All the Survivors, now you too can say I am Free, I am Free, Thank You Jesus I am Free! This book is dedicated to my mom and grandmother: "The Virtuous Women".

ACKNOWLEDGEMENTS

Thanks to Class 18, Norris Road, and Horn Lake at Levi Church of Christ congregations for all their prayers and support. Okay let's see if I can do this right!

I give thanks to you, God, for sending your darling Son to die on the Cross for me.

I give thanks to you, God, for loving me in spite of myself. It is only by your Grace and Divine Mercy that I am here today to tell my story, a story filled with Your Love of mankind.

I give thanks to Jesus, my Savior, my Comforter, my Best Friend; I give You Thanks for redeeming me.

I give thanks to my family and friends for enduring me during a dark journey of my life.

I give thanks to my children: Angela, Jerimea, Jimmy, and Dominique, for loving me.

Chapter Contents

The Prodigal Daughter

The Prodigal Daughter

Introduction

Led

She was led to a personal walk with Jesus Christ the night she surrendered her life to Him, an autumn evening in 1994, a day she would never forget. Jesus said "***When the Spirit of truth comes, He will guide you into all the truth.***" God told her through scripture that He would never leave her or forsake her, and He did not – she left Him and forsake Him. Ten years had passed, and still she used crack cocaine everyday.

As the early morning sun shone through her bedroom window, the phone rang. She answered, "Hello," a familiar voice replied, "Hello back at you." She knew him all too well. He was a man who wanted sexual favors from her in exchange for money. They confirmed their arrangements for him to visit in thirty minutes.

When he arrived, her children and their daddy were still asleep in the upstairs bedrooms. She and her guest stayed downstairs in the living room to quietly take care of their business on the couch. He gave her $50 and quickly finished his business with her. When he left, she ran upstairs to inform Nicko of the money she had just made for crack cocaine fare. He was already awake as she returned to the bedroom. She knew she had to immediately give him money whenever she had it for whatever purpose he chose. The children were awakened by the sound of their parents' voices in the bedroom.

The Prodigal Daughter

They were talking about getting high on cocaine. Their oldest son, who was three years old, entered the bedroom with his two year old brother. Their six month old son lay on his stomach in his baby crib, staring at everyone.

Patience ran its course on this September morning in 1994. Everyone was fed, bathed, and clothed before they took a journey in life that would change their lives forever. The oldest boys were buckled up in the back seat, and the youngest was in his car seat between her and Nicko in their 1984 blue and white Cadillac. The car did not have a radio, and carbon dioxide slightly filtered through to the inside of the car.

Their first stop was to an apartment house in south Memphis. They bought crack cocaine and smoked it in the car, while their children watched. The first rush of crack cocaine is always the hit crack cocaine chase, one after the next. They never got that first rush again, so the chase was on until darkness covered the skies.

Their last stop was to a neighborhood corner where they had lived many years ago. The drug dealers who were not dead or in jail hung out on this corner. Nicko parked the car to ask for gas money. The night lights twinkled and shone brightly in the sky. A young man gave him two dollars, and he bought a piece of crack with it.

She got out of the car to get a hit, but there was none left for her. She got angry with Nicko when he kept the drugs from her, and this night was not any different. Back at the car, they realized they were completely out of gas. She got the boys out of the car and proceeded to walk to her friend's place of business, a nearby laundrymat in the same neighborhood. Her friend was not usually there after dark. God was with them as it began to rain. A group of men sat inside the Watermark Scoreboard.

"Is Mr. Nelson coming back?" Enez asked. They did not know. As so many nights, God waited on her this night too. After about five minutes, Mr. Nelson arrived and he kindly took her home. Finally at home, she fed and bathed the children, tucked the oldest boys in their beds, rocked the baby to sleep, and began to pray. God heard her prayers; He wrapped His Loving, Forgiving arms around her as she fell into a peaceful sleep.

On Saturday morning, she woke her children for breakfast, and they had a glorious time with Him all day. She invited Him to come into her life and restore her soul. She gave herself over to Him on this day, but she had done this over and over again in her life.

The sun had set upon this part of the world. She and the children were watching TV when the test arrived at her front door. Nicko knocked on the door, and she let him into her house, along with a drug addict associate of his named Robert. She remembered a scripture, "***He is mine and I am His.***" She ran upstairs with the children and began to pray faithfully because she knew he had drugs with him. The only time Robert ever came around was to use drugs. Nicko did not come upstairs.

Instead, she heard the screen door close and Robert's car leaving. They were gone! She thanked Him for His Courage, Patience, and Love for her.

In this story, she must confess her fallings, share her victories, and be glad for His Mercy and Grace that saved her from herself.

* * *

Hopeless

Enez once thought she was a hopeless case, but in Jesus Christ she was not a hopeless case. She was the kind of case He wanted, the one He died for.

The sounds coming from inside her parents' bedroom were not sounds of laughter and fun. The cussing, crying, and shouting words filled the ears of the child who lay in bed, shivering in the night. This was not the first time she heard the drunken stupor of her daddy. More often than not, Enez would awaken from her night's sleep to find a frustrated and emotionally battered mother. She learned unhealthy behaviors as she watched her parents' interactions. Many women in her mother's generation, and generations before that, stayed with their abusive husbands. In her young tender mind, Enez thought this was love. She thought her daddy loved her mother if he hit her and shouted obscenities to her. She thought this must be love.

Enez also saw her daddy being kind to her mother after the outbursts. Her mother did not leave!

As Enez began to develop, both physically and emotionally, her self esteem was very low. She was a quiet girl, with no friends to call her own. She was short for her age, with brown skin, full lips, and an overbite that showed when she smiled. Her hair was long, thick, and dark brown. Enez was overweight, and she loved to eat. In her first year of elementary school, she went to a Catholic school. The children made fun of her looks, and she would cry. She was not particularly smart, and she had to study very hard to earn passing grades. At an early age, she longed for someone to love her. Enez did not know the One who gave her life loved her more than she could love herself.

One rainy, autumn day, Enez rode the bus on her way to the babysitter's house after school. She thought she had followed her mother's instructions for riding the bus, but Enez soon realized that she was a passenger on the wrong bus, going in the wrong direction. She told the nice bus driver that she was on the wrong bus and where she lived. When he reached downtown, he asked the waiting passengers at the bus stop if any of them were catching the 16 Forest Hill bus.

A young woman in a pink nurse's uniform spoke out, "I am waiting on that bus, mister."

The bus driver told Enez, "Wait next to that woman and look for the sign on the front of the bus that reads 16 Forest Hill."

The Prodigal Daughter

Finally, Enez was traveling in the right direction to the babysitter's house, and she arrived safely. Days later, she once again saw the woman in the pink nurse's uniform, walking to her house from the bus stop. She was a neighbor, who lived several houses down.

Enez's mother worked very hard to provide for her and her younger sister. Her mother liked to be among the elite, although her home was quite dysfunctional. She threw Christmas parties, Fourth of July celebrations, and Labor Day cookouts in their back yard. Every summer, her mother took Enez and her sister out of town on vacation. Every Easter Sunday, she sewed their Easter frocks and put ring curls in their hair for their visit to her mother's nearest relatives in Memphis to take pictures. The family never went to church on Easter, or any other Sunday, that Enez could recall. Momma did her best.

By the time Enez was thirteen, she was already having sex with an older boy who lived on her street. Her body was well developed – she had become a beautiful butterfly! He was a nice looking boy, with smooth, caramel skin and a masculine body. His black hair was wavy, and a mustache edged the top of his lip. The eagerness in his eyes complimented his thick eye brows. Enez had a 12-year old girl's crush on Sammy!

Sammy was the neighborhood stud. He sought the virgins to romance them and then leave them. Enez watched her neighbor visit Sammy's house every day after school. Hours passed before

Enez saw Lorie walking across the yard to her house with her panties in her hand. Enez, being young and naïve, she did not quite understand what was happening in Sammy's house. Enez asked questions, which were soon answered by Sammy. He was tired of Lorie because she was no longer a virgin. He wanted a new virgin, and he chose Enez. She was eager to allow him to take away the most precious gift God gave woman: her body.

One day, Sammy asked Enez to come to his house after school. This was the first time Sammy would attempt to have sex with her. Enez did not go home when she got off the school bus that day. She walked nervously to Sammy's house. She wanted to turn back and do what her parents asked of her – go straight home from school, but her feet continued to propel her to Sammy's house. As she approached the screen door, she peered into the living room and saw him sitting on the couch. At the screen door, Sammy looked into Enez's eyes, silently asking her, "Are you sure?" Satisfied, he opened the door to allow her inside. Acting like a gentleman, Sammy took her books and laid them on the coffee table.

"Would you like something to drink?"

"Yes, I would like a glass of water, please" she replied.

Enez followed him to the kitchen, noticing how nice and clean the house appeared. According to the neighbors' talk, she knew Sammy's parents were rarely in Memphis so she wondered who kept the house so orderly. Looking around the beautifully designed kitchen, she drank the water and handed her empty glass to Sammy. This time, Sammy followed her as she walked back to the living room and sat on the couch. Sammy turned on the stereo and selected soft music to break the silence in the house.

With the music playing in the background, Sammy reached over and kissed Enez on the lips. He removed her eyeglasses and gently pushed her into a lying position on the couch, as he continued to kiss her. Her mother had not talked to Enez about sex, so she only knew what her neighbor had said, "Girl, it feels good. He will like you when he finishes!" Slowly, he unbuttoned her blouse, one button at a time. Next, he slid off her bra to see her youthful breasts as he kissed them. He whispered in her ear, "I'll be gentle with you…it'll hurt, but I will be gentle with you." Finally, Sammy pulled her panties off, spread her legs, and began to penetrate her. Enez screamed hysterically, "Stop! Please stop! It hurts! I don't wanna do this! I'm too young!" He tried to comfort her, but she could not be comforted. She continued to cry and plead with him to stop. She apologized as she dressed to go home. He kissed her on the forehead as he sent her on her way.

One autumn evening, Enez's mother drove her to a restaurant near their home. How nice it would be to spend this time with her mother, Enez thought. They sat at a booth near the front window, and Enez picked up the menu to order. Her mom said, "We didn't come here to eat. I have something to tell you." Enez did not look at her, but she was listening. She could never look her mother in her eyes. Maybe she was afraid of her.

Her mother began to talk in a stern voice, "Enez, Marvin is not your real father. Your father's name is Dejoin Vonsure."

Searching the table for words, Enez found only what she believed to be true, "I know it."

"How do you know? Did someone tell you?"

"No. I could feel it."

There was only silence at the table. Enez thought back to a time when she was six years old, when they lived in an apartment near her grandmother.

Marvin came home from work and sat in a living room chair. Enez and her sister were with him, and her sister jumped into his lap. He gave the little girl a great big hug and kiss. Enez stood before him, waiting on her hug and kiss, but Marvin never acknowledged her. He continued to play with her sister. As she got older, Enez heard him say to her mother, "She's your child. She gonna end up just like you. Nothing!" whenever she got in trouble.

Her mother broke the silence at the restaurant table as she tried to explain the nature of her relationship with Enez's biological father. At eighteen, she desperately wanted to move away from her mother's house. Dejoin's parents were of the black well-to-do families. His mother was a school teacher, and he attended Catholic schools. Now, Enez's mother said, "I thought if I got pregnant by him, he would marry me. In those days, marrying the girl was the right thing to do if she was pregnant. Dejoin's mother had other plans for him, and it was not for him to have a child, marry me, or marry anyone else, for that matter. When Dejoin wouldn't marry me, I left town with my cousin until I needed to come back home to give birth to you. Dejoin's mother had sent him off to college."

The mother looked into her daughter's eyes across the table, "I thought I'd better tell you before one of my relatives did." They left the restaurant to enter a world of silence. Enez was not moved at all. It only confirmed for her that she was rejected of man even before conception. Rejection would follow her for a very long time. She would reject herself. She would reject Him who gave her life. They returned home, and things were as always.

Sammy was not finished with Enez. She was yet a virgin, and he was determined to be the one to enter her. After the restaurant conversation with her mom, Enez wanted to feel loved. She was lonely and felt so rejected. In the next few days, Sammy spotted her as she walked along the street. He noticed that she was not wearing a smile, and he asked her to come in for a while. She agreed. Enez sat in the living room, not knowing what to say. She was full of emotion and wanted to cry. She silently wished she could ask her father why he abandoned her. Tears flowed from the eyes of a young girl who felt so alone as she cried on Sammy's shoulders. He was there for her, and on that day he became her friend.

Weeks passed, and Enez became a frequent visitor at Sammy's house. She decided she wanted him inside her body. They made arrangements to meet at his house one winter evening, and she arrived at his door, as planned. They walked to his bedroom, and he removed her clothing, kissed her body, and gently pushed himself inside her. She moaned and groaned with pain, as he whispered, "I won't leave you." It would not have made a difference to her whether he did or not. She wanted the feeling of being loved for that instant. As the night crept on, Enez realized that it was getting late and she needed to return home before her mother and daddy arrived. She slipped her clothes on, kissed him on his forehead while he slept, and then quietly locked and closed the door behind her as she left. The short walk home was filled with silent thoughts for Enez.

Enez returned to visit Sammy a few more times, but he did not treat her any differently than he had the rest of the young girls in his life. The time she spent with him was for a season, and soon they went their own ways when he moved to California.

Enez's mother changed her career to become a public official. She drowned herself in her work. She had a meeting to attend every night. She was the president of many political organizations and a member of others. A black radio station had a late-night radio spot for her, so she was gone at night to tape her show. Enez learned how to cook dinner and wash cloths and was now keeping house for the family. There were no more parties, no more anything. Marvin, whom she always knew as her daddy, worked alternating shifts for American Airlines. Her parents were slowly becoming strangers to each other, as Enez's mom found a new purpose in her life. Her parents argued about her mother neglecting her obligations and responsibilities to her children and home. The arguments were no longer about his affairs with other women or not paying bills (while he kept $500 to $1,000 in his own pocket). Now, the shoe was on the other foot: Enez's mother had begun a career to satisfy her own purpose in life.

Enez's mother told her she had fallen out of love with Marvin and sought a new love, a political career. Her marriage and children had all gone wild. There was still hope in her new career.

The last night that Marvin slept at home with them would become the last night forever. Her mom left earlier that day in Marvin's new Electra 225. He loved his cars. She had an old orange station wagon that she had left in the driveway. Enez could hear her daddy calling around, looking for her mother. No one knew where she could be found. The night had come and she and her sister were in bed, trying to fall asleep. Their daddy was waiting on their mother in the den. As the door opened, Enez could hear the shouting begin and then her mother's screams.

She ran downstairs to see her daddy beating on her mother, hemmed in the corner. Enez screamed, "Daddy, please, stop!" He did not stop, and she ran back to the bedroom to drown out the sounds, but the crying and screaming still came through. She heard the front door open, and she just knew her mother had gotten away. But when Enez got up to look out the front door, she could see her daddy pulling her mother by the hair as she screamed to the next door neighbor, "Lillie help me, help me!"

Mrs. Lillie was a tall stout, lady and could probably have handled Enez's daddy. Her daddy pulled Enez's mom back into the house, and Mrs. Lillie came in behind them. Marvin stopped hitting on her mother and began to hit Mrs. Lillie, but she got away to her house to call the police. Enez's mother tried to run again, but he caught her. This time, Enez's little sister came running outside and jumped on their daddy's back to make him stop. Enez was afraid of him. She shouted, "Please stop! Please stop!"

Finally, he let her mom go, and they went to Mrs. Lillie's house. Her mother's small frame was covered with blood, and her tongue was split in half horizontally. She had knots on her head and face. Enez hugged her mother, and she hugged her back. The next morning, Enez walked to their house to see her daddy lying on her parents' bed. He said, "Enez, I am going to move out. I won't be coming back." He never did come back to live with them again.

Her mother became more active in her career. As for Enez, she began to look for love in all the wrong places and faces. She would encounter young men who said they loved her. She would become pregnant before her 14th birthday, but the pregnancy was terminated. She was too young to be a momma.

* * *

Growing of the Seed

Street life excited her. Riding by the women standing on the corner, she saw them as movie stars. In her eyes they were, because they received the attention Enez so desired. They wore big blonde wigs, mini dresses, and thigh-high boots or spike-heeled shoes. Their faces were made up with thick lipstick, red rouge, and bright eye shadow. The men blew their car horns at them, and women appeared to envy them when they passed.

Enez's neighbor, Lorie, described Johnny Nelson's son. She called him Nicko, an eighteen year old pimp and heroin dealer. His family owned several barbeque restaurants. He was a good looking man, with light brown eyes, 6 foot 2 inches tall, brown skinned and slightly heavy. He wore flashy clothes, permed hair, diamond and gold jewelry, and he liked to ride motorcycles and Cadillacs. Enez liked him from the moment she met him…he did not have to do anything for her. He was the kind of bad boy every wild, young girl would lust after. Lorie invited Enez to go to the movies with her, Nicko, and his cousin, Adam, and to sleep over her house after the movies. Lorie's date was Adam. The plan was set, and Enez told her mom she was going to the movies with Lorie and some friends. Enez's mother felt secure when she was with Lorie, and she never asked any questions.

There was a knock at the door. Enez looked through the peephole to see Lorie.

"Girl, are your ready?" Lorie asked.

"Yes, let me get my purse." Enez called out to her mother, "I'll see ya in the morning, Ma."

A green Cadillac Sedan De Ville was parked in front of the house. Enez spoke to everyone as she and Lorie got in the back seat for the short ride to the Bellevue Drive-In. Enez had never smoked weed before, but she knew the smell. When they arrived at the drive-in, Nicko and Adam got out for refreshments, and it appeared as if the car was on fire as they flung open the doors and the weed smoke bellowed out! The men did not exchange seating arrangements with Lorie and Enez when they returned, and the couples watched a Kung Fu movie, starring Bruce Lee. After the movies, they cruised the Memphis city streets.

The night lights, smell of weed, and fast talking surrounded Enez in a darkness that she was not familiar with. Eventually, Nicko parked in front of an apartment complex as a young man came strolling to the driver's side window. Nicko pushed the electric button to allow the window to roll downward.

"What's up, man?" the young man casually asked, as he reached the window.

"Hey man, what you got for me?" said Mister. Mister was another nickname for Nicko.

He handed Nicko several rolled up joints in a plastic sandwich bag in exchange for some money. Mister hesitated briefly, then lit up one of the joints. Before moving the car, Nicko glanced at Enez through his rear view mirror.

"Hey baby, come up here and sit with me. I wanna talk to you."

"Okay," she replied.

Quickly, she opened the back door to exchange places with Adam. She felt her heart beating rapidly as she sat next to him in the front seat. She stared at him as he drove through the parking lot and onto the neighborhood streets. The silence was broken by Willie Hutch crooning, "Choosing You Baby" over the eight-track tape. He turned the volume down and told her how beautiful she looked.

Her lips trembled, "Thank you."

"You ready to go home?"

Before she could reply, Lorie interrupted her thoughts, "It's getting late. We need to go home now."

Enez agreed, "Yea, it is late, and we do need to go home."

"Okay. Is it okay if I pick you up tomorrow?" Nicko asked.

"I'll call you tomorrow." Enez was not sure if she could leave home the next day. She was only fourteen years old.

The car was silent, except for the rock and roll music coming from the radio. Her house was dark as they passed by. Perhaps everyone was asleep. When they arrived at Lorie's house, he pulled her to him and kissed her on the lips. Lorie and Adam kissed each other good night while Enez stood outside, waiting for Lorie. The night was over, and Enez had fallen in love with Nicko. Lorie and Enez talked about the night until they fell asleep.

Neither Enez nor Nicko were overwhelmed with intellectual wisdom. Enez was a product of difficult family situations. She skipped school whenever she pleased. It was not because she did not have lunch money or because she wore Raggedy Ann clothes. She skipped because she wanted to be physically intimate with Nicko. In the following weeks, Enez frequently showed up at Nicko's house, and there was always someone there. He would either have a group of friends over, or sometimes it was his other woman. Enez would hang around, waiting to be noticed.

One early Saturday evening, the air was warm and Enez was lonesome for Nicko. She called him on his house phone.

"Yea," he answered.

The Prodigal Daughter

"Hi Nicko, are you busy?" she asked in a soft tone voice.

"Nah."

"Well, I am lonesome for you this evening."

"Oh yeah?"

"I'm at my cousin's house. It's not far from you. Can I come see you tonight?" she asked in a seductive voice.

"Okay, baby, I'll be waiting for you," he replied quickly. "I'd like that just fine."

Enez quickly hung up the phone and asked her cousin if she could walk to the store.

"Sure, but come right back," was the reply.

The sky was pale blue with white puffy clouds, and the air was still. Her fresh skin smelled of the bath beauty bar she had bathed with earlier. She wore denim shorts, a tight fitted pink blouse, and pink sandals. Her hair fell about her face and neck, and she wore clear polish on her fingernails and pink on her toenails. Her mind was clear as she happily walked to see Nicko, the man she had fallen in love with on their first date.

She knocked on the back door when she reached the house. She thought they were alone as she looked around after Nicko invited her in. She followed him to the bedroom and saw several men and two poodles standing in the bedroom. Enez was afraid. This did not look good at all.

Nicko locked the bedroom door and told Enez to take her clothes off. As she undressed, he pulled a camera from a dresser drawer, and the other men watched her undress. Nicko told her to lie on the bed while he took pictures of her and the poodles. At fourteen, the men in the room were much older than her. She did not want them to hurt her, so she did as she was told. One man undressed and got on top of Enez, as Nicko continued to snap pictures. She was raped; one man after another, and all the while Nicko continued taking pictures.

Suddenly, someone shouted from the other room, "Nicko, Shirley is driving up!" Nicko and the other men quickly dressed. They all went out the back door except for Nicko's brother, David. She lay in bed with him, but they did not have sex. Slowly, Enez put her clothes on and walked to the back door. When she reached the bottom of the steps, she walked in the shadows of darkness, filled with shame and guilt. Through her tears and shame, she wanted to feel invisible. No one said goodbye or offered to give her a ride home. She wanted the man whom she had fallen in love with to love her back. She tucked away those memories in her fourteen-year-old mind, and that evening did not stop her from seeing him again and again.

She told him whatever he wanted to hear, hoping to get him to want her. She called him one late summer afternoon. "Hi Nicko, what's up?"

He quickly replied, "Yeah, what's up with you? I hadn't talk to you in a week. Are you ready to go to work and get me some money from the streets?"

Enez had never worked the streets before, but she was willing to do what he asked of her. She hesitated for just a moment and said, "Sure, I'm ready."

"Are you ready right now?" Nicko asked.

She did not want to disappoint him. "Yeah, pick me up in 30 minutes." She wanted to be gone before her mother arrived home from work. Moments later, he pulled up in his Cadillac and blew his horn. Enez noticed that he was not alone as she walked swiftly to the car and got in the back seat.

Seated next to her was a tall, dark-skinned woman, wearing a blonde wig. Her breasts bulged out from the top of her blouse, and her huge hips squeezed inside her skirt. In the front seat was a light-skinned, thin man with relaxed hair.

Enez sat quietly as Nicko gave instructions to the woman. "Tamara, this is your new wife-in-law, and I want you to show her the ropes. She has never worked the streets before."

"Okay Nicko, I'll show her how to work the streets," Tamara answered in a soft voice that did not match her Amazon body.

The closer Nicko drove to the hooker track, the more nervous Enez became about her decision to work the streets. At the drop off point; Enez and Tamara got out of the car and walked to the corner.

Enez was filled with shame as she thought, "I've got to get outta here before someone sees me."

She asked Tamara to take her somewhere to use a phone to call a man she knew would give her some money. They found a phone at a rooming house on the corner of Latham and McLemore. She called her next door neighbor, Terry, to pick her up and take her home. Terry arrived and took Enez home safely.

A week passed before she talked to Nicko again. She knew before she could see him, she had to have some money, since he was a pimp. The next time Enez would conjure up another lie to see him. She phoned him and said, "I have some money. Come to my house and pick it up from me." She had her lie about the money ready.

When he arrived, he stood at the door with a friend by his side. She invited them into the house.

"Where's my money?" he asked.

"I left it behind the bar in the den, and now it's gone," she lied.

He walked behind the bar to see for himself. Of course, he did not find any money. She believed he knew she never had any money. He left with a smile on his face.

Enez sat in her bedroom, writing in her journal when the phone rang. "Hello," she answered.

She was excited to hear the familiar voice on the other end, "Is Enez home?"

"Yes this is me. How are you?"

"Hey baby, I'm doing good, but I want to see you. Let me pick you up, and let's ride for a while."

Enez thought he was not angry with her anymore for leaving the track and lying about the money. She quickly replied, "Yes, come and get me. I'm ready to see you too."

He arrived less than fifteen minutes later. She walked out to his car and saw his little brother, Tony, was with him. Tony moved to the back seat as Enez sat in front. They drove around for a while before Nicko started a conversation with her. He decided to stop by his friend's mechanic shop. Larry and his father owned a mechanic shop where Nicko frequently got his cars repaired.

When Larry got in the car, Nicko told him what had happened several weeks ago when Enez left the street track. Nicko drove to one of the family's barbeque restaurants. It was not in operation, and he had the keys to the restaurant. In the back room, he made her take off her clothes and forced her to have unusual sex with Larry. For hours, they used her body as if it was not hers. Nicko asked his twelve-year-old brother if he wanted to have sex with her too. Enez was afraid to scream. She was afraid to say no. She was afraid to do anything but what he wanted her to do with them.

Once again, she went home with her heart filled with shame and guilt. The cries into her pillows pushed the event down to the deepest part of her subconscious, and no one would ever know about these events until she put it in print.

At fifteen, she did not understand this was the beginning of her self worth. She constantly came and went to his cruelty to validate who she was becoming in her own eyes. Each day, she obsessively rode the streets, looking for him, longing for a moment's glance of his face. He may have realized she was only toying with him about being a street woman for him. Enez was still too young to be taken from her mother's den, so he left her alone.

One hot summer night, her neighbor loaned her his car to attend a party. She went to the party but was bored and lonesome for Nicko, so she drove to his parents' house to look for him. He was not home, so she and her friends decided to drive back to the party. At a traffic light, she pulled up next to a black Cadillac. As she looked at the driver, her curiosity was aroused. He smiled at her, and she smiled back.

"Where are you going?" he asked as the window rolled down.

She motioned for him to follow her, and he did as she suggested.

After returning to the party and parking their cars, he suggested Enez sit in his car. Her first glance was at the big diamonds he wore on his fingers and around his neck. Then, she examined the tall, dark, and handsome piece of human art work. His voice was a smooth baritone that could talk the mink off the mink.

"A smooth operator," she thought. "What's your name?" she asked.

"Joshua Taylor."

Enez had heard about Joshua Taylor. He was a big-time pimp in Memphis.

As he got a closer look at her, he asked, "How old are you, baby?"

She quickly responded, "I'm eighteen."

He looked at her with bedroom eyes and said, "You ain't hardly over sixteen."

"I am eighteen," she lied quickly.

She was only fifteen, but Enez looked like she was older because her body was well developed, so Joshua believed her.

He asked, "What do you call yourself?"

"Enezi is my name, but I like being called Enez," she smiled.

"Well, Enez, where do you live?"

With her face turned towards the street she replied, "South Memphis."

"You are a very pretty woman, and I'd like to get to know you. I want you to call me tomorrow." He raised his wrist towards his eyes, looking at the diamond watch he was wearing. "Hey baby I gotta make a run right now, and I'm already late." He gave Enez a pen and paper, "Write my phone number down."

She accepted the number and tucked it away in her purse. "Have a safe night. Call me around noon tomorrow," Joshua said.

"Good night," replied Enez as she walked towards her friends, standing near the party. A young lady standing with the group said, "You don't want to get involved with him. He likes to beat on his women. Girl, don't you know who he is? He ain't nobody to play with." Enez looked at her and smiled.

The next day, Sunday, Enez could not wait to call Joshua, hoping to take her mind off Nicko. The morning passed slowly for Enez. She constantly watched the clock on her bedroom wall. At ten minutes to twelve, she gathered her thoughts together because she did not want her conversation to sound immature. At two minutes to twelve, she had his number in her hand and moved towards the phone. She had just about reached it when it rang. "I got it," she voiced to her mother. There was silence in the house as she picked up the phone, "Hello."

"Is Enez in?" asked the voice on the other end.

She quickly replied, "This is she."

"Hey baby, this is Nicko. I heard you were looking for me last night. You got something for me, baby?"

She was startled to hear Nicko's voice on a Sunday afternoon, and Enez was lost for words.

"Hello? Are you there, Enez? Did you hear what I said? Do you have my money?"

"No, Nicko. I don't have any money," she said.

"Enez, why were you looking for me then?" Nicko said angrily.

"I wanted to see you, that's all, Nicko," she answered in a whisper.

Nicko cussed and screamed at her, "If you don't have any money for me, don't come lookin for me cuz I'm a pimp." He slammed the phone down so hard, Enez heard the clang as she laid the receiver down on its cradle. Enez stared at the scrap of paper with Joshua's number, which she still held in her hand.

Her mother's voice startled her, "Enez, your sister and I are going to the grocery store."

"Okay, momma."

It was now thirty minutes past noon, and she made another attempt to call Joshua. The phone rang three times before a woman answered it, "Hello."

Enez was silent for a second, thinking she may have dialed the wrong number, but Joshua answered the other line, "Hello." The woman hung the phone up, and Enez begin to talk.

"Hey Joshua, I apologize for being thirty minutes late calling you."

He replied in his baritone voice, "Why were you late?"

She did not want to lie to him, but how could she explain that she had been talking to another pimp? She made it plain and simple, "Josh, the phone was tied up." Their conversation did not last long.

"Baby, I am getting dressed to go out and eat breakfast. Give me your number, and I'll call you back later."

"Okay, are you ready?" she asked.

"Hold on a minute. Let me get pen and paper." They said their "see ya laters" after Enez called out her phone number to him. Two days passed before Enez heard from Joshua again. She tried calling him but did not get an answer.

The morning came with rain in its clouds. As she looked from her bedroom window, a tear of loneliness fell from her face. She wondered why Joshua had not called back. Enez began to write her most secret thoughts in her journal. Just as she finished her last stroke with her pen, the phone rang. She did not dare to answer it because she could not bear the feeling of disappointment. The ringing stopped, and she heard her mother's voice, "Enez telephone." She quickly looked at the phone on her bedroom table, as her heart filled with excitement. She hoped it was Josh. She answered in a sweet, sexy voice, "Hello."

The Prodigal Daughter

"Hey baby, I apologize for taking so long to get back with you, but I had some important business to take care of, and it took me longer than I expected. You're not angry with me, are you?" His deep voice caused Enez to tremble with exhilaration.

"How could I ever be angry with you?" There was silence on the other end, and she could hear his breathing. She thought even his breathing was sexy, and she wanted to be with him. "Josh, can I see you today?"

He cleared his throat, "I won't have time to see you today, but I'll pick you up tomorrow and take you out for lunch, okay?"

"I would love to go to lunch with you, Josh," Enez quickly replied.

"Okay then, baby, you got a lunch date with me. I'm a little tired baby, and I need some rest. I'll pick you up around noon. Is that okay with you?"

"Yeah," she answered.

"Talk to you later, baby. Have a good day," Josh said in a tired voice.

As they ended their conversation, Enez was full of excitement, anticipating the next day. . Enez shampooed and curled her hair, then polished her fingernails and toenails a pretty shade of pink. She laid out her favorite white, silk mini-skirt, which hung from her hips and accentuated her beautifully shaped legs. She matched the skirt with a pink chiffon blouse with butterfly sleeves. Enez matched her underwear also, a pretty pink bra and panties.

She picked out pastel colored, strapped, high-heeled sandals to complete her outfit.

The morning sun peaked through her bedroom window blinds the next morning. Her hair managed to stay in the rollers throughout her sleep. She looked at the clock on the wall, and it was almost 9 a.m. She knew before she could leave, her mother's house had to be straightened. Enez took a long stretch before her feet hit the floor, grabbing her robe on the way to the bathroom. She smiled at herself in the mirror before she cleaned her face and brushed her teeth. Her mother was getting dressed for work when she asked her, "Can I have lunch with friends?"

"And what are you going to do with your sister?" her mother asked.

"Well, can she stay over to Mrs. Lillie's until I come back?"

"Let me call Lillie and ask her if she doesn't mind."

Enez could not hear the conversation between her mom and Mrs. Lillie, but moments later her mother announced her decision. She agreed to lunch and reminded her to do her chores before leaving. Enez heard her mother's voice while she walked back to her bedroom, "I have a meeting this evening, so I will be home late tonight. Take your sister to Mrs. Lillie's house before you leave. There is dinner in the fridge for you to heat up at five o'clock. And, Enez, don't stay with your friends all day for lunch, okay?"

The Prodigal Daughter

The phone rang, and Enez answered, "Hello."

"Hey girl," a girl's voice came from the other end. "What's up for the day?" Enez knew this voice, and did not really want to talk with Lisa, a jealous girl who once had a crush on Nicko and spread lies about Enez.

"Hey Lisa, my mom wants to use the phone. I'll talk to you later," Enez said.

The two girls hung up, and Enez proceeded with her chores.

Later, Enez took a bubble bath as her favorite song artist, Willie Hutch, sang "Color Her Sunshine" over the radio. She stepped out of her bath and fragranced her body with lotion, thinking about Josh. She thought he was a man of class, unlike Nicko. Enez wanted to smell and look her best for him.

As she walked into the bedroom, her sister sat on one of the twin beds, staring at the television. "Hey! Big Sis, where are you going? Can I go with you?"

"None of your business, and no you can't go with me. I am taking you to Mrs. Lillie's house," she quickly replied.

The Road Runner chased the rabbit on the television as her mother announced, "I am gone . See ya'll later."

"This is good," Enez thought to herself. "She's gone now. I won't have to answer any questions about Joshua." She hummed to "Color Her

Sunshine" while looking in the mirror to shape her full lips with lip gloss. "Hmmmmmm," she said to herself, "You are a knock out."

"Come on, Lil' Sis, let me take you to Mrs. Lillie's house."

"I don't need you to take me just next door, Enez. I know how to take myself."

"Girl, come on here, before my ride comes," Enez said quickly.

Joshua blew his horn just as Enez knocked on Mrs. Lillie's side door, "Just a minute Josh," she called out to him.

Mrs. Lillie came to the door with a friendly smile on her face. "Hey little one, come on in. I have some milk and cookies for you."

Enez did not oblige, afraid of the questions Mrs. Lillie might ask about Joshua. "Hey Mrs. Lillie, my mom told me to bring my sister to your house until I come back from having lunch. Have a good day, everybody." Mrs. Lillie closed her door, but Enez felt her eyes watching from the kitchen window. Enez did not look back.

She rushed back to the house for her purse and to lock the door. Joshua stared at her as she walked toward his car and slid onto the black leather seat next to him. She crossed her legs as she closed the door.

"Hey baby, how are you?" Joshua greeted her.

The smell of his cologne almost took her breath away as she answered, "I am feeling good. How about you?"

He looked at her, never answering her question. "You are one fine woman. I see you don't shave your legs, I like that. It looks sexy on black women," he said with a smile. "Are you ready to eat? I'm hungry. Where would you like to eat?" he asked her as he turned onto the interstate.

Enez had not been to many fine restaurants. As a matter of fact, she had not been to any. She did not want him to show her inexperienced, so she pretended to be thinking and then said, "Oh, I don't know. Why don't you decide?"

Immersed in his thoughts, he placed a tape into the cassette player. The sounds of "My Girl," by the Temptations, crooned from his car speakers. "Oh I love that song," Enez said, but she was too embarrassed to sing along with the tape. She tapped her foot to the beat of the music and swung her crossed leg.

His Cadillac cruised off the interstate and yielded onto a major city street. He made a left turn, then a right to a restaurant parking lot, where a few cars were already parked near the entrance. Enez stared at Joshua's body while he parked and exited the car. She thought to herself, "This man is fine." He opened the back door to retrieve his navy blue double breasted suit coat, which hung on a hook near the back window. Tall, dark, and handsome – he was all that and some! He wore his laundered baby blue shirt, alligator belt, matching tie, and alligator shoes with class, along with the diamonds and gold that hung from his neck and fingers. A diamond and gold pendent clasped his tie. Any woman would love to walk into a room with him.

He held the door open for her as they walked in to the restaurant, where a hostess met them. "Hi Mr. Taylor, we have your favorite table waiting for you. Your waitress will be with you soon," the hostess said as she walked them to their table.

Enez was not surprised the hostess knew him. "He is a ladies man," she thought to herself. The couple followed the hostess to their table, where Josh pulled the chair out for Enez. "Thank you," she said as she sat down. The hostess gave each of them a menu.

"I really don't need a menu. I already know what I want, but I'm sure you need time to look over the selections," he said.

Her mind was racing. She had never been treated with so much class before, and she was nervous. "Josh, do you mind ordering for me? I admire your taste," she said as her eyes met his.

He looked into her eyes with a smile. "Yes, baby, I'll order for you. I'm sure you'll like what I'm having, but how do you eat your steak?"

"Oh no, he's asking the steak question. We don't eat steak at home. Mom can't afford it," she thought to herself. She said aloud, "I will have my steak like you have yours, Josh."

"I eat my steak medium rare, just a little pink in the middle."

"Oh, no, then I'd like mine well done, please," she said quickly.

Their waitress appeared, a pretty, white girl in a black and white waitress uniform and white laced apron. She wore her brown hair in a pony tail, and her pretty white teeth flashed as she directed her conversation towards Josh. "Hello, Mr. Taylor, are you ready to order?"

"Yes, I am Miriam," he said, "I'd like two T-Bone steak dinners, one well done and the other medium rare, two baked potatoes, and green beans."

"And what would you like to drink?"

Josh turned to Enez, "Baby, what would you like to drink?"

"Just water is fine for me," she replied quickly.

"Water it is for her and iced tea and water for me, please. I believe that's all for now, Miriam," he said as he returned the menus.

"I was beginning to think you weren't going to call me back, Josh. I was so happy to hear your voice," Enez said as she straightened her blouse.

"How could I not call you, baby? I wanna get to know you. I believe you could be someone special for me. I got plans for us. Enez, I want you to understand I have business with other women. You won't hear from me everyday. Are you sure you telling me the truth about your age? You are eighteen years old, right?" He asked her as he stood to take his suit coat off and hung it on the back of the chair next to him.

She did not hesitate to answer him with a lie, "Yes, I'll be eighteen in a few months." Saved by the waitress, she thought. "Here are your beverages, and your food is coming soon. Is there anything else I can get for you while you wait?"

Josh looked at their waitress, adding sugar to his tea. "No, Miriam, we're okay for now," he quickly replied.

"She acts like she likes you Josh," Enez said with a wink in her eye.

"Yeah she wants some of this PIMP'IN. I told her she better stick to what she knows, because I aint no play toy," he boasted in a whisper.

Enez thought about the lie she had just told him and wondered how long it would be before he found out her real age. "Oh well," she thought, "better make it last while I can."

Moments later, Miriam brought their food. Enez sat nervously as she watched Josh confidently cut his steak and mix the butter and sour cream into his potato. He tasted his green beans with his fork and looked up to see that Enez had not touched her food. "Are you going to eat or watch me?" he asked jokingly. She was embarrassed to cut her steak because she had never cut steak before. She thought she would cut it and it might fall to the floor.

Slowly, her confidence built as she watched him take his knife and fork again to cut another piece of steak. She began to enjoy her food as she copied him.

"I am full, baby! Is there anything else you want to eat or drink?" he asked when they had finished their meal. Miriam came back to clear the table as she placed the check near Josh.

"Did you enjoy your meal today, Mr. Taylor?" she asked, looking into his eyes with her baby blues.

"Yes, Miriam, I did, and the company too. How about you, baby?"

"Yes" Enez said proudly.

"I believe we are done here. Am I right, baby?" He reached into his wallet to take care of the check and a tip for the waitress. Josh stood to get his suit coat, and Enez pushed her chair back. Josh said, "I'll get that for you, baby." She waited for him to finish slipping on his suit coat. As he helped her from the table, she turned to look into his eyes, wishing the moment would never end.

They rode in silence in the car. Tunes played on the radio by artists such as The Emotions, Earth, Wind and Fire, and Lamont Dozier. Just before he made a right turn onto her street, he said, "I wanna see ya again before I leave for New York City in a couple of days. I'll be away for two months, and when I come home I want you to be ready for me. Like I told you, I got plans for us. Enez, I know you've had that wanna be pimp, Nicko, but now you have a chance to be with a real pimp, one who will treat you right."

She wanted to tell him the truth about her age, but she wanted him even more and did not want him to leave. "Okay Josh, whatever you say is fine with me."

He smiled at her with his pretty white teeth, "That's my baby, and that's what I like to hear. I'll call you Friday afternoon." He popped the car lock, and she opened the door, but first he pulled her back to him and kissed her on her lips. Her body temperature rose, and she began to stutter, "I'll see you soon?"

He replied, "See ya later."

Enez switched up the driveway, hoping he was watching her. Not looking back, she heard his car leave. She looked at her watch as she ran upstairs to her bedroom to write in her journal. As she finished writing the last words on the page, she heard a knock on the front door. She ran downstairs, looked through the peep hole and saw her little sister. She opened the door to let her in the house. "Girl," she said, "I was coming to Mrs. Lillie's to get you. You couldn't wait!"

"No," her little sister answered.

"Well you're home now, okay." Enez said calmly. She walked to her bedroom and thought about Josh. She smelled her clothing to remind herself of his kindness towards her. She thought to herself, "Oh, I may never want to wash this blouse again."

"Enez, its five o'clock, and I'm ready to eat," the little, light brown-haired girl said. She was Enez's baby sister. Although they were only three years apart, Enez had to take responsibility for her little sister when their mom was away. They called her Dusty because she always looked dusty. The two sisters were like two peas in a pod until Marvin left home for good.

"Okay Dusty, let me heat the food momma cooked for dinner. It'll be ready in a minute. You'll be eating by yourself cuz I'm not hungry," she said as she thought about her lunch date.

Dusty looked at her sister and asked, "Why aren't you hungry?"

She shrugged her shoulders and said nothing. Dusty went to the bedroom to wait on her dinner until Enez called loudly from the kitchen, "Your dinner is ready."

Dusty ran to the kitchen. "Thank you, Sis," She took her plate to the family room to eat her dinner at the table.

The phone rang just as Enez walked to the bedroom. She answered, "Hello."

The voice on the other end belonged to Nicko. "What's up with you? A fellow told me he saw you with Josh today. Was he telling the truth?"

Surprised, she caught her breath, "Nicko, you told me not to call unless I had some money to give you."

He yelled in her ear, and she moved the phone away from her face. "So, you'd rather give him your money? You know that man is pimp. You gonna lie to him like you lied to me? Well, guess what? I'm not gonna sweat the small stuff. He can have you." Nicko hung up the phone.

As she lay in bed in the dark, she wondered what Josh was doing, or if he was even thinking about her. She did not notice that her mother had come home until her bedroom light came on, and she saw her mother standing in the doorway with a look of concern on her face. "I need to talk to you, young lady," her mother said. Anytime Enez's mother used that tone of voice, Enez knew that she had done something wrong, and the consequences would not be nice.

Her mom went into her bedroom and disrobed. She called out, "Enez, I am ready to talk to you now." Enez walked into the bedroom, looking straight ahead. "I thought you told me you were going out with your friends to lunch."

"Momma, I did go with a friend," she said.

"Enez, don't play me crazy, girl. You know what I mean. Mrs. Lillie stopped me in the driveway and told me a man in a black Cadillac picked you up. Is this true?"

The Prodigal Daughter

"That old nosy neighbor needs to mind her own business," Enez thought to herself. She was caught red handed. "Momma, it was just a lunch date. I won't be seeing him anymore. It was just a lunch date," Enez said in a convincing tone of voice, but she could not fool her mother. Her mother had enough of her lying and sent her to bed.

A day and half passed before she heard from Josh. This was probably good timing for her mom to cool down.

"Hey baby," the voice on the phone said.

"Hey back at you. I was hoping it was you calling. I'm so happy to hear your voice," she said romantically.

"Enez, I want to see you tonight before I leave in the morning. I know you're gonna make it possible for me to see you," he said.

Enez had to think quickly. "How can I get out of the house? Should I meet him, or should I have him come late when mom's asleep?" "Josh," she said aloud, "Can you come around ten o'clock?"

"That sounds good, baby. I'll be there."

She quickly hung up. "Oh no, what am I going to do?" she thought. "What if he comes before Momma gets home?"

It was nine o'clock, and she could see her mother's headlights through the living room window before she heard the car door slam. Enez thought, "It's too late for Mrs. Lillie to stop her in the driveway tonight! And there's nothing to inform her about anyways." She heard her mother unlock the door and waited patiently while she entered the house. Her mom walked upstairs to her bedroom. "I'm tired and I'm going to bed early," she announced. After a quick bath, her mother slipped into her pajamas and relaxed in bed.

It was 9:45 at night, and Enez was nervous about Josh coming to her house. She sat in the family room, watching Robert Blake in "Baretta" while she waited. He still had not shown up at 10:15, and she finally fell asleep waiting on him all night. The next morning, Enez called his house, and a woman answered in a sleepy voice, "Hello."

"I'm sorry to wake you. May I speak to Josh?" she asked.

The woman replied, "Honey, Josh is gone to New York, and he won't be back for two months. Please don't call here again, looking for him. Thank you." The woman hung up the phone before Enez could say another word, as her heart sank to the pit of her stomach. There just had to be a good reason why he had not come by to visit her the night before, she thought to herself.

The weekend came and went. The telephone rang, and Dusty answered. "It's for you, Enez."

"Hello."

"How is my baby?"

Enez was so happy to hear from Josh that she forgot how disappointed she was that he had not come by that night.

"Hey Josh, I am fine!"

"I know that you're fine, baby; I asked how are you doing," he said with laughter in his voice.

"I called your house the day you left for New York. Your woman answered the phone," she said in a calm voice.

"I know you called, baby, and I apologize for not making it by your house to see you before I left. But you just make sure you're ready to be with me when I come back. I would have brought you to New York with me, but I don't want to start you off like that. This city may be hard for you. I told you I got plans for us."

She listened to his mesmerizing voice and wished she could jump on the first flight to New York.

"I don't hear you talking. You're not angry with me, are you?"

"No, no, I'm just thinking."

"I hope you're thinking about me, baby," he said in a sexy tone.

"Yes' it's you I'm thinking about, Josh" she said anxiously.

"Well, baby, I got some business to see about. I'll call you later, okay? You just keep in mind my plans for us."

Quickly, she responded, "Okay, Josh, I will. Talk to you later." She heard him hang up, and she held on to the receiver as she thought of them being together.

Josh called Enez every other day, reminding her he would be home soon and to wait on him. He knew from their conversations that she was becoming impatient and lonely. He never asked her to pack her things and come to him, but to wait on him.

****

One hot summer day in July, Enez decided to borrow her neighbor's car to take a trip down memory lane. As she drove past a South Memphis Street, she saw a familiar Cadillac parked at a corner store. Curiously, she thought to herself, "Should I turn around and go inside and pretend to buy something just so he can see me, or should I keep riding?"

Enez knew Nicko liked looking at her shapely, hairy legs and watching her hips sway from side to side. She saw him leaving the store through her rear view mirror and turned the car around to park. Nicko had not moved his Cadillac, and she parked two cars away from his. As she walked to the door of the store, she heard a horn blow. She turned to see him waving from the window, motioning her to come to him. She acted surprised to see Nicko. Her blue and white tennis dress moved as her body swayed from side to side, walking towards him.

Nicko looked at her with a smile on his face. His hair was freshly permed, and his face clean shaven. He wore a mahogany colored three-piece suit and a light mahogany colored shirt with ruffled sleeves and collar. He motioned for Enez to sit next to him in the front seat. She was a little nervous to get in the car with him, but she opened the door and got in next to him. His brown eyes laid upon her face as he said, "Hi Enez, what have you been up to? You sure are looking good to me, smell good too. How did you get up here? Are you driving?"

She looked at him with a smile on her face, "Thank you for the compliment! You're looking good too. I borrowed my neighbor's car. I'm parked right over there," she pointed. "Well, Nicko, I gotta go," she hurriedly said as she remembered her commitment to Josh.

"What's your hurry? I know Josh is in New York," he laughed.

"Yeah that's why I gotta go," she said as she opened the door to leave.

"You know I still want you, Enez. Hey, let's start over right this time. I'm a good man; I just want you to stop lying to me," he said quietly.

She felt her body becoming warm for him, as she wished he would ask her to stay. To her delight, he said,"Baby, come on and take a ride with me. I'll bring you back to your car." She looked at him, as she slowly brought her legs back inside the car and closed the door.

A tune by B.B. King, "The Thrill Is Gone," crooned from the car speakers as they drove through the South Memphis streets. Soon, they stopped at his parents' house.

Nicko drove up the steep driveway to the back of the house. "Come on with me. I want to change into something more comfortable."

"Okay, Nicko, that's fine with me," she said as she cleared her throat.

As they walked to the door, a man stood at the bottom of the driveway, motioning with his hands. Nicko motioned him away, and the man walked away. Nicko whispered, "He wants some dope." He unlocked the iron door and then a heavy wooden door to enter the huge carpeted kitchen. To the right, she saw a breakfast nook with a smoked glass table and gold cushioned chairs to match. As she stood in the middle of the kitchen, she noticed all the modern appliances were gold colored.

"Would you like something to drink?" he asked her.

"No, thank you."

He walked towards another room, "Come on, Enez, I'll be just a few minutes." They entered a small room with a desk and file cabinets along the walls. She followed him to the garage, which led to a set of iron stairs. At the top of the stairs, they came to another iron door, which he opened with a key. The cool air from the room rushed towards her face as she entered, and gold shag carpeting covered her shoes. "What a beautiful room," she thought to herself. Across the room was a bar with four stools, a king sized bed, and a glass topped night stand with an antique lamp setting on it. A round crushed velvet couch was placed under the window, overlooking the driveway. The windows were covered with custom draped in gold satin. A refrigerator sat near the walk-in closet.

"Have a seat, Enez. I'll be just a minute," he said softly. He chose a freshly starched blue jean outfit from the closet and laid it on the couch next to her. He took off his suit and laid it on the bed, "Enez, hang my suit up for me." She uncrossed her big brown legs and walked towards the bed.

He grabbed her and began to kiss her. She did not fight him…she wanted him. It had been a long time since she had been intimate with anyone, and Josh was not home. He unzipped her dress, and she slipped out of it as she kicked her shoes and socks off. Slowly, he pulled her undergarments from her beautifully shaped body. Nicko was gentle with her as he took her hand and guided her to unfold the covers over the bed as they slipped in between the sheets.

"Nicko, I know I haven't been honest with you in the past. I know pimps like to get paid, but I still live at home with my mom," Enez stated quietly.

"So what do think Josh is going to do with you? You know he is a pimp too. So you gonna play me.

I thought you really liked to be with me," Nicko stated coldly. They laid for a moment in silence, and she was afraid he was angry with her. She did not want to play games with Nicko. Suddenly he said, "Get dressed. I'm taking you back to your car."

In the car, she was afraid to say anything to him, afraid of his angry nature. When they reached the store, he parked his car behind her borrowed vehicle. "Enez, see ya later."

"Okay, Nicko, see ya later."

The summer months went by smoothly for Enez. She had stopped thinking about Nicko because there was no reason for it now. She was in Atlanta with her mother's sisters. Her last summer weeks in Atlanta gave newness to life. She talked to Josh occasionally while he was in New York He talked about the plans for them once they both returned home. Enez always agreed with him.

The phone rang, and she answered it before her mother reached it. "Hey baby," the deep voice on the other end said.

"Hey Josh, how are you?" Enez asked.

"I'm doing alright. I want to come by your house tonight."

She thought for a moment, then agreed with him. There was snow on the ground, and the moonlight made the snow look like crystals had fallen from the sky. When he arrived, Enez saw that he was draped in a full-length black mink coat and hat. She invited him in, and the room lit up like a rainbow from the diamond rings on his fingers. Too afraid that her mother would get out of bed to see who Enez had let into the house, she asked him to leave before her mom came downstairs. He left quickly.

Joshua called her when he arrived home. Enez explained to him that she was almost sixteen years old, but that did not stop him from calling or seeing her. He picked her up from school every day in his new plum Cadillac. Joshua had not put Enez on the streets. He bought clothes for her, he wined and dined her in nice restaurants, and made her feel special. He was never cruel to her.

After almost a year, they finally had sex. As she walked home from school one day, he pulled up next to her on the other side of the street. He winked and said, "Come on, baby, ride with me."

Enez teased Josh as she walked to his car, "How do you know I wanna go with you?"

He smiled, "Cause you wanna be with me."

She opened the front door and slid onto the plum leather seats. "Hi Josh! I'm glad you picked me up today because I wasn't ready to go home."

They rode in silence through the Memphis city streets. Suddenly, he turned into an apartment parking lot that she was not familiar with. "Come on, baby, I want to show you my other apartment." They climbed the iron stairs to the second floor and entered a lavishly decorated apartment. The living room was designed with glass, brass, and velvet furniture. They walked to the den and sat at the bar while he fixed himself a drink. He looked at her and motioned with his hand to follow him into the bedroom, where she saw a king-sized bed with a crush velvet spread and a redwood dresser and chest by the wall. She looked in the corner of the room and saw hat boxes stacked from the floor to the ceiling.

"Why are you so quiet, baby?" he asked as he guided her to his bed.

She stood over him as he positioned himself to lie down. "Your place is decorated so nicely," she said.

"Yeah, baby, come lay across the bed with me," he patted a spot on the bed next to him. Chills ran up and down her spine as he gently touched her. "Take your clothes off. I want to see what you look like without them."

She breathed softly as she removed her clothing and lay them neatly in a chair next to the bed. He looked at her and smiled at her teenaged, shapely body as they turned the covers back and lay between the satin sheets.

After what seemed like hours, he took her home. They rode in silence, except for the sound of romantic jazz playing on the stereo.

Enez had heard about how he mistreated women, how cruel he was to them, but she did not see that side of him. He seemed to always respect her. He did not plan to start her off on the streets while she was so young, no matter how much he wanted to. He knew she was jail bait for him.

One afternoon, Josh was parked in front of the school, waiting on Enez. She was astonished to see him as she walked out of the school. As she got closer to the car, she noticed another man seated in the front, a well known Memphis pimp named Mack who was also an associate of Nicko's. Enez hesitated to get in the car, although she had not seen Nicko in several months. She wondered why this man was riding with Josh. She got in the back seat and spoke to both men as they drove off.

Josh held most of his conversation with Mack, but he did not mind Enez listening in. "Man, that's my baby, Enez. She'll be ready just as soon as she is ripe. Isn't that right, baby?" he asked as he looked at her in the rearview mirror.

She agreed, "Yea, you're right." Enez knew Josh was not a man to play around with. She knew she had to get out of this situation before she became of age.

****

Enez's girlfriend, Ginger, was promiscuous in school. She was a small-framed girl with bow legs, pretty caramel complexion, dimples in her cheeks, and short, dyed black hair. She too was a young girl, often left home alone. Her parents owned a night club in Memphis. One day after school, she and Enez talked about working the streets. Ginger told Enez, "My man need a new girl in his flock. Let me introduce you to him. He's staying at the

Hotel Tennessee downtown." Ginger gave Enez the hotel phone and room number for her to call.

"Hotel Tennessee; may I help you?" the receptionist asked.

"Yes, may I have Room 210, please?" Enez said eagerly.

A man answered the phone, "Hello."

"May I speak to L.P., please?"

"You're speaking to him. Who is this?"

"Hi, this is Ginger's friend, Enez. I would like to meet you."

"Okay, how about tomorrow afternoon?"

She agreed to meet him as she hung up the phone. Ginger and Enez arranged to take the short bus ride downtown the next day after school. The hotel was not far from Main Street. It looked like an old landmark that needed renovations. The elevator doors squeaked opened, and Ginger pushed the button to go to the second floor. At the end of a long hall, they reached Room 210. Ginger knocked, and they heard a reply, "Who is it?"

Ginger replied, "It's us, baby."

A gorgeous, bare-chested man stood in the doorway. His face was smooth, the complexion of caramel. His jet black hair was long and silky. Enez's body became hot as soon as she laid eyes on L.P, and he looked at her lustfully. Her purple blouse pressed against her nipples, and her shorts wrapped around her hips tightly. Her high-heeled sandals accentuated her shapely legs, and her body smelled of perfume.

Ginger introduced Enez to L.P. He asked, “Is Enez what everyone calls you?”

“Yes, that’s what everyone calls me,” she said with a smile.

He looked at Ginger and said, “I’m hungry. Go down to the corner and get my favorite.” Ginger looked at Enez jealously because she knew that L.P. wanted to be with Enez. She obeyed L.P. He took advantage of their time alone and kissed her passionately. Before she knew it, Enez was in his bed. She knew he was a pimp and that pimps do not have sex with women for free, so she thought to herself, “Oh no, what have I done?” When they finished, she knew she had made a commitment to him.

Ginger returned while Enez was in the bathroom freshening up, and she could hear Ginger and L.P. talking. “Yeah, she gonna be your wife in law. Ya’ll come down here tomorrow and you show her the ropes. Don’t you run her off,” L.P. said aggressively.

Enez nervously came out of the bathroom. She thought, “This man ain’t playing. He knows both of us are under age, so I know he is ruthless under all that gorgeousness.” She looked at Ginger and said, “I’m going to get the bus back home. I’ll catch you later.”

L.P. looked at her, "What's the hurry? I'll send you home in a cab. You don't have to catch a bus back." He smiled at Ginger and told her to phone a cab and tell the desk clerk to call the room when the cab arrived. Ginger did as she was told. As Enez left, L.P. picked up a 20 dollar bill from the night stand and told her to come back the next day with Ginger to work the street track. "Don't have me looking for you," were his last words before she left.

Enez quietly walked to the elevator and did not notice the man in the elevator until he spoke, "Hello, little lady, having a good day?" She nodded her head. The doors squeaked open as the elevator stopped. As she walked down the smelly hall, she could see the cab through the faded window near the front entrance. The cab driver looked at her in the rearview mirror and asked, "Where are you headed, beautiful lady?"

With a smile she said, "546 LaCrage Ave." She was lost in her thoughts, and the dispatcher talking to other cab drivers was the only sound in the cab. When she arrived home, she noticed that her mother had not come home. She and her sister were alone. Enez took a hot bath and wrote in her journal before she fell asleep.

The next day was a school day, Friday. She did not see her mother the night before. As she left for school, she asked for permission to stay over her friend Anne's house that night. Her mother allowed her and did not call Anne's mom to confirm.

Enez chose a life she knew very little about. Joshua had protected her from it because she was a minor. L.P. was unlike Joshua – he was a professional pimp. Enez returned home from school, quickly finishing her chores before walking to Ginger's house. They rode the bus to L.P.'s, and he was waiting in the hotel lobby for them. Enez was nervous as they waited for the cab to take them to Fourth and Vance. She had only walked the street track once and had quickly left that same day. She kept her thoughts to herself, and minutes later she was standing on the street corner. The stars were shining, and the moon peeked from the night clouds.

Ginger said, "I'll introduce you to the man who runs the rooming house where we turn our dates."

Enez walked with her to a dingy looking place. The man wore a dress and make-up, sitting in the window as he hollered at the men outside. Other women used the place to turn dates also. Outside, several veteran hookers stood at the corner, flagging down cars. Enez pretended to know what she was doing, chasing cars like an eagle looking for her prey. Ginger finished dating and was coming downstairs. She tried to show her the ropes and get L.P.'s money too.

Enez looked across the street and saw Joshua's plum Cadillac turn the corner towards her. She ran to his car to talk to him. He asked her, "Girl what are you doing down here?"

She replied quickly, "I'm getting some money."

He looked at her, "Baby, go home."

Enez backed away from his car proudly, and he drove off into the night.

She turned to see L.P. and Ginger walking towards her. As he approached, L.P. smacked her so hard, she fell to the ground. Enez did not know the law of the pimping game: a hooker is never to talk to another pimp unless she is choosing him. She got up, dusted herself off, and tried again.

The other hookers chased a familiar car, wanting the man inside to choose one or all of them. Enez hung back and watched the other women. She looked the other way and noticed a man sitting in his car, stopped at the traffic light. She walked to his car, "Are you looking for a date?"

"Yeah, where can we go?"

She wanted to run from the earlier embarrassment and get money for L.P., so she quickly got in the car without telling anyone she was leaving. Enez did not understand the dangers of the streets. He drove away, and she trusted that he was being honest with her.

They rode to the back parking lot of an apartment complex. The man said, "We can go inside my sister's apartment and do our business." She believed him, glancing around to get a bearing on her surroundings. He parked a few spaces from the other cars. As Enez opened the car door, he pulled her back inside.

"Where the hell you think you going?" he asked as he hit her again and again. He forced her into the back seat and pushed her head into the door as he raped her and held his hand over her mouth. He raped Enez for what seemed like hours before he finally told her he would take her back where he had picked her up. He drove her close enough, and she began to walk until she recognized the area: Vance and Fourth Avenue.

As she reached the corner of Fourth and Vance, Ginger and L.P. walked towards her. L.P. said, "Come on, let's go." They walked back to the hotel room. Enez locked herself in the bathroom and cried softly as L.P. shouted, "Come out of there and give me my money!"

Her thoughts were still fresh on what had just happened to her, and she tried to explain what happened when she came out of the bathroom. L.P. did not believe her and began to beat her again. He put her out of his room in the early morning hours. It was very early in the morning, but night still covered the sky.

Walking aimlessly, Enez had no idea where to go or what to do. Her walk ended right back at Fourth and Vance. Sitting nearby was a cab, and she asked the driver to take her home. Sunlight began a new day as the birds chirped and early morning noises rang out. The cab driver agreed to take her home if she would have sex with him.

Without money, Enez agreed, "We can have sex at my house." She gave him the address, and when they arrived she told him, "Wait here, and I'll come back to get you."

God was with her that night, He looked down upon her. God allowed Satan to have his way with her, but He would not let him kill her. That morning, God sent her safely home. She unlocked the door and saw that her mother was still fast asleep. From the den window, Enez could see the cab driver still waiting outside. He finally gave up and left after a while, and Enez's mother never knew about that night her daughter made an unhealthy choice to become a hooker. There was a lesson for her that night, but she had not yet learned.

God did not see a pitiful case. He saw a little girl, all twisted out of His plan. He saw the nature of her sin and the sadness of her heart. The Savior saw one of His creatures walking in darkness, seeking the Light.

Enez's thoughts about herself were very negative. Her self-worth was allowing people to use and abuse her. She did not know how to love herself or how to love like Christ loves everyone. At night, she wept into her pillow crying, "If only someone would love me." She did not stop seeking human love long enough to hear Jesus say to her "***I love you, trust m***e."

* * *

The Prodigal Daughter

Longed to Change

Her life was quickly eroding downward to the pits of Hell. She did not know her purpose in life. She did not have any positive goals for the future, and she had poor grades in school. The people she surrounded herself with were all hustlers. Enez had started drinking at home whenever her mother was away. This binge did not last long because the alcohol made her sick to her stomach, and she would wake up in the mornings with a headache.

Aaron was very popular in high school, and all the girls liked him. He was tall, dark, and handsome, drove a nice car, and wore nice clothes. He came from a middle classed family: his daddy was a car dealer and his mom a nurse. He had several brothers and sisters. When they were younger, Enez did not like him for a courtship, but she began admiring him when they got older because of his popularity with the girls.

Aaron pretended to admire her. He knew she would have sex with him. Maybe the other girls would not do this with him, but he knew Enez would. They started having sex in his parents' garage when she was 16 years old. He never wanted normal sex – it was always unusual sex, and Enez went along with it because she thought he liked her.

He called her several late nights after he and his friends had been drinking. She snuck out of her mom's house and walked down the street to Aaron's house. When he finished with her, he walked her to the end of his driveway and turned away to go inside. She walked home by herself in the lonely, dark night, feeling hurt each step of the way. She thought to herself, "What am I thinking? Did I think having sex with him was going to make him love me?" She knew he would never love her, yet she continued to have sex with him.

Enez's mother organized a group of young college students majoring in political science to rally them into politics. Enez began to see a different group of people, and she admired them because they were going places in their lives. They discussed ideas and goals for young black politicians. These college students did not wear big diamond rings or mink coats or even drive fancy Cadillacs. Their lives had purpose, and she sought to have the same for herself.

One cool, winter evening, as her mother prepared dinner, Enez talked about attending UCLA. "Mom, I would like to attend college at UCLA," she said excitedly.

"Well, Enez, you have to really start studying hard to bring your grades up. We'll see about getting you there, and if that doesn't work, we'll try other colleges," she said with a smile.

Enez began to study hard to bring her grades up, and she attended summer school. She was able to finish high school a year early.

After graduation, she lost her way. Her life was back on the downward course. She did not have a guide for her life, and once again, she surrounded herself by those who only wanted to use and abuse her. Her dream to be someone positive was shattered.

****

One hot summer day, she walked to the bus stop with her head hanging low. Feelings of hope were gone. Enez did not notice the short, gray-haired woman sitting on the bus stop bench until the woman spoke to her, “Hi, young lady. Why are wearing such a long face today? You have such a pretty face. Let me see that beautiful smile.”

Enez looked at the woman and began to smile, but she did not mention why she had held her head down while she walked. Their eyes met, and the woman broke their silence. “Don’t ever walk around with your head held to the ground. You are somebody, and always remember that. Without Faith and Hope, the work is dead. They must work together. It becomes your shield against all principalities of this world. Remember, God loves you, and He keeps us safe.”

A bus turned the corner and came to a stop to pick up the two passengers. The woman boarded the bus first and picked a seat at the front. As Enez sat in her seat, she told the woman, “Thank you for those encouraging words, Ma’am.” She never saw the wise woman again.

Autumn’s season mixed in the summer’s final air. Enez began her first semester at Shelby State Community College, but she was still confused about her purpose in life. She had not seen or heard from Josh in several months, and Nicko was in prison for selling and distributing heroine.

As the last weeks of classes approached, Enez found out she was pregnant. This time, she was 18 years old and made the decision to keep her baby. Enez's decision to not give the baby up for adoption was immature and selfish. She thought having a baby would give her love and make the father love her.

That winter, Aaron and Enez occasionally had sex whenever he came home from college. In January, Aaron came home for winter break. She walked to his parents' house and rang the doorbell. Aaron stood in the doorway and asked, "What's up, Enez? You look upset. What's the matter with you?"

She pushed past him as she entered the house. "I have something to tell you," she said as he looked at her anxiously. "Aaron, I'm pregnant, and it's your baby,"

He looked at her with a frightening stare, "Naw, that ain't my baby. I've been away at school. I think you better leave now. I'll talk to you later," he said as he escorted her out. She heard the door close behind her.

Her knees felt weak, but she did not look back. She stepped strongly and courageously as she walked home. Her great aunt had told her long ago, "Only Him Who died on the Cross for our sins guarantees His Love for us. Enez, how can you expect any male to have respect and love for you if don't find it within yourself?"

Aaron went back to school to complete another semester. His family knew Enez was pregnant, and they were not happy about the situation. Aaron and Enez communicated very little during her pregnancy. He dated a young woman from their high school years, and he planned to marry her. Throughout her pregnancy, Enez lived in disillusion. She did not complete her second semester at Shelby State.

Looking for love, she started dating another guy who lived in the neighborhood, Stanley. Stanley was a short, slim guy with beautiful, big eyes and a brown complexion. Stanley's mother was married to a preacher. She tried to live a dedicated mother's life and exemplary for her children. Her first set of children with her first husband were dysfunctional. Stanley's oldest brother was an alcoholic and drug abuser. Stanley had been in and out of juvenile hall and jail since childhood. He got his high school diploma while in jail. He found jobs that paid minimum wage. He drank alcohol every day and smoked weed.

Enez told Stanley, "I am three months pregnant."

"That's okay with me. I'll stay by your side." He really did not mean it, although he was there for the second and third terms of her pregnancy. They had lots of laughs together. He accompanied her to the doctor and acted like he was the father, waiting on his baby to arrive, but he changed during her third trimester. He did not see her after work as he had before, and he was always angry for no apparent reason. He did not want her around anymore. She was crushed!

One warm, summer night she walked up the street to the house he was renting. Enez saw a blue Cadillac in the driveway as she knocked on the door. His younger brother answered the door. She asked, "Is Stanley home?"

He quickly replied, "No, he isn't."

Enez pushed past his brother and walked into Stanley's bedroom. There he was, lying in bed with another woman and her three children. Enez started to cry, and he told her to leave.

The woman, Lois, had moved in with Stanley along with her three children. Enez did not have a clue. Time would move on, and Lois would too. Eventually, Enez went back to Stanley to endure more self infliction to her mind, spirit, and soul even though he started dating another woman close to Enez's age, Leah. She was also pregnant with another man's baby, Still, Enez's days with Stanley were not over. He moved into a small apartment above a garage on the next street in the same neighborhood. Leah's baby was born a few days after Enez's baby was born. Enez did not know Stanley and Leah were still dating.

Enez walked around the neighborhood all day looking for Stanley. Darkness fell upon the sky, and the stars twinkled like small flashlights. She was angry with him as she walked through the neighborhood with her infant daughter under the moonlit sky. As she climbed the stairs to his apartment, she noticed a light on in the front room. She reached the top of the stairs with her baby in the stroller and knocked on the door as she took a deep breath.

He answered abruptly, “Who is it?”

She replied loudly, “It’s me, Stanley, open the door.”

Stanley opened the door to allow Enez and her daughter in. She removed the baby from the stroller and braced herself on the edge of the couch for support as she sat down next to Stanley. He looked at Enez, “What do you want? Why are you here?”

Angry tears pushed their way through her eyes as she sniffled, “Stanley, you said we had a future together, but you are still seeing Leah. You don’t want me anymore, do you?”

Stanley looked at her with hatred in his eyes. He stood in front of her and said, “No I don’t want you anymore, and you need to leave.”

Enez rose from the couch. She was almost his height, and she looked him in his eyes with tears flowing down her face, screaming like a woman in pain. He pushed her out the door, and she fell down the stairs. As she landed at the bottom of the stairwell, she noticed Stanley at the top of the stairs with her baby in one arm and the stroller in the other. It appeared he was going to throw the baby, so she ran up the stairs and begged him not to hurt

Amara. She walked home with her baby that night, never to return to him again.

Amara's father was very supportive of his daughter. He came from a good family who loved Amara in spite of her mother, Enez. Enez was grateful for the family's support. By the time Amara turned two, her father had almost finished college in New York and had decided to return home to work.

Enez had outgrown Aaron, and they split from each other. Enez started attending business college to learn to type and take short hand. She wanted a professional job to support herself and her daughter. She worked part-time at a diner.

Early one Saturday morning at the diner, she looked into the eyes of a customer. When she took his food order, he said, "The enemy sees you reaching forward to Originality and his keen tactic will try to pull you backwards to self destruction."

Enez noticed his Bible in front of him. He quoted the Scripture in red ink, "***I am the way, the truth, and the life. No man cometh unto the Father but by me…whosoever believeth on me, shall have everlasting life…he who hath the Son hath life.***" The gray-haired man stared at Enez and said, "I am reading from **John 14:6.**"

Enez thought to herself, "Do I know the Way, the Truth? My life is very confusing. I have always wanted what I wanted, and I want to have it quickly."

Her thoughts were broken as he placed his order, "I would like a cup of hot tea and dark toast, please."

Soon, the diner became very busy, and Enez brought the older man his order and check. She continued to check on his table, and he continued to read the book that lay open in front of him. Just as she was carrying food to another table, she noticed he had left the diner. She placed the orders on the table that she was serving, walked to the empty table and found a small book with her name written under the title "Holy Bible." Enez put the book inside her waitress apron, along with straws and napkins.

After her work shift, she remembered the book in her pocket. As she flipped through the pages, she noticed a twenty dollar bill pressed tightly in its binder. On that page, these words were underlined, "***Seek ye first the Kingdom of God and His righteousness and all these things shall be added to you.***" Enez read the underlined words. They held no meaning for her, so she took the money from the page and closed the book.

Attending school and working part-time was not working fast enough for Enez. She quit her job at Gridiron Restaurant, and she quit school.

* * *

The Prodigal Daughter

Still Lost

It was a sizzling summer day, and Enez stood at her front door, watching a man and woman moving into the house across the street. The man drove a fancy Cadillac and wore a wide brimmed hat. His woman wore a big, blonde wig, a short dress, and high heeled shoes. Enez knew right away this was a hooker and a pimp, and she was interested in meeting the woman. It turned out to be the man she met first a few weeks later.

As Enez took Amara for a walk, a car pulled up beside her. It was the Cadillac she had seen across the street at the new neighbor's house. The man watched her over his tinted shades and said, "What a pretty baby girl you have. She takes her looks after her mother."

"She sure does," Enez smiled, as she continued walking.

He slowly followed in his car, trying to catch her attention. Enez stopped in her tracks, "I am not interested in a pimp." She did not give him a chance to say another word as she and Amara began running. They did not stop until they reached home.

There was only one man in her life who truly loved her with all his heart, her grandfather. He was her PoPa. His face wore strength, and his eyes were filled with compassion and love. His dark complexion was a sign of freedom. She lost him before her twentieth birthday.

The Prodigal Daughter

As Enez entered the house, she found her mother on the phone. "Lillie, let me call you back. Enez, come here I need to tell you something," her mother spoke softly. Enez walked into the living room. "Enez, PoPa died today."

Her mother explained, "Your grandparents were in the hardware store, and PoPa passed out in an aisle. The store manger called an ambulance, and PoPa probably died in the ambulance. They said he had a heart attack."

Enez looked into her mother's eyes, searching for words. She cried out, "God, why did you take the only man who really loved me away?" Her grief for the loss of her grandfather lasted many months.

Enez's mother was really getting on her case about doing something with her life. Enez knew she wanted to get out of her situation. One Sunday evening, she noticed the woman across the street standing in her driveway. Enez crossed the street to introduce herself. "Hi, my name is Enezi, but everyone calls me Enez. I grew up in this neighborhood. Are you from Memphis?"

The woman looked nervous as she answered, "Yes, I'm from North Memphis. I saw you talking to Ponny."

"Who?"

"Ponny – my man," the woman said. She looked at Enez as though she knew who Ponny was.

"Ohhh, that's his name. Naw, I don't want a pimp," Enez said.

"Well, he's out of town for a couple of months anyway. Enez, you want to come in the house?" Enez accepted the offer. "By the way, my name is Arabella," the woman said as she opened the front door.

Although they had only been there a few weeks, the place was decorated as though she had lived there for years. Her living room colors were greens, pinks, and mauve, and Enez noticed the Victorian furniture as they walked through the dinning room and passed expensive wood furniture, beautiful crystal, and brass china. Enez walked to the kitchen with Arabella as they talked about earning some fast money.

Arabella asked, "Enez, would you like something to drink? I have wine, champagne, water, Coke. What would you like?."

Enez looked around the beautifully decorated kitchen and answered, "Coke, please."

They walked on shiny hardwood floors as Arabella escorted Enez to the den. Enez sat on a black, leather chair, and Arabella sat on the matching couch. Arabella placed her glass on a coaster on a glass topped table with gold legs. Underneath the table was a bear rug. They talked more about earning some fast money.

"Enez, have you worked the topless clubs?"

"No, I haven't. I tried, but they wouldn't hire me."

"Well, let's go out one night and try our luck."

The Prodigal Daughter

Enez went home after her talk with Arabella. She was met by her mother as she entered the house. "I hope you aren't planning to go out tonight."

Enez walked to her bedroom. As she sat on her bed, playing with her daughter, she noticed the small book that she had received from her customer at the restaurant. She remembered, "***Seek ye first the Kingdom of God and His righteousness and all these things shall be added to you.***" But she continued to seek what she thought was important, things given to her by sinful acts. As she flipped through the pages, her eyes fell upon these words, "***What does a man profit by gaining the world and losing his soul?***" She was headed for the darkest time of her life, and she was not wearing a life jacket.

The stars were shining brightly in the sky, and the air smelled like morning dew. Enez left her mother's house this warm, summer night, about to enter into a den of Hell.

Enez walked across the street to Arabella's house and knocked on the door. Arabella looked at Enez, "Girl, I know you not going to audition in that outfit! I got an outfit that will knock you out! You'll really like it, and so will the men."

Enez followed Arabella to the bedroom. She had not seen this room before. She noticed the king sized bed with matching ten-drawer dresser, oval mirror, and chest. The huge lamps were draped with fancy blue and gold tassels. Arabella pulled a sheer, tiger print dress from the closet. Enez looked at the dress, "Yea, I like this dress. Let's see if it fits."

Enez removed her clothing, including her bra and panties before she slipped the beautiful dress over her 34 inch hips. The fabric fit snugly around her waist and perfectly rounded breasts. She put her high heeled shoes on as she waited for Arabella to finish dressing.

A knock on the door let Enez and Arabella know their ride had arrived. Enez had recently met some of Arabella's friends; a preacher's daughter, two single women, and a married woman. Enez opened the door to the four women, waiting patiently on the other side. They looked jealously at Enez as they filed past. Arabella offered everyone drinks. "Not tonight, Arabella," the women said. Arabella finished putting on her make up and dressing, while the women conversed among themselves, and Enez filed her nails.

"I'm ready, girls, let's go," Arabella said.

All six women piled into the Chrysler, three in the front and three in the back. Their first stop was a club on Raines and Elvis Presley, but they were not hiring black girls. Enez had been there before with a high school classmate. They said the same line to black girls back then. Their second stop was a club called Donny's on Airways Boulevard. Enez went in first and asked a short, bleached blonde-headed man, "Are you hiring?"

"Yeah, baby. Why don't you audition for me? Walk over to the D.J.'s booth and tell her your name and what song you wanna dance to."

Enez strolled over to the D.J.'s booth with a sexy walk and used her stage name, Red Foxx. She asked the D.J. to play a Smokey Robinson tune for her audition.

The D.J. called out, "The lovely Red Foxx will be on stage next, gentlemen."

Enez walked onto the stage. She noticed the bright fluorescent lights under the flooring and the lights shining overhead. Men sat at tables around the stage, watching as Enez danced seductively to the music, slowly revealing her body as she undraped each piece of clothing. When the music ended, the men screamed wildly for her as she walked offstage. Enez put on her clothes as she stood at the table where Arabella was seated. Arabella and the other women waited for the short, blond haired guy, but he never returned. They decided to leave without any further auditions.

As they reached the car, Enez heard a man call out, "Red Foxx, Red Foxx!" She turned to see who had called her, while Arabella kept walking. This man was much taller and more handsome than the short, blond guy.

"I'm Donny. Would you like to work for me?" he said.

Enez replied, "Yes."

"Be at the club at 7:00 p.m. tomorrow night."

She walked swiftly to the car, and the other women sat quietly as they rode off. Arabella broke the silence, "Enez I told you that dress was a knockout." Before she went home, she stopped at Arabella's house to change back into her own clothes.

Amara had spent the night with her father's parents. Enez's mother was asleep on the couch when she came home. She quietly walked through the house without waking her mother and turned on the lap on the nightstand when she reached her bedroom. Her little sister was asleep in her bed.

As she undressed, she looked in the mirror and smiled, thinking about the events of the night. She thought to herself, "I can work at Donny's for a while…just enough time to buy a car and get a place to live other than my mother's house."

The next day, she set her plan into motion as she borrowed cab fare and a costume from Arabella. Amara was with her father again. She waited for evening to approach with anticipation. Finally, the cab arrived at six o'clock, and she soon found herself before the tinted glass of the club doors. Inside, she did not spot anyone to greet her. She waited at the door until an older woman walked swiftly toward her. "Are you Red Foxx?" she asked with authority.

"Yes I am," Enez answered nervously.

"Well, follow me. I'll take you to the dressing room to meet the other ladies."

A line of men stood wall to wall as the loud music played, and the smell and smoke of cigarettes permeated the air. A nude, white woman was on stage, dancing to a rock and roll song as the men cheered. Enez and the older woman reached a small room with lockers covering three sides of the walls, and a mirror covered the fourth wall.

The red headed woman finally introduced herself, "I'm Franny, your house momma. I don't allow my girls to touch the men or to be touched. If I catch you, there's a fifty dollar fine. This here is Doll Baby," she said as she patted the woman on her shoulder. "She'll show you around. Now get dressed because the evening shift will start soon."

Doll Baby looked just as her stage name represented. She was slim black girl, with Betty Davis eyes and long hair, just a few inches taller than Enez. She sat with her legs crossed, looking through the mirror as Enez changed her clothes. "Have you ever danced in a topless club before?" she asked.

Enez shook her head no in response as Doll Baby continued to watch her in the mirror.

"Well, there's nothing to it. You dance on stage to a three minute song. When you get off stage, walk around and ask the men if they want a table dance or if they'd like a drink. Table dances are seven dollars, but you know we ask for more than that because the house gets two dollars out of seven. Mike, the table dance keeper, walks around after each song to mark your name if you're table dancing. Keep up with it yourself cause he's been know to cheat you. I pay him after every dance and watch him mark it off the sheet. You order your own drinks from the bar. The customer can't order the drinks because we pay one price, and they pay a higher price. The beer is $3.50, and we keep 50 cents. Cokes are $2.00. You got it? Everybody knows some of the men like to date a girl and want her to leave before her shift is over. You have to give the club forty dollars if you leave early. I always make them wait on me so I can keep all my money. Well, are you ready for me to show you around?."

Enez was eager to get started. She and Doll Baby walked to the D.J.'s booth to submit their names and song selections.

"Hey Robin, this is Red Foxx. Red Foxx, this is Robin," Doll Baby introduced the two women. As they walked away, Doll Baby said, "Yeah, I forgot to mention: always come to the D.J. booth to give your name so you won't get a fine for being late. Now let me show you the bar and the kitchen."

She introduced Red Foxx to a man with a toothpick hanging from his mouth. "This is our bartender, Larry. Larry tries to be mean, but he's an okay guy," she said, smiling. They continued to walk to the kitchen, and the aroma of fried chicken, fried corn, greens, candied yams, and cornbread filled the air.

A gray-headed woman prepared a place at the table and smiled at Doll Baby, "Who is this beautiful, young lady you have with you, Doll?"

"She is one of the new girls, Mrs. Flow."

"Hey, little lady, and what your name be?" she asked.

Enez almost told the woman her real name, but she quickly said, "Red Foxx."

"Well, I am Mrs. Flow, and I'm pleased to meet you. I'm the cook. Everybody calls me Momma, and you can too." Enez looked at her with sadness in her heart, thinking "What is a sweet woman like her working in a topless club?"

"It's show time!" they heard the D.J. call out.

Baby Doll exclaimed, "Come on, Red Foxx. When the D.J. calls show time, that means a shift change, and the entire new shift enters the stage so the men can see new faces."

They quickly left the kitchen without saying goodbye to Mrs. Flow to get on the stage for the shift change. Afterwards, Doll Baby met her at the bar to set up their trays.

"Red Foxx, here is a towel to put on top of your tray, and here's a glass. I use the glass to keep my lipstick, pen, paper and other items. Well, good luck tonight. You're on your own now. See ya later. Oh, you need to ask Robin about who you follow on stage. Always do that so you won't be late for stage, cause they'll fine you."

Enez's first night working at the club was monetarily rewarding, and she returned to dance night after night.

One afternoon, Enez went to visit Arabella, who came to the door with swollen, black eyes. Her right arm was in a cast, and her lip was swollen and busted. She had been thoroughly beaten. Tears flowed from her closed eyes, and the smell of alcohol was on her breath as she invited Enez in.

"What happened?" Enez asked her.

Arabella walked to the kitchen and offered Enez a drink as she took a sip of her own drink. She told Enez, "I have to leave him. He's crazy. Whatever you do, don't get yourself mixed up with a pimp. He's leaving town this weekend, and I'm leaving too, but not with him. I'm glad you came over today so I can tell you goodbye. I hope to see you again someday but in a better life." Enez never saw Arabella again.

Enez used cabs for transportation and saved her money for an apartment and new furniture. Amara spent most of her time with her father and his parents. Enez's mother was busy with her career, but she did notice that Enez was leaving late at night and returning early in the morning. One morning, she woke Enez from a deep sleep. "Enez, where are you going late nights until the wee hours of the morning?"

Enez looked at her mom through sleepy eyes, "I have a waitress job at a club."

"Okay," satisfied, she left the room.

Suddenly, Enez's eyes flew open. It was almost five o'clock! She jumped out of bed and stumbled to the floor. The house was very quiet, as she walked around looking for her sister or mother. No one was home; she was all alone. Enez jumped in the shower and decided to get a bite to eat at work. She called a cab before quickly getting dressed. Just as she put her costumes in her bag, she heard the cab's horn and rushed outside.

Enez did not recognize the driver. He asked her, "Where you going, little lady?"

"To Donny's, near the airport."

The cabby turned the meter on as they started the ride to the airport. He looked at her through his rear view mirror. Gospel music played from the radio, and the cab driver turned it down to speak to her. "I have a daughter about your age. I bet you're about twenty years old. What are you doing working in a place like Donny's? You don't have to run to evil. Did you know God said that? He says, '***Their feet run to evil***'."

Enez thought to herself, "Yes, my feet have run to evil. I don't know the way of peace."

He interrupted her thoughts, "***The way of peace they know not; and there is no judgment in their goings. They have made crooked Paths; whosoever goeth therein shall not know peace…we wait for light, but behold obscurity; for brightness, but we walk in darkness***," he quoted. "My child, you've been blinded to the ways of the enemy." He continued reciting God's word to her, "***We grope for the wall like the blind, and we grope as if we had no eyes: we stumble at noon day as in the night: we are in desolate places as dead men.***"

Enez looked at his reflection in the mirror. He smiled at her, and she smiled back. They rode in silence as he continued to drive towards the club. Finally, they reached the parking lot. Enez knew the cost of the fare from previous rides. She told him, "Seven fifty," as she gave him a twenty dollar bill. "Keep the change." She opened the door to exit the cab and turned to look in his eyes, "Thank you for caring about me, but I don't plan to work here very long." She closed the car door and went through the glass doors to the club. She did not consider those moments of caring words from a stranger and went through those glass doors many more times after their conversation.

After a year of dancing, Enez was finally ready to move from her mother's house into a two-bedroom townhouse, The Lofton Town Homes. She paid over $5,000 in cash for new furniture and later paid cash for a red Pinto. She was looking for Peace, but it was only a temporary peace in her life.

Her daughter's father briefly stepped back into her life to use her for his car note payments, but she soon became bored with him. She only knew one kind of man to have relationships with: Pimp, Hustler, Mack Daddy. That is who she was looking for. This kind of man would not be ashamed of her. He would tell her what she wanted to hear, not what she needed to hear. Later on, she learned that being a lady of the evening came with a price. Her life with Aaron was short-lived. As Enez put it, "That dog could not hunt." But there was a dog that had been in her life who did know how to hunt.

Enez read a plaque in a store one day. It said, "We have found out we only have to be empty in order to receive Grace. Grace is a gift." It was a Gift that she refused to accept.

* * *

Emptiness

He came in the image of a man she would not turn away from. She had seen a gray Cadillac parked near the entrance of her apartment complex on many occasions. It had a signature plate on the front with "Nicko" inscribed on it. Enez was familiar with that name, but she did not recognize the car, and she had not seen the occupants of the car.

Enez had a day off from work on this warm, Thursday night. Her daughter was visiting her grandmother for a few summer nights, and Enez was home alone watching television when she decided to drive to the corner store for snack items. Just as she approached the corner, she saw headlights facing her and the plates Nicko. The driver of the car turned into the parking lot, and

Enez noticed the driver was not Nicko. She asked the driver as they walked to the store's entrance, "Is that Nicko Nelson's car?"

"Yeah, this is his car," he answered. The man was very slim, and most of his front teeth were missing. "Nicko's brother-in-law, Jerrod, lives in the Lofton Town Homes. Do you know Jerrod?"

"Yeah, I know him."

"My name is Luther. What's your name?"

"Enez," she softly replied.

"Would you like me to take you to see his brother-in-law?"

Anxiously, she said "Yes!"

After they paid for their items, Enez followed Luther to the townhouse. Nicko's brother-in-law opened the door. He did not recognize her at first, so she started to identify herself. Suddenly, he remembered her and gave her a big hug, "Come on in, Enez! Have a seat. I haven't seen you in a long time. Woman, you are looking good! What are you doing with yourself?"

She thought as she looked at him, "Yes, he's still a long-haired, fast-talking man." Enez could never get a word in edge wise.

"Nicko is out of prison; he's on parole. He goes to a halfway house on the weekends."

He continued to talk like a road runner, and Enez was about to say, "Well, it was nice seeing you again," when he suddenly blurted out, "Do you want me to give Nicko your phone number?"

Enez held her lips tightly and wondered how many more nights she would be lonely like this. She trembled slightly as she thought about her answer. "Yes, let me write my number down," she responded before she left.

Home again, she put away the snacks she had purchased. She heard the phone ring just as she reached the top of the stairs. Short of breath, she answered, "Hello."

"Hi, is Teresa home?" a man's voice asked on the other end.

"You have the wrong number," Enez replied. She lay across her bed, looking up to the ceiling as she thought to herself, "I haven't seen him in a long time. I wonder what he looks like now." Sadness crept into her heart as she remembered their past. She heard that he had married Shirley, his son's mother. "What am I doing?" she whispered to herself before she fell asleep.

* * *

"Seek Ye First the Kingdom of Heaven"

Nicko phoned her two days later. "Hello, is Enez home?"

She recognized his voice immediately. "Oh! Hi, Nicko! How are you?"

"I'm okay, baby. I heard you're doing really well since the last time I saw you. I want to see you, baby. Do you think you can arrange that?"

She blurted out, "Yes! Why don't you come by tomorrow morning? I'm off on Mondays. Let me give you my address. It's 1240 Loft, apartment two. You got it?"

"I'll see you first thing in the morning. You be sweet until then," Nicko said shortly.

"Okay." They ended their conversation, and Enez turned on the television. A preacher talked to a crowd of people, "Where He Leads me, I will follow…" Enez thought, "Where who leads? Follow who?" The preacher now mentioned lost sheep, and Enez thought, "Am I one of the lost sheep?"

The phone rang again. "Hello," she answered. "Oh hey, John. You're here in Memphis? I can be ready in an hour. I'll meet you at our favorite restaurant." She showered quickly and dressed in one of her favorite outfits to meet him. John was a regular date, and he paid quite well for her company.

The Prodigal Daughter

It had been a long day for Enez. After she left John, she cruised home, feeling very satisfied with her life. She took another shower and fell into a deep sleep when she got home. She dreamed that someone knocked on her door. Enez answers the door and a tall, brown complexioned man is standing there with brown eyes of fire looking at her. *She tried to close the door, but he stood in the way, intending to hurt her. She heard a voice warning her, "It is I who you hunger for, hunger to fill and quench your thirsty soul. But you do not know Me. You only know men who will quench your physical thirst, men who don't know how to love you, because like you, they didn't know how to love Me."* She woke from her dream, feeling nervous and frightened. Sweat covered her body. She was afraid to fall asleep again, so she stared at the ceiling for a long time. She did not realize when she finally fell asleep again.

The next morning, she heard a knock on the door as she finished her breakfast of bacon, eggs, and toast. She asked, "Who is it?"

"Nicko," was the reply. Enez opened the door. There he was – tall, course hair,, overweight, and trickery in his smile – just as he had appeared in her dream. She let him in and sat on the couch in her gown and matching robe. He walked around the room as if he was searching for something, but he finally sat next to her on the couch. He kissed her as he eagerly groped her body. Enez moved his hands away, "Stop." She remembered hearing that his mother had died from cancer, and his father was murdered while doing time in Federal prison.

"Nicko, I was sorry to hear your parent's have passed on," she offered her condolences. "I have to pick up my daughter. I'd better get dressed." She hoped he would respect her privacy and stay downstairs while she dressed, but he did not. He appeared in the bedroom doorway as she slipped out of her gown.

"Just as I remembered you, girl. You are still fine," he said as he admired her body. "So, you have a daughter now. Where is her father?" He walked closer to her and put his hand on her breast. Before she could answer, he put his lips over hers, filling her mouth with his tongue. She returned the kiss and did not resist him. They had sex that morning. Afterwards, he asked her for money, and Enez gave him what he wanted. She hoped that she would be able to resist his attempts next time.

Days and nights turned into weeks, and Nicko became verbally abusive in his pursuit of Enez. She was afraid of him. She gave him her money every night after work…she had once again fallen into the hands of a pimp. He controlled her. He took her car so she would not have transportation. Yet, every night, he went home to his wife and son, while Enez cried into her pillow, alone. She was afraid of what he would do if she left him.

It was a starry, late fall night when Nicko picked Enez up from work. She gave him her money as soon as she got in the car. As they arrived at her place, he said "I'll see you in the morning."

The Prodigal Daughter

Enez lay in bed, tossing and turning without sleep well after midnight. She thought about ending this unhappy relationship, and she was determined to act upon her thoughts. Enez called a cab as she got dressed. She gathered all of Nicko's possessions and waited. When the cab arrived, she told the driver, "3859 Leatherwood, please." Enez saw Nicko's Cadillac parked near the curb as the cab pulled up. She was nervous, but she got out of the cab with his things in her arms and put everything on the front porch.

The next morning, Enez felt satisfied that she had decided to bring closure to the relationship. She wanted out! She was able to sleep. Later, she was awakened by a knock on the door. As she peered from her bedroom window, she saw Nicko's Cadillac. She hesitated to answer the door, and he knocked again. She saw Nicko and his brother, Tony, looking towards her bedroom window. "Oh no, he sees me now," she thought frantically. Enez rushed downstairs to let him in. "Good morning," she called out.

"Good morning. I want you to work a double today. Get dressed," he demanded. She was startled and nervously got dressed to leave. In the car, Enez found it strange that he got in the back seat with her. She looked down at the floorboard and saw the 8-track case she had left on his front porch earlier that morning. Suddenly, he grabbed the case and repeatedly hit her over the head with it as he called her everything but her own name. He told his brother, "Man, I thought she was going to be a good girl, but I see she ain't. She put my things on the porch! Man, if you hadn't said anything I wouldn't have seen the tape case." Enez went to work with knots on her head and bruises all over her body many times after that day. She tried to get out of the situation. He beat her almost everyday.

Now, Enez worked the day shift at one of the five clubs Donny owned. She worked 14-hour shifts, leaving one club to work at another. She had worked her regular day shift on this day, and she was tired. Nicko and an associate drove up to the Luck Lady club to pick her up.

"I don't believe I want to be with you anymore," Enez told Nicko. He immediately hit her in the eye, then dropped her off at Donny's club. Once again, she walked into the club with a black eye, which she covered with make-up. The pain from her eye became excruciating after she had worked long enough to earn a couple of hundred dollars. She paid her dues and called a cab to go home.

As she walked into her house, she saw Nicko's friend sleeping on the couch. Nicko stood at the top of the stairs and said, "You better have my money."

She nodded as she walked up the stairs and gave him her money. In the bedroom, she spotted the small silhouette of a child lying in the bed. She crawled to her child and hugged her tightly. Nicko left abruptly, without saying good bye. Enez cried herself to sleep that night as she did most nights. She was no longer in control of herself or her daughter. Many days, she did not know where her daughter was, or who she was with.

The Prodigal Daughter

Enez talked to her mother on the phone late one evening. “Hi mom, how are you?”

“Honey, I’m okay, but I know you and my grandchild are in trouble being with that awful man. I believe Amara is left alone in the car for many hours or locked inside the house while she is asleep.”

“Momma, why do you say that?” Enez was sad because she knew in her heart that what her mother said was true.

“When she is here with me, she won’t let me leave the room. And when she wakes up, if no one is in the room with her, she screams and screams at the top of her lungs. She won’t let me out of her sight. Enez! I want you to think about what you are doing with your life and your little girl.”

One Sunday morning, Enez woke up to see her daughter lying next to her. She looked into Amara’s brown eyes and smiled when she saw the love that filled her daughter’s face. Enez said with a smile, “Honey, it will all be over today. I am yours, and you are mine.” Enez once again made up her mind to leave Nicko. She wanted to do the things she used to do for her daughter and herself. The afternoon approached quickly.

Enez and Amara sat in the living room, watching television when they heard a knock on the door. “Who is it?” Amara said in her baby soft voice.

"Tony," a gruff voice answered. Enez walked to the door to open it. Tony stepped into the living room, "Nicko sent me here to take you to work."

Thoughts raced through her mind, "Usually, I would work on Sunday at one of the clubs, but I wanted to spend time with my baby on this day and for the rest of my days." Abruptly, she said aloud, "Tell Nicko I'm not going to work today. I'm spending time with my daughter." Tony said nothing and left.

Enez looked at Amara, "Let's get dressed and go across the street. We'll ride the go carts and play putt-putt at Al's Golf Haven." After all their activities, they were hungry. Enez said, "Amara, I'm going to cook a pot of spaghetti and meat balls." Enez always gave Nicko all of her money, and he never bought groceries for her, so she searched for change to buy dinner.

Enez and Amara were happy to be together. They walked and ran to the corner store, and it started to rain before they got back home. As they reached the top of the hill, she saw Nicko's car. He noticed them and reversed to the end of the driveway to pick them up. They got in the car, and he took them home.

Enez walked to the kitchen to put the groceries away as Nicko followed her. He asked, "Why didn't you go to work when I sent my brother to pick you up?"

She stared around dully, looking for empathy. "I wanted to spend time with my daughter." He walked closer to her and hit her in the stomach, knocking her to the kitchen floor. He kicked her like she was a soccer ball, and he the athlete, reaching for a field goal.

With each kick, Enez heard Amara screaming for her. Enez begged Nicko stop, "Daddy, please stop! Please stop, Daddy!" As she lay on the kitchen floor, she saw Nicko's brother in the doorway, holding her child back. She could hear the sound of her own ribs breaking within her body. Her breasts and legs were numb.

Finally, he stopped. "Get ready for work," he ordered.

Painfully, she climbed the stairs and went to her bedroom. Amara stood in the doorway, crying.

Nicko gruffly said, "If you don't hurry up and get ready, I'll beat you again in front of your daughter."

"Okay," she said slowly. Enez got dressed for work as quickly as she could, afraid he would hurt her again, or worse, harm her daughter. Nicko dropped Enez off at work and left with Amara.

In the club, she looked at herself in the mirror that covered the walls. On stage, her body started to turn black and blue from her neck to her ankles, but the colored lights helped conceal some of the bruising. No one mentioned her emotional distress or the bruises on her body, perhaps because it was not the first time. It was painful to dance, but she knew Nicko would beat her again if she did not give him what he wanted. The pain was unbearable after she had danced long enough to make one hundred dollars. She called a cab to go home.

The cab driver was familiar to Enez. As she crept inside the cab, the driver looked at her with pity. The short, slim guy with a bald head helped Enez get into the back seat. He looked at her from the rearview mirror, "***Seek ye first the Kingdom of Heaven…and the burden will be light.***" The cab ride was quiet as she thought about the cabby's message. As they arrived, he said, "This one is on me. "He parked the cab at her front door and escorted her in. No one was home, and Enez took a hot shower and fell fast asleep.

It was yet autumn. The leaves had turned a beautiful orange, brown, and yellow, falling like rain drops from the sky. Amara lived with Enez's mom, and she did not spend any time with Enez. Most of the furniture in Enez's apartment had been moved to Nicko's house. She was about to be evicted from her home, and the electricity had already been cut off. Her body was worn and torn from the constant beatings and the long hours she worked.

One day, she arrived at her mother's doorstep, looking for monetary refuge. Enez was too tired to work on the street the night before and had no money to give to Nicko. She was distraught. She had no place to live, and she had been fired from her job at Donny's.

The Prodigal Daughter

Enez and her mother sat in the living room, discussing Enez's life when they heard a knock at the door. As her mother opened the door, Nicko stood at the doorway. She said aggressively, "She don't want to go with you."

Enez heard him say, "Tell her I said come out now." Enez walked to the door.

"Come on, baby, I need you to come home. I've been looking for you all night. You had me worried."

Her mother looked at him with hatred in her eyes, "Get off my porch right now."

He looked back at her, and the whites of his eyes burned with anger. "B…., do you know who you are talking to?"

Enez stepped in between them to keep him from hitting her mom. He pulled on Enez's arm as her mother grabbed the other arm. Enez went with him to keep him from hurting her mother. She did not know what else to do. Her self esteem, courage, and pride were all stripped from her. He was all she knew. She walked away with him, leaving her mother standing in the doors of defeat.

As she reached the front door, she saw Tony in the back seat of the car. Enez sat quietly, while Nicko drove down South Parkway towards his home. As he crossed the interstate, he punched her in the stomach. She curled over in pain. "Where is my money?" he asked her.

With tears in her eyes, she said "Daddy, I don't have any money." As they approached his house, he hit her in the stomach once again before she could shield herself. Nicko had hit Enez so often that she jumped if he merely raised his hand. If he yelled and used obscene language, she knew a hit would follow somewhere on her body. Inside the house on Leatherwood, he got a baseball bat and threatened to beat her with it.

Tony was nervous, "Hey man, the police may be coming. Just make her go to work on the hooker track." Nicko agreed and decided not to beat her again. Instead, he made Enez walk the streets of Midtown in Memphis. The body which consumed her spirit was in a physical mess and so was her spirit. Nicko drove Enez to the corner of Cleveland and Jefferson to work the hooker track even though she was in great pain. It had only been seven days since he had beaten her profusely.

There was a hospital at the corner, and Enez admitted herself into the emergency room. The x-rays showed that she had fractured ribs and head injures caused by severe blows. A friend of her mother's was at the hospital, visiting a sick friend, when she heard a doctor call Enez's name and asked to see Enez. A nurse asked her, "Would you like a visit from Latisha Farmer?"

Tears fell from her eyes, "Yes, please, tell her I am in here."

Mrs. Farmer walked into Enez's room and smiled, "***My God shall supply all your needs according to his riches in glory by Christ Jesus.***"

Enez said, "I want to believe in Him. I want a better life, but I don't know how."

"He has been here for you all the time, waiting on you to allow Him into your life. He wants to direct you from the darkness of your life to His Marvelous Light."

"I am blind. I can't see. My eyes are filled with hurt and shame. I wander in the wilderness of sin. How can God want somebody like me?" Enez asked sadly. Mrs. Farmer prayed with Enez, and Enez cried and cried.

Without health insurance, she was released from the hospital the very next day. The only thing she thought of was returning to Nicko. A week later, her mother filed a petition to take Amara into temporary custody. "Enez, maybe if I take Amara, you'll come home and straighten out your life for your child," she said in her aggressive voice. Enez wrestled with a situation she thought she had no control over.

Finally, the court date for temporary custody arrived. Nicko dropped her off at the courthouse. She was nervous, but she knew it would be best for her mother to take control of Amara's life. She walked to the red, brick building and entered through the glass doors. At the custody hearing, she noticed Amara's father, her mother's cousin, and her mother seated in chairs against the walls. Enez stopped to talk to Aaron. "I am so sorry to do this, but I'm afraid that if she stays with me, something might happen to her. Let my mom take care of her. I am sure you and my mother can work things out in her best interest."

She signed the papers without hesitation. She said goodbye to everyone and walked outside to wait on Nicko.

* * *

Longing for Patience

Enez did not know anything about being patient or waiting upon God. She lived in the here and now. She only thought about finding a place to rest her head, not her soul. She did not realize there was a resting place for her at the foot of the Cross. An older woman told her long ago, "There is rest for the sinner, when Jesus died on the Cross and sat on the right hand of God, our sins were purged, and we rest with Him." Enez would not listen when the older woman also quoted, "***Come unto me, all ye that labor and are heavy laden, and I will give you rest.***"

Her heart sought physical rest and what she thought man could give her. She stayed with Nicko every night in a hotel, with no rest. Her mother had given up on her, and Enez had given up on herself. She started dancing in the clubs again.

Enez did not know God, and she lived in fear. One night, one of the dancers at the club told her, "I saw Nicko's wife. Shirley is having a baby." Her heart fell to her stomach, and she could not manage her emotions. She ran from the club, intent on finding Nicko. When she finally reached him by phone, she asked, "Nicko, is Shirley pregnant?"

"No, she's not having a baby," he lied.

She wanted to be satisfied with Nicko's lie, but she knew better. Later, he picked her up from the club, and they rode around. He explained, "You know me and my wife have sex. Did you really think I'm not having sex with her? What are you thinking?" Still, Enez had sex with Nicko. He was gone before morning. She assumed he went home to his wife and son.

One night, he turned her on to powder cocaine. Up until then, Enez had not gotten into the drug scene. She was always working or too tired to think about drugs. Nicko picked her up from work, "Hey baby, we're going to stop by my oldest brother's house for a few minutes before I take you to the hotel." She nodded in agreement.

They entered the house, and several men were in the back room. Nicko escorted Enez to a bedroom and turned on the television. In a few moments, Betty, Tony's woman, walked in and waved hello. Nicko pulled out a glass pipe, a wire with cotton wrapped around the tip, and an empty bottle of mouthwash. "Baby, I want you to try this," he said to Enez as he put a small white ball on top of the pipe. "Hold the hole on the side, and I'll hold the torch." He dipped the cotton-tipped wire into the bottle of mouthwash and lit it with his lighter.

Enez obeyed. She pulled from the glass stem, covering the hole as he had instructed, and a cloud of white smoke filled the inside of the bowl. He snatched it away from her and continued the process himself. She had no idea that she had just smoked cocaine.

Nicko left the room and was gone for hours.

Just before the break of dawn, Nicko woke Enez from her sleep. "Hey baby, you gotta go get some more money. I don't have money for your room."

She had given him $300 that night, so she looked at him in anger. She knew the hotel would put her things out if she had not paid the rent by noon. She freshened herself and rushed to make the rent money. Nicko left her on her own. She made her rent money and took a cab to work.

****

Enez became pregnant. She felt very weary, and she wanted to turn her life around. She asked her cousin, Joe, to protect her from Nicko. Joe lived in their great aunt's family home. Enez and her aunts sat on the porch when Joe arrived.

"Hey Joe," she said as he entered the screen porch.

"Hey girl, what's up with ya," he smiled.

"Joe, I need your help. I'm pregnant. I've saved some money to get my own place, but I need protection."

"Protection from? No, let me guess. Nicko."

"Yes," she admitted sadly. "I found an apartment near here. The resident manger didn't do a background check because she knows me. But it's near Nicko's house."

"And you really think he's going to leave you alone, and you him?"

"All I can do is hope for the best. I don't want to live in and out of hotels any more. Will you please help me?" A tear fell from her eyes as she pleaded.

"When are you moving into your apartment, Enez?"

"In two days. It's a two-bedroom apartment with a huge kitchen and living room, the Sillett Apartments. I already have my bedroom and den furniture and kitchen pots and pans. I have everything I need to move."

Over the next two days, Enez avoided Nicko, and Joe helped her move into the new apartment. Nicko walked around the apartment complex as she unloaded her clothes from Joe's car. She heard his voice.

"What's up?" he reached over to touch her face. She moved away from him, saying nothing. Her heart began to beat faster, and she moved closer to the door of her apartment as her cousin walked out.

"Man, what do you want?" Joe asked.

"That's my woman. Who are you?" Nicko asked sharply. He looked at Enez, "Isn't that right, baby!"

Enez did not reply as she walked into the apartment. She heard her cousin say to Nicko, "I'm her cousin, Joe. She said she doesn't want to see you again. Did you know she's pregnant?" There was silence, and then she heard the door close.

"Joe, what did he say when you told him I was pregnant and didn't want to see him anymore?"

"Enez, he walked away saying nothing." Joe plugged the radio into the electrical socket near the hallway, and they both sang along to a tune by Al Green.

A few weeks passed. Enez had not seen Nicko, and she was feeling safe but cautious. She arrived home from work and stood at her apartment door to unlock it. Suddenly, Nicko grabbed her and pushed her inside. She tried to run to the bathroom to lock the door, but he caught her. She jerked away and tripped on the edge of the bathtub. Nicko grabbed her by her hair, dragging her to the bedroom to rape her. When he finished, he grabbed her purse and searched for money. "Where is the money, Enez?" he asked angrily. Before she could answer, he found it and put the bills in his pocket as he walked out the front door.

Her body was numb as she staggered from the bed to lock the front door. Suddenly, a sharp pain in her abdomen caused her to bend over. The pain became more intense as she walked. Blood trickled down her leg as she walked to the bathroom. She knew she had just miscarried her two-month pregnancy. She rocked in her chair, moaning from the rape and loss of her unborn child. A night passed before she called Joe to take her to the hospital. When she was released from the hospital, she went to Joe's house to heal her broken heart and body.

Three days passed, and Enez decided that she needed to go home to face her fate. As they neared her apartment, she saw a broken window and a screen placed over the window. Joe parked the car. Enez stayed in the car while Joe walked to the apartment. Joe unlocked the door and walked through the apartment to find no one inside. "Come on in, Enez. No one is in here."

Enez walked in and searched her bedroom. She looked in a corner of the closet where a paper bag with drug paraphernalia had been kept. The empty bag was on the floor, and she knew that Nicko had broken in. Other valuable items were still there. Enez and Joe cleaned up the glass, and Joe promised to stay with Enez for as long as she needed him to. As time passed, Nicko slowly made his way back into Enez's bed and her heart. She told Joe she could make it on her own now, and she began smoking crack cocaine with Nicko.

Joe knew Nicko had come back, and he had a few words to say to him. "Nicko, I know you're seeing my cousin. I hope, for your sake, you'll treat her right, man," Joe said as he left the apartment for the last time.

After several weeks, Nicko convinced Enez to give up her apartment to his brother and woman. Tony and Betty stayed at the triplex on Cardington Street. They were selling cocaine, and the place was hot for them. The police were sure to come at any time. Enez agreed to make the switch. They were to pay the rent for her apartment. Tony and his woman lived there for one month, and they also smoked cocaine. Enez lost the apartment but continued to live in the triplex with Nicko. A few weeks later, Nicko and his brothers rented the triplex to a couple.

It was the weekend, Saturday. Donny had moved her to his new club, and Enez was the only black girl working the day shift. She loved it because she had no competition. After several nigthts of not having a place to rest her head Nicko decided he would bring Enez to his house to live with him and his wife. "Baby, I'm going to move you into my house on Leatherwood. You'll have the efficiency above the garage for a while with my brother." Enez agreed with him, as she had always done. Enez believed his wife knew about the arrangements, since she knew her husband was a pimp.

One day, Enez came downstairs. As she walked through the garage, she noticed all her stored furniture from the apartment was gone. She entered the kitchen to find Tony, David, and Shirley preparing breakfast. Enez looked around for Nicko.

Suddenly, Shirley came after her with a knife, and Nicko immediately stepped between them. Nicko and Enez walked back to the efficiency above the garage. He explained that his wife did not know Enez had moved into the house, and he would take care of everything. She never had a chance to ask him about her furniture. She thought to herself, "What point would that have made?"

David slept in the bed, while Nicko and Enez slept on the floor near the fire place. It was a cold winter in 1982. Enez continued to live in Nicko's house, and Shirley moved to her mother's house until the baby was born. Enez occasionally smoked cocaine with Nicko, Tony, and Betty.

The night Shirley's baby was born, Enez was upstairs in her room. Shirley had come to the house to be with Nicko while she was dilating. Enez could hear a commotion going on in the driveway from the bedroom window. Nicko was in the house, getting high with his associates. She heard Shirley yelling, "It is time for me to have the baby." Her brother, Jerrod, said, "Man, let's go." Nicko did not move. As Enez watched from the bedroom window, she saw Shirley and Jerrod leave. Soon, she fell asleep.

At dawn, Enez walked downstairs to see Nicko still sitting at the dining room table, and his associates were gone. Suddenly Nicko's brother-in-law came into the house. "You have a little girl," he told Nicko. "You need to go see her."

Nicko was nervous. He turned to Enez. "Go to the corner store and buy a bottle of Jerri Curl lotion for me."

Enez obeyed. When she returned, he looked at the bottle of lotion and said, "This is the wrong brand." He pushed her in the closet and began to beat on her. When he finished, she ran upstairs and cried. Shirley still had not moved back into the house, and Enez continued to live upstairs. Nicko had left, and she thought she was alone. Later that morning Enez came downstairs to take a bath.

Suddenly, Shirley rushed into the bathroom with a pot of almost boiling water. Enez jumped out of the bathtub. Shirley tried to fight her, but Enez refused. Eventually, Shirley pulled up a dining room chair and sat in the hallway. She instructed Enez on what to tell Nicko. "Tell him you want to move from this house." Enez could not tell Nicko anything – perhaps just like Shirley. Finally, Shirley left the house, and Enez wrapped a towel around herself and went upstairs.

A few days passed. Nicko picked Enez up from work. She noticed her clothes lying on the back seat as she sat quietly waiting for him to explain, "Baby, you know my wife just had a baby, and she wants to be home with our baby. She is my wife." Enez was not surprised. She continued to look at him as he spoke, "I have rented a room for you at a house off McLemore. You'll like it. I'm going to take you there now." Enez did not say a word. She was happy to leave Nicko's house. He drove her to her new place, and she was happy about it although his severe drug habit would not allow him to be responsible for her rent. Shirley and their children returned home.

One early morning hour, the rent lady came knocking, and Enez was hungry for food. She walked to Nicko's house, where she saw many cars parked in the driveway. Shirley answered the door. "What you want?" she asked angrily.

"I need to see Nicko, please."

"He is busy right now."

Nicko's brother, David, came to the door just before Shirley closed it. "Hi Enez, what's up?"

"I need to see Nicko. The rent lady is asking for her money. Last night, Nicko said he would pay it. And I am hungry," she spoke bitterly, as she shivered from the cold wind.

"Well, you stay right here. I don't want his wife to hurt you."

Enez stood outside, hungry and shivering. David said, "Nicko said come on in the house."

She entered the kitchen, and David led her to the middle bedroom. Nicko sat on the floor, smoking cocaine with Big D, Honey Boy, and other men she had never seen. She looked at him as a tear fell from her face. She turned to walk away with an aching heart. The cold wind froze her tears, and the hunger pains from her stomach were now growls. Once again, she was out on the street with no place to go. The landlord put Enez out that afternoon. She was two weeks behind on the weekly rent, so she had to move back into the house on Leatherwood. Nicko's wife was not happy about that situation. Shirley moved back in with her mother.

A few weeks passed, and the Christmas holiday approached. Enez did not have gifts to give to her daughter, and she was ashamed. She did not try to communicate with her family. On Christmas Eve, she walked downstairs and saw Nicko and his wife with their new baby girl and son, enjoying their Christmas together. She thought about what he told her earlier that day, "Why don't you go over to your mother's house to see your daughter?"

"How can I, Nicko? I have no gifts. I'm ashamed to see my family and pretend like everything is alright."

Enez did not bother Nicko and his family. She went back upstairs and cried in her pillow until she fell asleep. Morning came, and it was Christmas day. She got up, thinking she would find him up and about, but he was asleep in bed with his wife.

Enez had no place to go, no family to call her own. Shirley soon moved back with Nicko permanently to be with her family. It was time for Enez to move out again.

* * *

The Prodigal Daughter

Peace

She longed for Peace but was ashamed to find it. The triplex was empty from tenants, and now she had a rent-free place to live. Enez was fired from her job. She had no family, low self-esteem, and no interest in living. She occasionally worked the streets, standing on a corner to earn money for Nicko's ever increasing drug habit. He smoked cocaine every day. She was tired of her life and was seeking a way out.

Enez had not seen Nicko for several days, but she knew he was around, smoking cocaine. She paced the house, filled with thoughts of leaving him. Suddenly, she thought, "I can phone my friend, Madelyn. She will help me get out of this situation." Enez searched the drawers and closets for change. She found some coins in an old coat, hanging in the closet. Her heart beat quickly as she walked to the corner store to use the pay phone.

While she was dialing Madelyn's number, she noticed a pamphlet near the phone. She picked it up as Madelyn answered, "Hello."

"Hi, Madelyn. This is Enez," she replied with a crack in her voice. "I'm in trouble. Will you please help me? I need to get away from him."

"Yes, Enez where are you?"

"I'm at Mississippi and South Parkway."

"Enez, you're near my home. If you get here, I'll take you were you need to go."

"Okay, Madelyn. I need to get a few items from the house, and I'll walk to yours," Enez said in relief. They both hung up the phones without saying good bye.

She looked at the pamphlet in her hand. She saw a picture of Jesus on the Cross on the cover. Inside, it read, "***Peace is not something the Lord left for us in a package. Peace cannot be put into a package or a book…now in Christ Jesus ye who sometimes were far off are made nigh by the blood of Christ. For He is our Perfect Peace.***"

She walked faster to the house, as tears rolled down her small face. Before she reached the house, she saw Nicko and his brother-in-law driving in the wrong direction on the one-way street. He parked his car and followed her into the house. When they reached the bedroom, he saw her packed suitcase on the bed. "B…., where do you think you are going?"

Before she could answer, he hit her, and she fell against the wall. His tennis-shoed foot came down and struck her a vicious blow. Pain exploded along the side of her head. She passed out for a moment, but she could hear his voice, "You better not pass out, or I'll hit you again. Get up from the floor and walk outside to my car."

Enez stumbled to the car, groping the air with her hands to find her way. Both her eyes were swollen shut. He pushed her inside the car down to the floorboard. She lay in pain, while he continued to beat and kick her. She heard him say to the driver, "Take her to Leatherwood." Next, she heard the motor roaring up the steep driveway. With the engine still running, he said angrily, "B…, get out of the car."

Once again, she groped the air, feeling her way up the stairs. At the top of the stairs, Nicko kicked her inside the room where she had once lived. He karate kicked her over her entire body until he grew tired. She lay whimpering on the carpeted floor in a fetal position. He forced her to stand as he pushed her into the half bathroom and closed the door. She lay on the concrete floor by the toilet, and she could hear him pushing the refrigerator against the door. Enez lay on the floor for hours without moving, listening intensely to the sounds outside of the room. She could hear music, people talking, and the sound of water hitting against the car in the driveway.

Before the sun set, he came to her prison and released her. He forced her to lay on the bed next to him. "Look at what you made me do to you." He blamed Enez for beating on her. She fell asleep in his arms. It was nightfall before they woke up, and he was trying to get her out of his house before his wife came home. When they reached the kitchen, David's wife entered through the back door. She looked at Enez in pity.

Nicko drove to the Dixie Queen to get them something to eat. They did not speak in the car. Nicko brought her back to the place where he had first beaten her. Enez opened the car door and slowly walked up the driveway to the house as she heard the sound of his car pull away.

Her body and mind were torn and she lay on the bed in pain. It was hard for her to breathe. She walked to the bathroom and looked at her reflection in the mirror through one eye. She was unrecognizable. Her left eye was closed shut. The right pupil peered from under one lid. Her face was swollen and in severe pain. As she bent over to run her bath water, she gasped from the pain of breathing. She peeled her bloody clothes from her body. It hurt to move. She stepped gingerly into the full bathtub. The warm water soothed her aching body, and she fell into a trance as she read from the pamphlet she had found at the phone booth earlier. "***We cannot think our way to peace. We can only know peace when we allow Him to do away with all enemies of peace. And when we begin fully to walk in the light as He is in the light…his blood will keep us cleansed, minute by minute of the sin of even understandable or non understandable self pity.***"

* * *

Peace, Perfect Peace

Two weeks after Enez's face healed, she was back to walking the Midtown streets for money. A new topless club, Charlotte's, had opened on the corner of Jefferson and Cleveland. Enez walked into the club one late afternoon and saw her old friend, Jane, from Donny's, standing behind the bar. Jane immediately recognized Enez, as she came from behind the bar to give her a warm hug. Jane was a beautifully shaped, white woman, with long, blonde hair. She walked with grace and pride. Her weakness was an old, rugged motorcycle biker.

"Hey Red Foxx, how are you doing?" she asked with a smile. It was dark inside the club, and Jane could not see the bruises that still marked Enez's face.

"You know, girl, I'm okay," Enez was glad that someone thought enough of her to even ask.

Jane walked back to the bar as Enez followed, "You know, I'm looking to hire a dancer/ waitress for the night shift, but I need someone who is dependable. Are you still working for Nicko?"

"Yes, Jane. I'm living on his property too," Enez said as she reached out for the Coke Jane placed on the bar for her.

Jane took a closer look at Enez and saw that her face, arms, and hands were swollen. "Enez, you gotta get away from him. He's going to kill you. You remember the biker guy I was dating when I was working at Donny's? Well, the last time he beat me, I was in the hospital for two weeks. He smashed my skull in with his steel toed boot and broke several of my bones. He brutally beat me to where I will never have children."

Enez stared into Jane's baby blue eyes, and a tear fell from her cheek as she reached for Jane's hand.

Jane said, "I have a two-bedroom duplex I can share with you. You can work for me. But I don't want Nicko nowhere around. Don't worry about your clothes. Come home with me tonight, and while you're here tonight you can waitress for me, okay?"

Enez did not hesitate to take Jane up on her offer. She waitressed in the club that night and went home with Jane. After a few days, Enez had earned enough money to buy a bed for her room. She was happy to be able to make money and keep it all. She was no longer afraid that Nicko would find out where she was working or living. She had finally taken responsibility for herself, she thought.

One night, Nicko hid in the dark as he waited for her outside the club. The club had closed for the night, and Jane, her male friend, and Enez walked to the car. They noticed a car parked in the dark. As the car door opened, they saw a familiar silhouette walking quickly towards them. In the dim light, Nicko called out Enez's name. She recognized his voice, and her heart began to beat fast. She was nervous as he walked closer to her. Jane pulled out her pistol and commanded him to stop.

He stopped walking and spoke to Enez, "What are you doing, baby? I need you to come home. I won't hit you anymore. I'm going turn myself in to my parole officer. I'm going to drug rehab. You'll see."

"Enez, get in the car," Jane instructed Enez. "Don't step any closer," she said to Nicko.

Jane's friend told Nicko, "Man, look, I don't know the story but the ladies don't want to be bothered, okay? So, let's all leave quietly."

Nicko silently returned to his car, and they caught a glimpse of his headlights as he disappeared into the night. Enez sat in the front seat next to Jane, thinking of another time Nicko had tried rehab.

They were living in the triplex. Enez was in the house with Nicko, when his wife came over one afternoon with Nicko's cousin and his mother's sister. Nicko was not surprised when he answered their knock on the door.

His cousin walked in, as his wife and aunt stood in the driveway. "Man, are you ready to go?"

Nicko looked anxiously at Enez, "I promised Shirley I would go to rehab. Her job's insurance is paying for it."

Enez was not sad about his decision. In fact, she looked forward to the break. Nicko packed a few belongings and joined his wife outside. Shirley looked at Enez with hate in her eyes.

A few days later, Enez came home from work and noticed the television was on. She did not remember leaving it on before she went to work. Something moved in the closet. The door opened, and Nicko stood to greet her, "I thought you were the police! I couldn't do it." He told Enez, "They were taking us to a drug meeting in the area, and I just walked out to come home."

Now, Enez laughed as she thought about how ridiculous Nicko had looked coming out of the closet. Jane asked, "What are you laughing about?"

"Just had a thought." Enez did not want share her thoughts.

Nicko did not try to pursue Enez for a few weeks, and she and Jane had become very good friends. Later, Enez would find out that Jane was doing more than managing a club. Jane took frequent short trips to Florida, and Enez kept the house in order while Jane was away. Jane did not elaborate with Enez about her out-of-town trips. Jane's last trip to Florida was supposed to last a couple of days, but a week passed and then another before Enez finally heard from Jane. Enez rushed to the phone as she got out of the shower. "Hello," Enez answered.

"Hello, Enez." Jane did not sound very happy.

"What's the matter, Jane?"

"I can't talk long, but I'll discuss things with you when I return home. A few people will come by the house to gather some items for me. I hate to take the car from you, but I need to sell it. I have someone who will help you pay my share of the bills. I'll call you back another time. Take care, and I'll see you later." Before Enez could respond, she heard a dial tone.

Enez thought this was a good opportunity to file petition to gain permanent custody of her daughter. She now had a nice home for Amara to live in, and she was no longer with Nicko. But it was not meant to be. As time would have it, Enez started seeing Nicko again. He came to the club with his friends one night just before it closed. Nicko wore a suit, white mink coat, and a brimmed hat – he had not sold everything he possessed. Nicko looked good to Enez. He and his friends sat at a table, and Enez was their waitress. As she returned with the drink orders, Nicko gazed at her with his soft, brown eyes. "Hey baby, are you ready to come home now? Stop all this craziness. You know you're my baby, and I miss you." Enez smiled at him and gave him her phone number. He called the next morning, and she invited him over for breakfast. The relationship started all over again. It was not long before Nicko was spending nights with her and demanding her money.

Two months passed before Enez heard from Jane again. "Enez, I heard Nicko has stayed with you at my house. I'll be home in two days, and you'll need to find another place to live. I am moving in with Sam, my boyfriend."

Enez's heart sank, and she was silent. "Oh no, where will I go? I have filed a petition for custody of my daughter, and now I don't have a place of my own to live," she thought to herself. Aloud, she said to Jane, "Okay, I will find a place."

True to her word, Jane came home two days later. She walked in and found a comfortable seat in the living room, facing Enez. "Enez, I've been in jail for the past two months. I got caught transporting drugs. Have you found a place to live?"

"Yes, Jane, I have somewhere to go". Enez did not want Jane to be concerned about her. "When will you move in with Sam?"

"The end of the week." Jane walked to her bedroom and lay across her bed and fell asleep.

By Friday, Jane had moved from her house, and Enez had rented a room for the weekend. She and Nicko were still involved with each other, and she no longer had control of herself. She was once again dependent on him to take care of her with her money. She did not realize the utilities had been turned off on Leatherwood, and his wife had moved out again until one night there was no rent money for the next day. Enez followed Nicko to the house on Leatherwood to discover that the electricity, water, and gas had all been turned off.

The court date for petition of custody arrived, and Enez was not prepared. She dressed nervously, knowing that things had not improved in her life. Still, she hoped for the possibility that she could win her daughter back. Nicko dropped her off at the courthouse. She stood alone, filled with shame and guilt. She walked into the court room. The presiding judge was a man. Her mother and her mother's cousin sat together, and Enez took her seat on the bench across from them. The bailiff called out Enez's name and her mother's name, and they walked together to face the judge.

"I see you are here today to gain custody of your daughter."

"Yes, your honor, I am,"

"Do you have a place to live?"

"Yes, your honor, I have a residence."

"And what is your address?"

She gave Nicko's address to the judge.

He looked at her angrily, "Is that Johnny Nelson's house?"

Enez looked surprised. "Yes, sir."

"Do you honestly think I am going to award you custody of your daughter to live in the Nelson's house?" he asked angrily. "Mrs.Brown, I hereby give you full custody. You are no longer a temporary custodian of said child Amara Nichole Stone." He looked at Enez, "To you, I hereby state your petitioned denied."

Enez could not look at her mother. She did not blame her mother for what had happened. She knew she had lost custody of her daughter because of her own fault. Enez had just lost all parental rights to her daughter. She left the courtroom, feeling all hope was gone forever.

Enez went back to work at another of Donny's clubs, Shirley's. Nicko was seeing Janice Bond Cupper, a woman from his past before he was imprisoned and before his parent's death. The triplex where Enez had lived was sold, and the utilities were still off on Leatherwood. She worked long hours to support their crack cocaine addiction. Some days, Nicko pawned his wife's car and then showed up at Enez's job for money to retrieve the car.

One winter day in 1982, Enez was arrested for Public Lewdness for dancing in a topless club and allowing men to touch her body while she touched theirs. She was working the Pink Garter that night. The day shift was changing over to night shift when the police came in with arrest warrants. The women sat in the dressing room as the officers called out the names on the warrants. Enez sat nervously, hoping her name was not on the list. She had not yet changed into her street clothing. The officer called her, "Red Foxx, come with us."

She was escorted to the paddy wagon, wearing only her dancing costume, and TV cameras and newspaper reporters filled the parking lot. Enez looked around and saw Nicko watching as she entered the paddy wagon. Although he immediately posted her bond, it took several hours for her to get out of jail.

She lived once again from motel, to hotel, to inn. Nicko came to her job many times to retrieve her money. She would only have enough left to the pay the club. She was alone, hitch hiking rides, and spending her nights on Leatherwood in the cold. Occasionally, Nicko sent his brother to pick her up from work. This night, Enez walked out of the club when her shift ended, and she saw Nicko's brother in a familiar car in the parking lot. He rolled down the window, "Enez, Nicko told me to pick you up tonight."

She walked her tired body to the car and noticed Betty sitting in the front seat. She got in the back seat as she asked, "Where is Nicko?"

"I don't know, but he told me to take you over to our friend's house to stay the night. We know a man who has an empty apartment. He's going to let us stay there until his broad is released from jail."

Enez did not ask any more questions. Soon, they were inside the apartment. A man she did not recognize was asleep on the couch in the living room. Tony and Betty retired to bed. Enez went to an empty room and found a blanket in the corner. She made herself a pallet on the floor to sleep.

When she woke the next morning, the house was empty. Everyone was gone. The doors were locked, and she could not get out. She was about to panic when Nicko opened the door.

"Why would you lock me in this apartment?" she asked him angrily.

"I told Tony to make sure he locked you in here so you can't leave. Where is my money?"

She gave him her money. He pushed her to the floor and lay on top of her, roughly pulling her panties off. She did not resist him because she knew what the consequence would be. Afterwards, she bathed, and Nicko left without saying good bye. He locked her in the house again.

Nicko arrived later to take Enez to work. She was sitting in the living room when he opened the door. "Why aren't you ready for work?" he asked angrily.

"I am ready, Nicko." Enez knew not to say anything else for fear of inciting his anger. She gathered her work bag, stepped out and saw Janice sitting in the front seat of the car. Her heart skipped a beat, her legs became very weak, and she wanted to run away from Nicko. Enez did know of Janice's appetite for cocaine and drug dealers. She dated a dealer from Florida, a married man with an appetite for rock cocaine. One day, Janice and the dealer went out of town, and he died in a fatal car accident. Janice was left with his antique Cadillac and the Memphis apartment he rented.

Now, Nicko said, "Baby, this broad got big connections with some Florida drug dealers. I want to get in that connection. You know I gotta stick around her, so I will be at her apartment for a while. You just keep doing what you're doing."

Another evening, Enez rode to Janice's apartment with Nicko. Nicko said, "Baby, you will stay here with me tonight." Enez saw Janice, Nicko's son, and Janice's sister, Lynn, in the house. Enez sat in the living room, and Nicko called out to her.

"Yeah Nicko?"

"Come here. I got something for you."

She walked into the room to see Nicko smoking cocaine from a glass pipe. Janice came from the bathroom, followed by her sister. Nicko put some cocaine on the pipe for her. She inhaled and exhaled the smoke once and refused to do it again.

The night was late, and the cocaine was gone. Nicko decided everyone should go to sleep. Janice gave Enez a gown to wear to bed. It fit her shapely body perfectly. Janice prepared a place on the floor for Enez to sleep next to the bed. Nicko fell asleep on the floor with Enez. Later on in the night, Enez turned over to hold Nicko, but he was not there. She looked up to the bed and saw that he was asleep with Janice. Enez got up from the floor and slipped in the bed under Nicko. He held her throughout the night. The next morning, Janice was very angry to see Enez and Nicko in the bed together.

During the winter months, Enez slept in a cold house with no running water or heat. The neighbors allowed her to use their water hose to flush the toilet and take a cold bath. Other days she rented a room before Nicko could find her. If he found her without money, he severely beat her. Nicko continued to live with Janice, until their cocaine addiction caused her to lose her apartment.

It was spring time. Enez sat in the driveway of Leatherwood, looking for Nicko to show up soon. She had given him all her money the night before. She was hungry and needed a bath. Her aunts had always welcomed her to stay with them. On this cool, breezy day, Enez made a decision to do just that. She gathered her few belongings and walked to her aunts' house. She remembered the house from when she was a child. The red and white-frame house with the screened in porch sat near a corner on Ethlyn. Enez walked to the porch and found her Aunt Enezi, whom she was named after, sitting in a rocker.

She smiled at Enez when she saw her with her bags, "Well, I see you've had enough of that life, huh? Come on in, child. Are you hungry? I just fixed your Aunt Les some lunch, and there is plenty."

They walked inside the house. Les sat in the living room, watching television. "I knew it wouldn't be long before you would come to stay. Don't hold your head down, child. Always hold your head up, no matter what," she said with a smile.

Enez took a hot bath before eating lunch. Her aunts welcomed her unconditionally. She sat on the couch while her Aunt Enezi held her close, as a mother holds her child. A tear dropped from her aunt's lined face, and Enez fell asleep in her arms.

She still worked at the club, but now she kept her money in between the floor and the carpet at her aunts' house. Nicko was busy smoking cocaine with Janice, and he did not show up at the club, much to Enez's relief.

Aunt Les was in the last stages of cancer. Her body was weak, and she could no longer hold her urine. The last time Enez saw Les alive was as she was taken to the hospital in an ambulance. Soon after, Aunt Enezi also started having health problems, and Enez took care of her at night and some days.

On one occasion, Nicko caught up with Enez just before she got off work. He was in the car alone. He asked her for money, and she gave it to him. He dropped her off at her aunt's house and told her he would come back for her later. She waited for him until the early morning hours.

Enez walked to Leatherwood and saw Nicko's car parked in the driveway as she approached the house. The back door was unlocked, and she walked to the front bedroom to find Nicko and Janice lying in bed. Janice was fully clothed, but he was naked. Her heart raced as she touched his foot. She noticed the floor model television was gone. Nicko began to scramble for his underwear as Enez left them in the bedroom. She returned to her aunt's house.

Enez's appetite for cocaine had increased. She met a man who lived down the street from her aunts. His brother was a drug dealer, and he was a smoker/dealer. Thad visited Enez at night to cook up the cocaine while her aunt slept. Thad brought a cocaine pipe, mouthwash, and home-made torch with him, and he gave the cocaine to Enez freely. One night, she wanted cocaine and asked him for it. Thad was happy to oblige her because he wanted to make money and smoke. "Thad, I want to spend fifty-dollars," she said to him. He pulled out a bag of white powder to cook it in a spoon. When it cooked into a rock, he put it on the glass pipe for her. Enez smoked cocaine until the morning light. She knew it must have been more than what she had spent.

Over the next few days, Enez broke away from Thad. Her aunts' health had gotten worse, and she had asked for her friend from Chicago to come take care of her. Enez stopped smoking crack and continued to dance and keep her money. The woman from Chicago came to live with them.

One afternoon Enez was running errands, and Nicko came by the house. The woman from Chicago answered the door. When Enez came home, the woman said, "I just saw a demon. His eyes were fire red and his voice filled with anger. He said he was your man. I told him you were not here, and he left."

Amara spent the night with Enez. They were now awake and talking in bed when they heard a knock at the door. Enez peeked from the window and saw Nicko standing on the porch. Her aunt was asleep, and the woman from Chicago was at her friend's house. Enez opened the door and asked, "What are you doing here?"

He replied pulling her arm, "I came to get my money you been saving for me."

Enez became frightened, and Amara shouted, "Leave my momma alone," as she stood behind Enez.

Nicko looked her straight in her eyes and said, "Give me my money, or you will have some problems." As Enez gave him the money, a police car pulled up.

"Ma'am, is there a problem here?" the officer asked, looking at Nicko. "We had a call from a neighbor about this address."

Enez thought to herself, "This would be a good time to get my money back." She said, "Sir, he has three hundred dollars that belongs to me."

The officer pulled Nicko by his arm, "Do you have some money that belongs to that lady?"

Nicko said defensively, "Yeah, but she told me to come and get it."

"Well I advise you to give it back to her."

"She only gave me two fifty."

"Okay," the officer said patiently, "Give it back to her."

Nicko returned the money to Enez and left.

Nicko called Enez a week later to tell her one of their friends had passed. He wanted Enez to attend the funeral with him, and she agreed to go. The day of the funeral, he picked her up. His son was in the front seat, and Janice and Shirley sat in the back seat of Janice's antique Cadillac. Shirley got out of the car as Enez approached, "I don't want to sit in the middle," she said bitterly. Enez got in the car and sat between the two women. The women talked to Enez but not to each other. "Your hair sure is pretty, Enez," Janice said. Enez wore her hair in a long bob, accentuating her low-cut black dress. Nicko distanced himself from all of them except for Janice.

After the funeral, everyone rode in the procession. As they arrived at the cemetery, Janice pointed to the graves, "Enez, how many people do you think are dead over there?"

"Oh, maybe several hundred."

Janice said with a smile on her face, "Everybody is dead." Janice and Enez chuckled.

Nicko took Enez home after the funeral. He said, "I'll return later." This time, Nicko did return later that evening to spend time with Enez.

In the meantime, the woman from Chicago went back to Chicago, and Enez's aunt moved in with Enez's mother. Enez was alone in the house. Nicko spent several nights with Enez, and she continued to work at the club. Enez knew Nicko was still seeing Janice.

One night after he had gotten her money, he promised to come back. As she waited, she became very angry with him. Enez knew which hotel Janice and Nicko visited frequently, and she called the front desk of the hotel. She informed the clerk that people were smoking cocaine in Janice Bond Cupper's room and hung up the phone, feeling both stupid and satisfied.

She heard a knock at the screen door. Tony's voice asked, "Enez, is Nicko over here?" As she was about to open the door, Nicko came through the kitchen window, enraged. "B…, why did you call the hotel, telling those people we were smoking drugs in the room? You better be glad they didn't come to the room, b…! They called and told us someone had called. I came over here to beat your a…"

Enez ran to the bedroom, and Nicko lunged after her. She fell to the floor as Nicko kicked her face. Her nose began to bleed and swell. Nicko took her to the bathroom and held a cold towel to her nose. Suddenly his brother said, "Man, let's go. This woman is crazy." Nicko and Tony left the house. Another week would pass before she would see Nicko again.

Her relatives from out of state were visiting for the holidays. Christmas Eve came with a big surprise. The phone rang, and it was Nicko, wanting to come over. "I have a surprise for you."

She agreed to see him and waited patiently for him to come. When he arrived, he rushed to the bathroom and used it without closing the door. Enez stood in the hallway as she stared at a sandwich sack filled with white powder. Still in the bathroom, Nicko said, "Baby, go and get me that bag I bought in with me. Put on a pot of water." Enez obeyed. He finally came from the bathroom and walked to the kitchen. Enez had seen the cooking preparations for cocaine to become its rock form many times. Nicko did not stop until it was all in rock form. "Baby, get me a plate," he said with authority. She reached in the dish rack to retrieve a plate as Nicko dried the rock cocaine and cut some of it into small pieces. He tried it out for himself before giving a piece to Enez. They smoked rock cocaine until late Christmas morning.

Enez was glad that she had gone shopping for her relative's and Nicko's gifts days earlier. When the drugs were gone, she wanted more. She pulled out three one hundred dollar bills from under the carpet, Nicko was too high to be angry with her. He tried to call several drug dealers, but they were with their families. It was late in the afternoon, and Enez needed to get ready to visit her relatives at her grandmother's house because she knew they were expecting her. Enez gave Nicko his presents and said, "Merry Christmas." Nicko left as Enez wrestled with her intense high to get dressed before walking the block to her grandmother's house.

A few weeks later, her Aunt Enezi was taken to the hospital, where she spent her last days on earth. Enez's days of living at her aunt's house came to an end when her mother bought the property. "Enez I am going to buy Ethelyn.. I don't mind you living there, but you must pay rent, utilities, and I don't want Nicko living there," she said with authority. Enez knew Nicko had no other place to rest his head. He and his wife were now separated although she still allowed him to spend some nights with her on occasion. The utilities were still off at the house on Leatherwood. She continued to live at her aunt's for a few more weeks.

The Prodigal Daughter

****

It was a year before a trial date came for Enez's Public Lewdness case. Enez stood trial just after Thanksgiving. She pled not guilty. Enez was on trial with two other dancers, Linda Lewinski and Utah Undbavoc. Linda was a Southern girl from Mississippi, trying to work her way through school, and Utah' was a German exotic dancer. They also pled not guilty. Each woman hired an attorney, and Enez gave her attorney whatever money Nicko did not get his hands on.

The trial went on for several days, and the women pled their innocence and proclaimed their character to a jury. Enez saw Donny sitting in the lobby area several times. The jury of men and women did not believe their innocence and found them guilty. Enez was to return the next week for sentencing. The judge gave all the women a week to get their business in order before turning themselves in to the authorities.

Enez sought help from her grandmother. Over the next week, she stayed with her grandmother and did not call Nicko at all. Enez's sister came to their grandmother's house to drive her to the jail at 201 Poplar. She took the walk of consequence with humility. The judge ordered the sentence to be 60 days in the city jail to begin the sentence that very day. Enez looked at her sister nervously as she walked into a room to be escorted to the tunnel that led to the jail. Reality set in as she heard the sound of cell doors closing. She looked through the bars like a frightened child.

Suddenly, her daddy's sister appeared. "My dear niece, I am here to help you. Would you like to be a trustee?"

Enez had no idea what it meant to be a trustee, but she said, "Yes."

"Someone will be here to get you soon."

For the first time, Enez looked up and prayed, "***Take my yoke upon you, and learn of me; for I am meek and lowly in heart: and ye shall find rest unto your souls.***" She became a trustee on her first day, and Enez never saw the main population. Every day she spent in jail counted for two. Enez saw God's Marvelous Power working through others who loved and cared for her.

Enez called Nicko collect at his brother's house. He answered the phone, "Hello."

"Hey Nicko, you haven't been here to see me. I need some money too. Will you bring me some?"

"No, I ain't bringing you nothing." He hung up the phone.

She spent the rest of her sentence reading a Bible another inmate had given her and praying for God to help her change her life. She was to be released a few days before Christmas, but the release date was incorrect. She was delayed until the authorities made the necessary corrections to her paperwork. She saw her sister waiting for her, pacing impatiently, as she walked through a set of glass doors. They walked to the property room to retrieve Enez's property, and her mother stood in the lobby, waiting for her oldest child to walk towards freedom. God allowed Enez to see the face of a mother's love, yearning for her daughter to come home.

Inside the car, Enez exclaimed, "I'm hungry! I'd like some Kentucky Fried Chicken." Everyone in the car laughed.

"Enez, your grandmother said you can stay with her for a while, and your Aunt Lola is coming from Atlanta to take you back with her to live, if you really want to change your life."

Enez was silent as they made their way to Kentucky Fried Chicken. Her mother continued to talk after the meal was ordered. "After you get yourself straightened out, get a job, and a place to live, I'll give you custody of Amara."

Enez knew this was a wonderful opportunity, "Yes, I'll move to Atlanta," she said eagerly.

Enez's obsession with Nicko was worse than any drug addiction. The hardest thing she ever did was to leave Nicko. "***Seek ye first the Kingdom of Heaven…and the burden will be light***."

The two days before her aunt arrived were crucial. She sat in the den, watching television when she was startled by the doorbell. She was not expecting anyone, and her grandmother was out grocery shopping. She walked quietly to the front window and slowly pulled the golden drapes back to see a slim man wearing an outdated, plaid tri piece suit. He turned his head as if he had seen her peeping. It was Nicko, and she was frightened.

"How did he know I was here?" she asked herself. Enez opened the door as Nicko smiled at her through the locked screen door. Nicko's oversized body was now a skeleton. His cheeks were sunken into his face, and his beautiful, brown eyes were bulging.

"Hey baby, how are you?" he asked, looking into her eyes.

"I am okay, Nicko, but I really don't want to talk to you. I was in jail for 30 days, and you didn't give me any money or even visit me. As a matter of fact, you said you had nothing for me. I know why you're here, Nicko. I don't want to live like that anymore. I'm through smoking crack." Enez did not give Nicko a chance to reply as she closed the door.

Enez aunt arrived, and the Christmas and New Year holiday passed without any problems. The day before Enez was to leave, Nicko tried once again to get Enez to return to him. He called her grandmother's house. Her grandmother, aunt, sister, and mother sat at the kitchen table talking while Enez packed her clothes. Her grandmother answered the phone, "Hello," Enez heard her grandmother say. After a moment of silence, she said "She is not available." Enez's grandmother slowly placed the phone on its cradle and returned to the table trembling.

"Momma, what happened?" Enez's mother asked.

Her grandmother looked at Enez, who now stood in the hallway. "That man just called me a b…" Enez apologized for his outburst before she returned to the bedroom to complete her packing.

She was awakened by the morning sunshine coming in through the window adjacent to her bed. She lay in bed for a moment, excited about her new life. She smelled bacon frying and coffee brewing. Enez jumped from bed and walked swiftly to the kitchen.

"Good morning, Momma Hattie," she said with enthusiasm.

"Good morning, Enez. This is your day, honey. I hope you really get your life together this time."

Enez nodded her head as her grandmother finished the last scramble on the eggs and said, "Yes, I am really ready this time." She turned to get herself cleaned up for breakfast when she noticed a pot of grits on the stove. "Momma Hattie, I am really going to miss your grits," she said in a child-like voice.

The family kissed and hugged her goodbye as Enez waved until she could not see them any more. She and her aunt drove through the long, back country roads of Mississippi. Enez listened to jazz as she thought, "Is my burden light? Am I running from me? I can't run from me. I must put God first in my life to fall in place with Him."

It was nightfall by the time they arrived in Lithonia, Georgia. Enez had never been to her mom's oldest sister's house. The garage door opened as she drove up the driveway and parked the car. Enez's aunt said, "Here we are," as she unlocked the trunk for Enez to get her suitcase. "Don't worry about mine. I will get it in the morning. I am tired."

With her suitcase in hand, Enez walked into the basement of a beautiful, three-story house. Aunt Lola led Enez to her room. "This is your room, Enez. I'll give you a tour of the house tomorrow. Good night," she said, walking to the end of the hall. Enez heard the door close behind her Aunt Lola. She saw a bathroom across the hall from her room and decided to take a hot bath. Enez stepped into a warm bubble bath and relaxed her mind and body. When the water turned cool, she stood to turn on the shower. As she stepped out of the shower, she realized she was about to start a new life once again.

A few days after she arrived in Atlanta, she called Nicko at his cousin's house.

"Yeah," the man answered on the other end.

"May I speak to Nicko?" she asked nervously.

"I guess you can, Enez," the man replied.

Nicko answered, "Yeah what's up? Where are you?"

"I am out of town."

"Oh, you left me, huh. So why are you calling me?"

"I really don't know, Nicko. Maybe I missed you. But I think I'm better off here without you." She placed the phone on its cradle.

"The enemy is cunning, baffling, and a destroyer of life. The Lord is trying to show you how to trust, be peaceful and have comfort with Him," the preacher said in his Sunday sermon. Enez began attending Sunday service with her cousin. She wrote Nicko on several occasions, trying to convince him of God's goodness, but he never responded to her letters. Finally, she gave up and moved forward with her life.

She was determined to change her life. One cold, winter morning, Enez got dressed again to job hunt. She had already lived in her aunt's home for several weeks, and employment seemed to be scarce. She took a long walk towards the main street, away from the subdivision where she lived. She saw a "Hiring"sign in the window of Church's Chicken.

Enez walked into the fast food restaurant to apply for the job. She had seen the sign before, but she had not been interested. Now, she was desperate for a job. The woman at the front counter said, "Welcome to Church's. May I help you?."

Enez thought, "If this is all I have to do, take food orders, I can handle that." She said aloud, "Yes, I am here to apply for the job posted in the window."

Enez noticed the woman at the counter was dressed differently than the other workers. She gave Enez an application, who always kept a copy of her resume and work and school history with her. She sat at a table to fill out the application and gave the paper to the woman when she finished.

"I see you are from Memphis. I have relatives who live in Memphis. You can start work tomorrow, I see. I'd like you to start in the morning, okay? The pay is minimum wage."

Enez agreed to her start time and pay. She left, feeling like she had accomplished something. For the first time in many years, Enez was about to work a respectable job. She woke up early the next morning to walk the long distance to work. She passed a group of construction workers and waved at them as she walked to work. Enez noticed women working on the crew, directing traffic.

Her first day at work, she had to cut chicken into parts in the freezer. Enez was determined not give up as she cut the chicken with freezing hands and shivering body. The next day, the manager said, "I want you to fry chicken today. Eddie is going to train you." Enez put on a cook's apron, and Eddie went to the freezer to grab a pan of raw chicken. Eddie showed her the egg coating mixture and seasoned flour for the chicken. He dipped the chicken in the egg mixture and then rolled it in the flour. Enez watched and listened as the process continued. The following day she was on her own, frying chicken for Church's Chicken. She was not ready for this task, and Enez made a mess frying chicken. The orders came fast, and the grease was too hot. Enez decided, "This is not for me. The freezer is too cold, and the kitchen is too hot." She applied for a position across the street at Captain D's.

The following week, Enez was hired for the lunch shift at Captain D's. Every morning, she walked the same long, winding road. Every morning, the construction crew spoke to her as she passed by them.

Spring time arrived in the beautiful state of Georgia. Her shift started, and the construction crew gathered inside Captain D's to eat fish for Friday's lunch. She noticed the tall, dark complexioned man who was never as dirty as the other fellows, staring at her. Enez walked over to their table and asked, "Would you like some more tea, gentlemen?" She walked around the table to fill their glasses. As she reached for the staring gentleman's glass, he asked her, "Aren't you that gal who waves at us every morning?"

Enez nodded her head, "Sure I am. Is there anything else I can get for you gentlemen?"

They all answered, "No, I am fine, thank you."

When her shift ended, it was time for the long walk back home. As she approached the crew, she saw a man sitting inside a huge machine, waving at her to come to him. She walked toward him and noticed it was the man who had stared at her at the restaurant. He wasted no time saying, "Hey, my name is Sprig. Would you like to work for the company? We need some laborers and women on our crew. We have two white women, and we need a black woman to make three. You won't do much, but shovel a few times and flag cars for traffic when the trucks come in and out of the site. The pay and benefits are good too. They start you with fifteen dollars an hour, sun up to sun down. You have to save your money because most of the work is in the hot days, and there isn't much work during the winter. I'll talk to Sam, our foreman, if you want the job."

Enez did not hesitate, "Yes, I want the job."

Monday, Enez had a day off from Captain D's, and she got a call early that morning. "Hello, may I speak with Enezi?" she heard a deep southern accent.

"This is she."

"I am Sam. Sprig said you would like to work with our crew."

"Yes sir, I sure would."

"I'll come by and pick you up on Tuesday at eight o'clock am. We can ride to the company to get your paper work for employment. You do want to get paid, don't you? You need to get yourself a pair of work boots. Now, where do you live?"

Enez was so excited, she almost forgot her aunt's address. She said, "1922 London Cove. It's not far from the work site."

Sam arrived on time, and Enez was ready. She wore jeans, shirt, and work boots that her aunt had bought the day before. She also wore a hat to keep the sun off her face. Sam was an old, country boy.

He reminded Enez of Fred Flintstone. He chewed tobacco and kept a spit cup between his truck seats. He was quiet on the ride to the company's office. Along the way, he asked, "Are you from around here? Do you have any children? Do you have a boyfriend?" They finally arrived at the office, and she filled out all the papers before they left for the site. The midmorning sun reached its peak when Enez and Sam arrived at the construction site. Sprig stayed cool from the morning heat, sitting in the cab of the construction company's machine.

"Enez, let me introduce you to my crew," Sam said as he stuck a piece of tobacco in his mouth. She walked with him to the far end of the site, where she saw a slim, gray-haired man standing near a machine with long blades on each side. "Hey Neal, I want you to meet our new crew member."

"I hope it don't get too hot for ya," Neal said with a pleasant grin.

A nice looking man walked towards Sam. "Sam, those dump trucks are due to arrive pretty soon. Where do you want them to dump first?"

Sam answered Billy, "Tell the drivers to start on the east side first. Billy, I want you to meet our new crew member, Enez. Enez, this is Billy. Billy, take Enez and give her a flag and an orange vest to wear. Show her how to direct the traffic when the trucks arrive." Sam turned his head to spit out tobacco.

The rays from the sun shined in Enez's eyes as she saw a tall, blonde-haired woman walking towards them. “Hey Billy,” she said in a heavy southern accent “Who you got here with you?”

“This here is Enez. She is going to help you ladies out, directing traffic and other labor jobs. Enez, I’d like you to meet Bobbie.”

Enez shook Bobbie’s hand. She noticed Bobbie’s eyes were heavy with eye shadow and mascara. “Hey ya, Enez! Let me introduce you to Linda.” They walked over to the water cooler where another woman stood.

“It sure is hot,” Linda said, wiping her forehead with a handkerchief. “Your name is Enez. Billy already mentioned your name to me. I sure hope you can stand the heat, Enez. My name is Linda, if Bobbie here hasn’t already told ya. Billy told me to give this to ya,” she said as she handed Enez a flag and orange vest. “The fist truck should arrive after lunch. We will probably have two trucks today. You got it easy today, but tomorrow will be a different story.”

As the sun set to the west, Enez finished her first work day with the construction crew. Many more days turned into weeks and summer months, as she faced the scorching rays of the sun, building roads and highways. Enez deposited her money in the bank every week. Her aunt helped her find a used car, and she taught her how to drive a four-speed car. Enez made plans to move into her own apartment soon.

“Hey Enez, I have a friend in Atlanta I’d like you to meet,” Bobbie mentioned one hot summer day during lunch. "Tonnie is having a girl's set at her house tomorrow. Would you like to join us?"

"Yeah, Bobbie. That sounds like fun! What are the directions to her house?"

"Why don't you meet me at the construction site tomorrow at noon and follow me to her house?"

"Okay that sounds cool, Bobbie. Tomorrow it is!"

The next morning, Enez woke to find herself alone in the house. She ate breakfast, showered, and got dressed to meet Bobbie. As she arrived at the site, she saw Bobbie in her red Mustang, motioning for Enez to follow her.

The drive to the city was very short, and they arrived at a duplex on time. Bobbie and Enez walked to the door together. They heard a reply to their knock, "Who is it?"

"Girl, this is Bobbie."

A young pregnant woman opened the door while a two-year-old boy ran behind her. "What's up, Bobbie? And you must be Enez, from Memphis. I am Tonnie. I have a cousin who lives in Memphis on Gaither Street. Do you know the Larry's?"

Enez looked puzzled, "No, I don't think I know that family."

"Well, come on in and have a seat. Make yourselves right at home while I put Little Terence down for his nap."

Bobbie and Enez were talking about their work week when Tonnie walked in with a sandwich bag partly filled with a white powder. “Bobbie, I got some good stuff this time.”

Enez looked at Bobbie. “Enez, you snort coke?” Tonnie asked.

“I have snorted before, but I didn’t like it. It makes my sinuses drain, and I don’t like that feeling. Me and my ex-old man smoked cocaine in Memphis.”

Tonnie smiled at Enez and said, “You know, I’d like to try smoking it. Do you know how to cook it?”

Enez’s stomach churned as she remembered the cocaine high. “Yeah, I’ve watched it being cooked enough to know the process, but I never really cooked it myself.”

“Well, tell me, and I’ll try to cook it,” Tonnie said as they walked to the kitchen. The three women sat at the kitchen counter as Enez explained the process of cooking the cocaine to its rock form and what to use to smoke it in. Bobbie volunteered to drive to the nearby head shop to buy the smoking utensils. Hours passed, and Tonnie, Bobbie, and Enez smoked cocaine for several of them. Tonnie’s phone rang. It was her baby’s daddy, and he was on his way to her house. Enez and Bobbie left for home as they said their goodbyes, but there would be many more weekends and nights of smoking cocaine together.

Tonnie introduced Enez to her drug dealer, Buster. He lived in College Park. Buster was his own best customer, with his plentiful supply. Enez felt comfortable around him, even when they were alone in his apartment. Sometimes, they relaxed and enjoyed candle light and wine as they smoked their cocaine.

It was not long before Enez's savings ran low. Her aunt was ready for Enez to make it on her own, and Enez knew she had to cut all ties with her new, crack-smoking friends. She started to worry that her aunt did not know how she was spending her money. As she drove down Wesley Chapel, she saw a sign on a corner post at the traffic light. It read, "***Take no thought for the morrow: for the morrow shall take thought for the things of itself.***"

Enez cranked up her car as she noticed the morning dew on the windshield. She stared at the wiper blades as they swished back and forth, thinking to herself, "Where do I go from here?" A few days earlier, the foreman had mentioned the workload was about to slow down for the winter months. She had nearly spent all her savings on drugs, and she had to move from her aunt's house by August. She looked at her watch and drove off to work.

Enez's old habits for making money returned when times were hard. She became friends with several of the male crew members and started asking for money from them. Her savings once again grew quickly as she made plans to move from her aunt's home. Periodically, Enez talked to her daughter in Memphis. She wanted to make a new life with her daughter, and she was determined to prepare a place for them.

In August, Enez traveled the streets of Dekalb County, looking for an apartment. One Friday evening she received a phone call from the resident manager of the apartments she was most interested in. “May I speak to Ms. Brown please?”

“Yes, this is she,” Enez replied.

“This is Mrs. Johnson from the Apple Gate Town Homes. We have run your credit check, checked your references and employment, and everything looks okay. I’ve approved your move into a one-bedroom apartment the first of next month.” The woman waited for Enez to respond.

“Yes, I‘ll be ready by the first of next month. Thank you so much, Mrs. Johnson,” Enez said with excitement.

“Great. This will give us time to clean and paint the apartment for you.” Both women agreed and said goodbye.

Enez prepared for her new apartment over the next two weeks. Her aunt gave her a full sized bedroom set, and she rented living room furniture and a dinette set. Enez paid for telephone services. The electric bill came with the rent payment. She was now on her own in her new apartment.

****

The Prodigal Daughter

It was late November. She sat on her living room couch, reading the classifieds in the newspaper. Enez needed a job because the construction company hours were dwindling down as Sprig said they would, and she had no savings. As she skimmed the paper, an ad for a clerk position caught her eye. "Internal Revenue Service Center is looking for reliable, dependable workers for the tax season. If you are an interested candidate, please apply at 1049 Mason Avenue. Applications will be accepted Tues-Thurs, 8:30-1:00 and 5:00-9:00 in Atlanta." Enez looked at the calendar near the phone and thought to herself, "The first day is next Tuesday, the week after Thanksgiving."

The air was cool, and the trees were beginning to lose their leaves. The rain poured down on her umbrella as she walked in to the Internal Revenue Service Center to apply for the clerk position. It was crowded with people applying for different positions. Enez filled out the application and chose morning and evening hours before she handed it to the lady behind a table. The rain continued for several days, and Enez could not work because of it. She became lonesome and frustrated because of her situation.

In her life, there had always been this one person, one habit, one desire that she clung to doggedly. As long as she clung to these things, she could never be free. He was cunning, baffling, and a destroyer of life, yet she called Nicko in Memphis, asking him to come to Atlanta and visit. A few weeks later, he came with his cousin. They drove his cousin's eighteen wheeler truck to Atlanta. Soon after, he left to return to Memphis, and she craved his body yet again. She asked him to come back, but he refused.

Some days later, Enez heard her co-workers discussing how they were going to apply for unemployment benefits. They too were only working two days a week. Enez tried to apply for benefits also. Enez rode the bus to the unemployment office and walked in to a room filled with people. Enez stood in line, waiting to talk to the woman at the receptionist desk. She was lost in deep thought when she finally heard the small framed woman sitting behind the glass window call out, “Next please.”

“Yes, I am here to apply for unemployment benefits,” Enez said in a soft voice.

“Okay. Your name please?” the woman asked without looking up.

Enez spelled out her name, and the woman gave her a form on a clipboard, “Fill out this application and someone will call your name to interview you.”

“Thank you.” Enez said as she found a seat in the back of the room to complete the application. Almost an hour later, her name was finally called by a tall man with a beard. “Yes, I am Ms. Enezi Brown,” she patiently said.

“Follow me.” She followed the man to his cubicle. “Can I have your application, Ms. Brown?” He looked at the application as he typed into the computer system. “Ms.Brown, I am sorry to tell you, you haven't worked enough quarters to qualify for unemployment benefits."

She sat in the chair for a moment before telling him thank you for his time. On the bus ride home, Enez's mind was totally blank. She walked home slowly from the bus stop. As she entered her apartment, she felt depressed and filled with despair. She sat on her couch crying, when the phone rang. "Hello," she said after clearing her throat.

"May I speak with Ms. Enezi Brown, please?" The woman on the other end said patiently.

"Yes this is Ms. Brown."

"Hey, I am Mrs. Johnson from the Internal Revenue Service Employment Department. I would like to schedule you for an interview on Wednesday, December fifth. I have an opening after lunch. Let's see, would one o'clock be okay for you?"

"Yes one o'clock is good for me, Mrs. Johnson," They both agreed to the date and time and said good bye until then. Enez called her mother's baby sister, Gladys, who also lived in Atlanta. Gladys and her family were a great support for Enez. "Hey Gladys, guess what? The Internal Revenue just called me for an interview next week!"

Gladys said, "Enez, the job is yours. God has blessed you. Let's pray together. Lord God we know you have said nothing is impossible for you. Hear our prayer for Enez tonight as she goes for her interview at Internal Revenue next Wednesday. Bless her, Lord, that she may receive your blessing. You have said, '***Now the God of hope fill you with all joy and peace in believing, that ye may abound in hope, through the power of the Holy Ghost: Roman 15:13.***' Amen."

"I love you, Gladys," Enez said as tears rolled down her cheeks and she sniffled through the telephone receiver.

"I love you too, Enez," her aunt said. "I am going to get some rest now. I will talk to you later."

The next few days passed very quickly, and finally the day for the interview arrived. She ironed her favorite navy blue dress and scarf. Her panty hose matched her complexion, and her black pumps accented her shapely legs. Enez drove her car, which she had repaired, to the interview. She walked into the office building with confidence. "Good afternoon. My name is Enezi Brown. I have a scheduled interview appointment with Mrs. Johnson."

"Yes, I see your name on her list. If you'll have a seat, I'll let her know that you are here, Ms. Brown," the receptionist said.

Enez sat down in a cushioned brown chair near the center of the room. She picked up a magazine laying on a table next to her and began to read for a few moments before her named was called out. "Yes, I am Enezi Brown," she said with a smile. Enez walked towards a short woman, wearing a dark brown pants suit. Her hair was gray, curly, and short. She stretched out her arm to Enez as she said, "Hi, Ms. Brown. I am Mrs. Johnson. We spoke on the phone last week. Follow me to my office." Enez followed Mrs. Johnson to her office. "Have a seat, Ms. Brown." Mrs. Johnson took a seat in a black high back leather chair as she picked up a folder from her redwood desk. "Ms. Brown, you are aware this is a seasonal position? I have looked at your application. You are from Memphis and you haven't lived here very long. Let me ask how IRS can benefit from hiring you?"

Enez replied without hesitating, "I am a reliable and dependable worker. I work with urgency and diligence, and I work well with others."

"Ms. Brown, we will start training Monday of next week. I see on your application you have mentioned both shifts. We need someone for the 3rd shift, eleven to seven in the morning. The pay scale for you is nine dollars an hour. Seasonal employees do not receive any benefits. Are you able to work those hours, Ms. Brown?"

"Yes, I can work those hours," Enez said.

"Do you have any questions for me, Ms. Brown?"

"No, I have been very well informed, Mrs. Johnson."

"Well, Ms. Brown, if you don't have any questions, our interview is finished. I look forward to having you on our team."

The Prodigal Daughter

Enez was so excited about her new job. She called the construction company foreman to resign for the winter months. "Hey Sam," Enez said excitedly. "This is Enez. Sam, you know I'm not getting enough hours with the construction company, and I didn't qualify for unemployment benefits, so I applied with the IRS, and they hired me today. I need to resign until the season change."

"I believe we can work that out for ya, Enez. Look, I will be in the neighborhood tomorrow and I can bring the necessary papers for you to fill out so you will have a job come spring, okay?"

"Okay Sam, that's fine with me. What time will you come by?" Enez asked.

"Oh, around noon," Sam replied.

Her training day began on Monday. She was very excited about the job. She no longer had to endure the weather. She was casually dressed as she went to work. She waited in the lobby for the trainer along with several other people. A thick-bearded man walked from the rear of the building and began calling out names from a paper that he held in his hand. All the names had been called, and he said, "My name is Mr. Jimmy Fisher. I am your trainer for this one night training session. At the end of each table in the training room, you will find your name. The tables are marked. For example, this table is for last names that begin A-D, and so on. Take a seat please, anywhere at that table. Follow me, please," he ordered sharply.

They entered a huge room with tables and chairs in rows. At the end of each table were two boxes. Enez sat at the second table, first chair. A woman sat next to her. "Hi, my name is Doris. What is your name?"

Enez replied, "My name is Enezi, but they call me Enez."

The trainer stood in front of the room, facing everyone. "May I have everyone's attention, please? As you may know, this is only a four-hour training session. Your schedule will begin tomorrow. Some of you may have been interviewed by Mrs. Johnson or Mr. Harper. You were told this is a seasonal position, but we have made some changes, and this position is now a full-time position with benefits. Before we start our training tonight, I will pass out a second application document that you need to sign, and it will be attached to your original application." Mr. Fisher said.

Enez's training night went like a breeze. She was now a full time employee with the IRS, and she had met a very nice woman. But her flesh was still in control of her being. She constantly acted upon the desires of her flesh and not of her spirit. Although she worked hard every week, she still longed for that one desire, Nicko. She did not communicate with her daughter or her mother on a regular basis, and she distanced herself from her aunts also. Now, she was on her own. She was at the IRS for almost three moths before she made a terrible choice with Nicko.

Enez called Nicko at his cousin's house in Memphis. "Hey, is Nicko there?" she asked.

"Yeah, hold on," the voice said on the other end said. Enez heard someone call Nicko's name.

He picked up the receiver, "Hello."

"Hey Nicko, this is Enez. How are you?"

He paused before he angrily replied, "How do think I'm doing?"

Her heart dropped because she hoped he would be happy to hear from her. "I am lonesome for you, baby. I just wanted to hear your voice," she spoke quietly.

"You know when you call me, I expect you to have something for me. You got something for me? Cause I am messed up pretty bad around here. I owe my cousin for a package he fronted me."

Enez shook her head as though he could see her. "No baby, I'm sorry. I don't have anything for you, Nicko. Nicko, why don't you move to Atlanta with me and get your life together? I'll pay for your airplane ticket. You don't have to answer now. Give me a call when you are ready, "she said softly.

She continued to work for the IRS as her communication with her family became more sporadic. Her car developed transmission problems, so her friend, Doris, gave Enez a ride to work while it was being repaired. Enez rode the bus home in the mornings after work. Soon, her car was repaired.

The Prodigal Daughter

Enez sat in a hot bubble bath when the phone rang. She reached for a towel to wrap around herself, and her wet feet made impressions in the beige, thick carpet. She stood near the night stand to answer the phone, "Hello."

"I have a collect call from Nicko. Would you like to accept it?"

Enez paused. She knew his call could only mean he wanted something from her, not to ask her how she was doing. She answered softly, "Yes, operator, I will accept the call." Enez sat on her bed, waiting to hear his voice.

"Hey baby, I've decided to come to Atlanta. When can you get that ticket to me?"

Enez stared around her bedroom wildly. She was hoping he had would not take her up on her offer because she knew this was a terrible choice. She opened her mouth to reply, "I will drive to the airport and pay for a ticket from Memphis to Atlanta in the morning. Call me tomorrow afternoon, and I will have the flight schedule, okay?"

"Enez, I really need to leave," Nicko stated.

"Good bye, Nicko. I'll talk to you tomorrow."

Enez purchased his ticket the next day. As she unlocked her apartment door, she heard the phone ring. She rushed to answer it, but there was no one on the other end. A few moments later, the phone rang again. It was Nicko, and he was not calling collect.

"Did you get my ticket like I told you?"

Enez sat on the couch and took a deep breath. She thought to herself, "Like he told me."

Nicko repeated, "Did you get the ticket like I told you?"

She finally replied, "Yes, I got the ticket. I scheduled you a flight on Delta Flight 210, Gate 30, departing at 1:45 p.m. this Friday. You'll arrive in at Atlanta 2:45 eastern time. Nicko, Nicko! You can't cash the ticket in for cash, so don't even try it!"

"Woman, who do you think you talking to?" She noticed a different tone in his voice today.

"Okay, Daddy." They both said there goodbyes.

Early Friday morning, Enez went grocery shopping after work. She was excited about Nicko coming to live with her. As she drove home from the grocery store, a thought crossed her mind. "What am I doing, asking this man to live with me? He's been nothing but trouble for me for many, many years. Maybe he won't stay long, and he'll go back to Memphis."

As the time approached to pick Nicko up from the airport, she had not heard from him to confirm his arrival. She arrived at the airport, wearing a blue jean suit and her hair in a pony tail. Enez sat at the arrival gate, waiting for Nicko. His flight arrived on time, and she was excited to see his handsome body exit the terminal doors. She walked swiftly to greet him, and he looked at her with hate in his eyes. She did not acknowledge his demeanor towards her. Instead, she smiled, "Hello, Nicko. I'm happy you made it here safely."

He nodded his head in silence as they walked through the airport to the parking lot . Nicko finally spoke to Enez when they were in the car. "Why did you leave me?" he asked angrily.

Enez's heart began to race as she was all too familiar with his behavior. She wanted to turn the car around and put him back on a flight to Memphis, but she had only paid for a one-way ticket. Enez was very quiet, not wanting to make the situation worse. He sat next to her, looking straight ahead. Perhaps he knew he was in a strange city and did not want any trouble. It took almost an hour before they arrived at the apartment complex. The beautiful plants and green trees on the front lawn painted a peaceful picture.

He smiled at her, and she smiled back as she parked the car. He kissed her and said, "Hello." When they entered the apartment, Nicko escorted Enez to her bedroom, and they made love all day long until it was time for her to prepare for work. Before she left, she told him, "Daddy, there is food in the fridge and pantry when you get hungry."

Weeks passed, and Enez started smoking marijuana. Her car was giving her trouble again, but this time she did not have any transportation. Doris had started a new managerial position on a different shift. Enez missed work, and she lacked motivation to continue working a real job. She was headed towards her old behavior with Nicko. It was not long before Enez quit her job at the IRS. Now, Enez had to really get busy. Her rent, utilities, and phone bill were due. She looked in the Yellow Pages for showgirl clubs. There, she found the phone number and address to a club called the Purple Onion.

"What you gonna do, baby?" Nicko asked her as he lay stretched out across the bed.

"I'm gonna give the club a call to ask if they are hiring," Enez said anxiously as she dialed the number.

A man answered, "Purple Onion, may I help you?"

"Yes, are you hiring any dancers or waitresses?" she asked quickly.

"Yes, I am. And who might you be, Miss?"

"My name is Enez ,and I am from Memphis, looking for a job."

"Well, come see me tonight, young lady. I am Roger, the manager. Do you know where we're located?" he asked kindly.

Enez looked in her lingerie drawer and found a sexy sheer black teddy. She slipped on the top and panties, then she packed a cosmetic case with make up and her costume. Enez did not know certain sections of Atlanta, so she called a cab to pick her up before seven o'clock.

Later that night, she walked into the club and asked for Roger. "I called this afternoon about a job," Enez said.

"Oh yeah," a slim, black man said. He took Enez by the hand and escorted her to a table. "What can you do, baby?"

"I'd like to waitress." Enez had gained many pounds since her earlier days dancing in the clubs, and she did not want to expose her body.

"Well baby, you can start tonight. I see you came prepared," he said jokingly.

Enez knew the club scene all too well, and she knew how to maneuver. Enez worked until closing. She made over two hundred dollars on her first night. She arrived home in the wee morning hours, and Nicko was on the phone when she walked in the bedroom. Enez listened quietly.

"Yeah man, you say the money is good in Texas. Well, me and Enez might just come try it out. Look here, man, let me get back with you. My woman just stepped in." He laughed, then added, "I'll see you soon." He turned to Enez and said, "Hey baby, you have a good night?"

She put the money on the bed and walked to the bathroom. Enez heard Nicko counting the money as he came in behind her. She bent over to run the bath water, and did not look him in his face. He walked out without saying a word. Enez finished her bath, and walked into the bedroom to find Nicko asleep. Quietly, she walked to the patio, sat down, and listened to the birds, perched on a branch of a magnolia tree. She thought to herself. Nicko was talking to his long time acquaintance, Greg, another pimp. He was discussing leaving Atlanta to meet him and his girl in Texas. "This situation has gotten out of control again. What can I do? I have no job. Nicko is talking about moving to Texas." She walked back into the apartment and lay quietly next to him. She held him, never wanting to be without him again.

The next morning, Nicko and Enez ate breakfast at the dining room table. "Baby, we need to leave Atlanta and get us some real money. You know this square stuff ain't for us. Greg's woman, Tina, will show you around town. I want you to sell your furniture. All we need is a suitcase with our clothes. We can stay at the hotel with Greg and Tina," he said, looking in her eyes. "What's wrong, Enez? Haven't I been patient with you?" He smiled, but his voice was very serious.

Enez did not brother to answer, and she knew it was pointless to disagree with him. Enez pushed some food on her fork to finish her breakfast.

Nicko and Greg had a close familiarity that only a long acquaintance could bring. They grew up in the same neighborhood, hustling women, gambling, and selling drugs. Nicko did not worry about a place to stay. He knew Greg would make that possible for him once he and Enez arrived. Over the next several days, Enez sold her furniture and other items. She did not communicate with her relatives about moving. She packed enough clothes to fit in one suitcase. They left behind many pieces of furniture and clothing in the apartment. On Thursday morning, Enez and Nicko took a cab to the airport. They had pre-rented a car for their arrival in Texas.

A red-headed woman sat next to Enez on the plane. "Hello," the woman said while stretching her hand out towards Enez. "My name is Becky, and yours?" she asked with a wide smile.

"My name is Enez."

"Where is your trip taking you, Enez?"

Nicko sat on her other side as she answered, "We are going to Texas." The rest of the flight was very quiet. When the airplane touched down in Texas, Greg met them at the airport. Enez and Nicko went to the car rental counter to pick up the rented car.

They rode through Dallas to get to the hotel. Nicko glanced at Enez as he followed Greg in the other vehicle. "When we get to the hotel, I want you to get dressed for work. You know we can't stay in the hotel with Greg and his woman. I believe their children are with them."

"Yes, daddy," she whispered as the car made a right turn into the parking lot of the hotel. She stared at the building silently for a minute, then let herself out of the car and started for the trunk to get their suitcases.

Greg, Nicko, and Enez stood outside the hotel when Greg's daughter opened it and acknowledged her daddy. She leapt into his arms and wrapped her tiny legs around his waist. He kissed her and brought her to her feet before yelling for Tina. "Tina, why is this baby in here by herself? Didn't I tell you to keep an eye on her at all times?"

A tall, mulatto woman walked out of the bathroom and said in a heavy Hispanic accent, "Okay daddy, I won't do that again." She steadily examined Enez.

Greg cooled down suddenly. "Tina, this is Enez," he said, pointing back over his shoulder towards the door. "Listen, Tina, I want you to show Enez around the city tonight, so you need to take care of the baby and get dressed for work."

"Okay, daddy," she replied meekly. Tina did as she was told. While Tina fed the baby, Enez took a shower. Greg and Nicko left the hotel room

Enez stood in the warm shower, thinking to herself, "Here I am again. There is something about evil, I feared no evil. '***Yea, though I walk through the valley of the shadow of death. I will fear no evil…***'" Enez felt refreshed after the hot shower.

Tina openly watched Enez get dressed. "You and I might have to ride downtown near the hotels," she said in a quiet voice.

Her words caused Enez to turn around and stare at Tina. "That's fine with me, Tina. I don't know the city, so I am with you." She ran her hands down her body, straightening the blouse and mini skirt she wore. Tina put her baby to sleep and showered before Greg returned. Greg and Nicko entered just as Tina was putting her high heeled shoes on.

"Are you ready, baby?" Nicko asked.

"Yes, daddy, I'm ready to hit the street," Enez said as she grabbed her purse.

"I stopped by the store and got condoms for you, baby."

She opened the box and put the individually wrapped condoms in her purse.

Greg called out, "Tina it's getting late. Hurry up, let's go. It don't take all night."

"Okay, daddy. I'm ready. Where are the keys?" Tina bent over to retrieve the keys as she kissed Greg good night. Enez leaned over and kissed Nicko.

It was a beautiful night. The stars were bright overhead. Enez knew she had to bring Nicko some money. Tina parked her car near an elaborate hotel. As they walked along the building, a drunken man stopped to talk to them. His breath was foul with the smell of alcohol.

With a smooth motion, Tina linked her arms into his as they walked down the street. 'Well sweetie, where is your car?"

The drunken man slurred, "My car is parked right over there." He pointed to a gray Subaru, parked on the street.

Tina and Enez led him to his car as the man pulled out his keys. Tina whispered in his ear, "Let me and my girlfriend take care of you, baby." He agreed and gave his keys to Tina as they piled into his car.

Tina said to Enez, "Hey, I'll take you back to the car and you follow me." Tina did not wait for an answer.

Enez started the car and followed Tina as they made a right turn at the next corner and then a left at the traffic light. They finally arrived at a parking lot of a weekly hotel suite. Enez parked the car and walked towards Tina. "Tina, what are you doing? Is he going to date both of us? I got to get Nicko's money," she whispered.

Tina slid her arm under the drunken man's arm and led him to his suite. In his suite, the man fell on the bed and passed out. Tina quickly went through his pockets and found his wallet. There were several 100 dollar bills and a package of powder cocaine in it. What happened next surprised Enez. Tina took the keys to his car, and said with a cold laugh, "Enez, that white man thought he was going to party for free. He will wake to find his money and car gone."

Tina and Enez walked swiftly across the parking lot. Enez got into Tina's car, parked next to the Subaru. Tina and Enez drove through the streets at a normal speed so as not to bring attention to themselves. Enez followed Tina to an alley to dump the car, and then Tina drove to the hotel where they lived. The morning light was upon them. Before they entered the room, Tina split the 700 dollars with Enez. The men were sleeping inside the room.

They changed their clothes and lay next to their men as the sun peered through the hotel curtains. Soon, the baby girl cried out for food.

Greg woke Tina up, looking for his money. "Tina get up. Where is my money?" She directed him to her purse. As he searched through her purse, he found the Subaru keys. "Tina, what are you doing with these keys?" Greg asked, harshly.

Tina stood near the dresser and explained what happened. When she finished talking, Greg reached for the iron which lay near the dresser and began to beat her over the head with it. She cried, "Please stop, please stop!"

He yelled, "I sent you out to show my friend's woman the Texas ropes, and you go stealing cars. What were you thinking, Tina?" Finally he stopped, got the baby dressed, and left with Nicko. A few days later, Tina was arrested. There was no money to bail her out of jail, so she had to stay until her time was served.

Enez tried to work the street track alone. She felt in her bra to make sure her money was still in place. So far, the afternoon had been good. She wanted to make Nicko happy, so she stayed longer. Enez had a thing for blonde, blue-eyed, white men. A car pulled up and stopped. She glanced over her shoulder to make sure the police was not approaching. The man talked to her from the opened car window.

"You're not vice, are you?" Enez asked, curiously looking at the white driver.

"No, baby, I'm not vice. I just want to see your brown thighs. How much would it cost me?" he asked.

"What do you desire?" Enez flirted with him as she rolled her tongue provocatively. She watched a gleam come into the man's eyes, not sure of his intentions.

"I got 50 dollars, baby. Can you handle that and give me around the world?" Enez knew what he was asking for. She agreed to take him to the room she worked from. He sat on the bed and suddenly pulled out his badge. "You're under arrest for prostitution." Her heart fell to her stomach. Enez was sent to a Texas jail for two days. Enez and Tina were on the same floor, and Tina was released one day before Enez.

Enez's days in Texas were short-lived. Greg, Nicko, Tina, and Enez paid for a flight to San Francisco, where they lived in and out of hotels. Sometimes the money was good, and sometimes it was not. Several weeks passed before Nicko decided to return to Memphis with Enez. They traveled by airplane to Ohio and rented a car to finish their journey to Memphis. When they reached Memphis, a twist of events caused Enez to go deeper and deeper into a lifestyle of unhealthy choices.

* * *

The Prodigal Daughter

Hope

***"Now the God of hope fill you with all joy and peace in believing, that ye may abound in hope, through the power of the Holy Ghost"* (Roman 15:13).**

She looked at the outside of the red brick building. Nicko reached in his pants pocket and handed Enez some money. "Baby, go inside and rent a double room for two nights," he said.

Enez went to the hotel office to pay for their room. The wood floors in the office were shining, and a tall, balding man stood at the front counter. "May I help you?" he asked.

"Yes, I'd like to pay for a room for two nights, please."

"Will that be a single or double room?"

"I need double beds," she replied.

"There is a $20 deposit to have phone service in the room. Will you need a phone?"

"No, I don't think so."

"With tax and two keys, that comes to $78, little lady." Enez gave him four twenties. In return, the desk clerk gave her two dollars and a key to the room.

Nicko watched Enez walk to the car and shut the door. She gave him the change and the keys to their room. Nicko looked at the key with the room number imprinted on it, 228. He pulled to the room and gave her the second key. "Get your luggage from the trunk and take it to the room. I'll be back later so you can get to work." Enez watched from the window as Nicko left in the rented car.

"But the wicked are like the troubled sea, when it can not rest, whose waters cast up mire and dirt." **Have patience with me…**

The stars in the night sky were glistening brightly when she opened the door to see Nicko with his daughter, son, and niece. Their small legs climbed the stairs to the hotel room. "Hey, little ones," Enez greeted the children. They rushed passed her without speaking, straight to the television, changing the stations.

Nicko walked in with pizza and said coldly, "I want you to feed my children before you leave for work. It's enough for them to get two or three slices a piece." Enez washed her hands and placed paper towels on the table near the window. The children washed their hands and ate pizza.

His coldness frightened her; she left for work without saying good bye. She walked to the car, hoping she would have a good night. Enez drove the rented car to her favorite spot, the parking lot at Donny's. A man approached the car, and she asked him, "Do you want a date?"

"Yeah," he replied. "Follow me to my hotel, and I'll give you $100."

Donny's was well known for high paying John's from the club, so she accepted his offer and followed him to his hotel room on Brooks Road. When they got inside the room, Enez used the bathroom and made sure no one else was in the room. When she returned, two men stood near the door – the man whom she had followed and a blonde haired man. The two white men were drunk, and they had no intentions of paying her for sex that night. They had their way with her until they were finished. They finally let her go, and she drove back to the hotel.

Enez had to be crazy to think Nicko would care if she had been raped by two white men. She walked inside the dark room. The television was playing, and the children were in the other bed, asleep. Nicko stopped her as she walked toward the bathroom. "You got my money?" he yawned. "I know you wouldn't be here if you didn't."

Her heart skipped a beat, and her throat was choked from tears. She had just been brutally raped. The words spilled from her mouth as she told him about the rape. He replied without any concern, "Well, now you can get back out there and get me some money."

She looked at him as he turned his back to her. She knew he was serious. If she did not have money when he woke up, there would be consequences. Enez left the hotel room, feeling lonely, afraid, and ashamed. She desperately needed to get his money now. Doing evil was not her fear; it was Nicko whom she feared. To her, Nicko was her god.

Donny's was the only place Enez knew of where men with money would come to satisfy their sexual pleasures. She returned to find a man looking for sexual pleasures in exchange for money. She spotted a young, white man staggering out of the club, walking towards her car like a magnet. She asked him to get in the car, and they agreed to get a hotel room. He paid for the room at the slinky hotel on Bellevue Avenue with a $100 bill. Life on the streets had taught her many things, one of which was to watch the billfold. The room was near the back of the hotel.

When they reached the room, he gave her $100, and they took care of business. He also gave her a small package of powder cocaine. Afterwards, she drove him to his hotel near the airport. She was satisfied that she now had Nicko's money. She drove back to the hotel in the morning darkness. The stars still glittered brightly, but there was a slight tint in the sky, warning of the coming dawn. Once again, she found him sleeping in the hotel room. She slipped into a hot bubble bath to relax her tense body. Then, she lay next to Nicko until the early morning dawn.

The sun shined through the window as Nicko rolled over. He climbed from the bed slowly, walked to the window, and stared at the bright sky. "Enez, where is my money?"

She rolled over to grab her purse. "Here baby, I got your money." Her words had the same refreshing effect as the morning sun to him. He walked back to the bed, put his hand under the sheets, and rubbed Enez's legs. The children stirred awake on the next bed, and their passion ceased. It was not long before the children were dressed and eating breakfast. Nicko picked up the money and tucked it inside his pocket. The morning passed quickly, and Nicko and Enez drove the children to their mother.

It had been a while since Nicko and Enez had used crack cocaine. Being at home aroused their disease of addiction, and they were ready to buy rock cocaine. They were silent while Nicko drove to a familiar apartment house. Enez looked at him as he dug in his pocket for a one hundred dollar bill. He looked at it with uncertainty as he began to pull away layers of crisp one hundred dollar bills. Nicko said, "Baby, this was more than one bill here. We have three more bills." Nicko tucked the other bills in his pocket as he proceeded to buy drugs.

Enez's stomach became nauseated as they drove to the head shop to buy a cocaine pipe, chore boy, grain alcohol, and cigarette lighter. Finally, they arrived at the hotel, and Nicko gave Enez enough money to pay for two more nights. When they reached the room, they smoked cocaine until darkness covered the sky. Enez's soul was in a sinful trance, and she was too ashamed with guilt to call home and tell her family that she was in Memphis.

A few days passed, and Enez was getting dressed for work when Nicko's pimp friends, Greg and Darnell, came to the hotel. She overheard them talking about a woman who lived in the hotel.

"Man, she is a plain-looking brunette, white woman who wears glasses. Her name is Stacy," Darnell said.

"Man, she wouldn't give me no play. She is staying on this floor on the other side of the hotel."

"Yeah, she won't break ice with me either," Greg said with a smile.

"You know, I am popular with the white women, but this one is hard to break." All the men laughed loudly.

"Pimping is my livelihood," Darnell said suddenly.

"Hey baby, it's time for you to get out here," Nicko spoke sharply to Enez.

Enez walked from the bathroom and finished adjusting her clothes in the mirror. As she looked at her reflection, she saw Darnell tossing a small package on the table. "Gentlemen, let's snort this little powder before we go pimping."

She stared into Greg's face but quickly shifted her gaze to Nicko. Greg stared at the package as though someone had just taken his last breath. "Darnell, you mean to tell me you been riding with me, carrying powder cocaine in my car today and me not even knowing about it?"

Enez walked over to Nicko. "Daddy, I'll see ya later."

"Yeah baby, have a good night and be safe."

As she walked to the door, Greg still argued with Darnell, "Man, you might think this is a little bag of powder, but I don't want anybody in my car or in my company, carrying drugs and I don't know about it!"

She walked out and closed the door behind her. It was a beautiful night. The stars were brightly lit overhead. She drove down Winchester Avenue to Airways and parked her car in front of Donny's. She sat waiting like an animal stalking its prey. She waved from the window when she saw a familiar face. The man walked over to the car and got in the front seat with her. Enez turned the car on, and they went to his home in the suburbs of east Memphis. The night was too early for her to return to Nicko. She knew he would be very pleased with her earnings of $700, so she stayed and enjoyed a good meal, wine, jazz music, and conversation.

She did not want the night to end, but Enez was aware of the life she had chosen, and it was time for her to leave. The man kissed her goodbye, "Be careful, until we meet again." Her heart was filled with joy as she thought about her time with him, but then her heart saddened with grief as she thought about the choices she had made.

She drove back to Donny's to see if there was anymore action. The parking lot was filled with cars and people going in and out of the club. Enez looked closely to see a man she dated back in her dancing days. She quickly approached the man with a wide smile. "Hey baby! You remember me? This is Red Foxx."

He looked at her with his aged, blue eyes, and the smile on his face drew wrinkles that had not been present before. "Oh yeah, my little princess. Where have you been, sweetie?"

Enez cleared her throat, hoping he had not spent all his money on table dances and drinks. "Oh, I moved to Atlanta for a while. What are your plans for tonight?"

"Well, I really didn't have any, Red. Would you like to follow me to my house? I would love to have your company, and as always I will make it worth your while."

She did not hesitate to accept his offer. He walked her to her car, and she waited for him to drive from the entrance so that she could follow him.

It was four a.m. when Enez arrived back at the hotel, and Nicko was asleep. She slipped into the running bath water, and her body relaxed from the excitement of seeing her old friends and knowing that Nicko would be happy with her when he woke up. She smiled as she lathered soap all over her body. Before she fell asleep, Enez tucked away $300. Her past history with Nicko taught her to stash some money for the rainy day, which was surely coming ahead.

The morning flew by Enez as she slept until afternoon when the growl from her belly awakened her. She found herself in the bed alone. Nicko had left and taken all but $20 of the money. She felt in her secret place to make sure the money she had stashed away was still in place. "Yes," she whispered as she rolled out of bed to get something to eat. The phone rang, and she answered, "Hello."

"Hey, baby! Get dressed! Come on and ride with me for a minute." Nicko did not wait for an answer as he hung up the phone. Almost two hours passed as Enez paced up and down, waiting for Nicko. She ordered food from the hotel restaurant while she waited. Finally, Enez decided to disrobe and relax. She heard men talking at the door, and then Nicko came in. "Hey baby, are you dressed? I have company with me." Enez quickly grabbed her clothes and entered the bathroom. She heard the voices of Greg, Darnell, and Nicko.

"Hey, Nicko, I think she likes you, man. I have never seen you with a white woman. Man, they pay like a winning slot machine. The woman says she is from Denver. She has the accent too, man. You better jump on that before one of these other pimps does."

Nicko's eyes locked with Enez's as she walked seductively to the door. The sun shone down on her, and she seemed to be a golden reddish color. Her skin had the same deep color of a brand new, shiny penny. Nicko stared at her as she said, "Daddy, I am going to get ice. Is there anything you want me to get you?"

Her words made him feel in control. "I am okay, baby," he replied with a slight grin.

As Enez walked to the ice machine, she saw the young woman who the pimps had described earlier.

It appeared she was trying to make her move on Enez's man. The late afternoon turned into another work night and the same routine for Enez. When she returned to the hotel, she found the white woman in the room, smoking cocaine with Nicko.

The door did not open completely as she turned the lock. To her surprise, the chain held the door. She called Nicko's name. He came to the door to let her in, and she saw the woman sitting in a chair by the window. She placed a crack rock on the pipe as Enez closed the door. Enez looked at the both of them and walked to the bathroom to gather herself.

When she left the bathroom, she did not say a word. She opened the door to the hotel room and ran to the car. Enez drove to the nearest hotel and rented a room for the night. Enez was caught completely off guard by the quick turn of events. It had been rude, she thought to herself, as she stared up towards the ceiling as she lay in the bed. Her mind and body fell into a trance, and she did not wake up until the next morning.

Without anger, she called Nicko at his hotel room. He answered the phone, "Hello."

"Are you alone, Nicko?"

"Yes, I am," he continued. "Baby, I'm sorry. I really don't have an explanation for myself, so I can understand you leaving last night."

Now it was her turn to talk. She said in a low, soft voice, "I don't work the streets, jeopardizing my life for us, to come home to my man and find a woman sitting in my room, smoking crack." She had his attention now because he knew what she was saying was totally against the game.

"Baby, come on home. I am waiting on you. Where are you now?" he asked.

She did not commit to him that she would come back, and she did not mention where she was staying, in case she needed to leave again. She quietly said, "I'll be home soon." Hours later, Enez parked in front of the hotel room. Nicko opened the door and stepped back, allowing her to enter. She stopped and stared around, looking dumfounded. She was quietly thinking to herself, "Why did I come back here? What am I thinking?"

Nicko stood next to her, studying her closely as she sat in a chair near the window. "Baby, you jump to conclusions fast, don't you? You didn't see me smoking crack, did you? But you've taken it for granted that I was smoking with her. Enez, leave the pimping to me."

His remark irritated her, and she replied sharply, "Oh? If that's the case, I can take it for granted you chose lily white women with a drug habit." Tension began to build between them, and Enez knew Nicko's temper all too well. She sat back and watched him rummage through a drawer and then lay several twenty dollar bills on the table. The tension disappeared, and Enez relaxed.

"You can pull your horns in, baby," he said with laughter. The sound of his laughter was rich and carried a note of excitement.

Enez lit a cigarette, crossed her shapely legs, and slowly inhaled. She blew smoke towards Nicko. “How do you know she is really for real with you, Nicko?”

Nicko looked at Enez through the evaporating smoke and said, “That ain’t no problem. All of us are riding near the Millington Navy Base tonight. It’s pay time for those good old Navy boys. Enez, she didn’t give me the impression she wasn’t a thoroughbred. The only way to judge her is by the money. You know an average hooker will go out on the streets and earn a few dollars, just enough for her night’s trap and play around the rest of the night.”

Enez looked surprise to hear Nicko. “You’re right about that,” she smiled. .“Baby, I’m sorry for last night’s reaction.” Enez walked to the side of the bed where Nicko was now lying. She went inside her bra and gave Nicko $300, “Here, Daddy” she said as she squatted next to him.

He stared at her for a long time before asking her to relax with him before night fall. The television lights blinked on and off as they consumed each other. “Hey baby, get bathed and dressed. I am going down the hall to wake this hooker, Stacey.”

As Enez walked from the bathroom with a towel wrapped around her body, Nicko returned with the woman. Enez gathered her clothes and returned to the bathroom.

“Enez, when you’re finished, I want to introduce you to Stacey.”

Enez dressed and entered the room. She saw a brunette, pale-faced woman, wearing thick, brown-rimmed glasses, sitting at the same spot where she had seen her the night before. Enez stood near Nicko as he introduced the two women. “Enez, this is Stacey, Stacey, this is Enez.” Both women nodded their heads in greeting.

It was not long before Nicko was ready to drive the two women to work. They were silent in the car until they reached the hotel. “Enez, go inside and pay for two rooms.” She did as she was told and gave Nicko the keys to the rooms. He told the women one room was for them to bring the Navy men to, and the other room was for them to stay the night. Immediately afterwards, Enez and Stacey went to work.

Before an hour had passed, Enez ran back to the car without Stacey. She had stolen several hundred dollars from a drunken sailor. She rushed to the hotel to tell Nicko she had to leave Stacey. Enez stayed in the hotel, and hours later, they heard a knock at the door. “Who is it?” Nicko asked abruptly.

“It’s Stacey, Nicko,” she said softly.

Nicko opened the door, and Stacey saw Enez sitting in a chair across the room. Stacey was not happy to see Enez. She pulled Nicko gently by his arm and asked him if she could talk to him privately. Enez excused herself. Swiftly, she passed Stacey and Nicko as she left to find the ice machine in the lobby. She walk back to the room, hoping that

Stacey and Nicko had finished their conversation. As she turned the key, she heard Nicko say, "Wait a minute, woman. You don't tell me how to take care of my business." Enez eased back slightly onto the walkway of the hotel and closed the door. Nicko was angry with Stacey. He yelled at her, "Get back out there and bring me my money." As Stacey walked past Enez, tears flowed from her eyes.

Later that morning, Stacey knocked on the door again. Nicko was asleep when she arrived. Enez opened the door. Stacey sat in a chair while Enez shook Nicko's foot on her way to the bathroom.

Nicko said, "What's up? You take care of my business?"

"Yeah," she said with a sigh of relief.

Enez walked out of the bathroom to see Stacey pull out a roll of money. Nicko told Stacey, "Go get a shower so we can leave for Memphis after breakfast."

Stacey really dug Nicko and wanted to give him her money. Enez was jealous when it came to Nicko because he was her god, lover, man. He was everything to her, and she did not want to share him. She pretended everything was okay with this new person in her life. Until, one day Nicko decided to drive them all to Atlantic City, New Jersey.

Greg and his woman, along with Nicko and his two women, were snorting cocaine. Greg watched Nicko as he rubbed his nose. "Man, let's take these women to Atlantic City." Nicko sat back in his chair and decided it was a good idea for them to travel to get some real experience and real money at the casinos. Enez looked at Nicko and thought to herself, "What could I lose other than my soul? I have already chosen him and this lifestyle."

The day was warm from the morning sun. Enez and Nicko sat in the front seat of their rented car. Stacey sat in the back behind Enez. Nicko had been up most of the night, smoking cocaine. As he drove, he placed a piece of cocaine on the pipe and tried to pass it to Enez.

"No, Nicko. I don't want to get high," she said.

Enez hoped Stacey would refuse also. Nicko reached back to give Stacey the cocaine pipe, and she did not accept it. As Nicko looked in the rear view mirror, a car suddenly stopped in front of them, and Nicko rear ended it. He quickly got out of the car since he did not have a valid driver's license. He did not want to go to jail, and Enez swiftly moved to the driver's side.

Greg and Tina followed behind in another vehicle. They finally reached the scene of the accident. They moved the luggage from one vehicle to the other, and everyone took off in Greg's rental car. Before they left Memphis, Nicko ordered Enez to rent another car for their trip. As always, she obeyed him. The almost 24-hour drive was filled with music, sleep, and silence. Enez and Nicko shared the driving. They finally reached the city of gambling and hustling. It did not matter to Nicko that the women had just arrived. He immediately warned them to get ready for work after checking into the hotel room.

Enez and Stacey drove to a casino, The Golden Nugget. They sat at a table in the lounge to have drinks, and Enez was not worried about making any money. She had set aside some money in Memphis for a rainy day. She drank until she was drunk and then began slurring her words as she poured out some of her secrets and Nicko's life situations that he had not discussed with Stacey.

Stacey sat across from Enez, listening intently. "I have some money left over from Memphis," Enez said sluggishly. "I have to make sure I am not out in the cold. Nicko is on crack really bad."

Stacey told Enez that she had come from Denver, Colorado. She came to Memphis with a man who was from Nashville and was now in jail in Memphis. Finally the two women at the table sat silently. Enez looked at her watch. "Well, I guess we better get Daddy some money." Both women separated and did not see each other until the next afternoon.

In the next few days, Nicko was quiet. Enez had not learned about his conversation with Stacy. They ate breakfast at a nice restaurant, went shopping, and lay about in the hotel room until night fall. When the stars and the moon were shining brightly against the earth's roof, Stacey and Enez began to dress for work in the casino's bars.

Enez drove the rented car inside the garage at the casino, and the women went their separate ways.

Enez said loudly to Stacey as she walked toward the busy street, "I'll be in the casino lounge." She entered the casino and heard the ringing bells from the slot machines and people yelling numbers. Different colored lights shone brightly as she walked excitedly through the casino floors to the lounge. She sat next to an older man at the bar.

The bartender approached Enez, "What are you having to drink tonight, little lady?"

Enez smiled at the bartender, "I would like a gin and tonic with a twist of lime, please."

"Coming right up." The bartender's name tag said Lenny. He quickly bought her drink order. "Would you like me to run a tab for you, Ma'am?"

The man sitting next to her spoke up, "Put her drink on my tab, Lenny."

She stirred her drink and placed the stick on a napkin as she tasted her refreshing drink. "Thank you!"

"Beautiful lady, my name is Eddie, but everyone calls me Ed. Are you from around here?" he asked in a deep southern accent.

She looked into his greens eyes and said,"My name is Natalie, but everyone calls me Nat. No, I'm not from around here. Atlanta is my home."

Their drinking, conversation, laughter, and touching each other lasted a while before he asked Enez to his room for a night cap. She watched him open his wallet to pay for their drinks, and she saw several one hundred dollar bills winking at her. "Yes, I would love to have a night cap with you," she said in his ear. They walked to a beautiful room in the hotel. A king-sized bed with a plush comforter was in the middle of the room, and the drapes were a Victorian mahogany with gold tones. She noticed a redwood table with cushioned chairs.

Seductively, she sat down in the chair, and crossed her shapely legs. Her black skirt moved up her thighs. As the man came to her, he placed three one hundred bills in between her breasts. "Would you like another drink, Nat?" he asked at the bar while he made himself a drink.

"No, but I would like you to come here to me when you finish."

He turned quickly to see Enez unbutton her blouse. Enez rocked Ed to sleep before she removed his arm from her upper body and gently slid from the bed. She quietly put her clothes on and walked over to his pants. She reached for his wallet and took all but a few hundred dollar bills. She tiptoed to the door and stuffed the money in her panties as she got on the elevator. When she made it to the ground floor, she went to the back of the casino and flagged a cab to the garage to her car.

When Enez arrived back at the hotel room, she gave several hundred dollar bills to Nicko. Stacey soon returned and knocked on the door. Nicko told her to go to her room, and he would see her in a minute. Nicko looked Enez in her eyes, and she could not understand why he had this look in his face. She thought he would be happy with her. In the hotel room, Enez began to touch him, and he jerked away from her before he drew back and hit her, "You played me for a sucker." She still did not understand why he was so upset with her. He walked out of the room and stayed away from her that night.

The street laws of a pimp and his hooker are, first she must show loyalty to him, especially when he has a new woman. Second, she must never look at another man, unless she is looking for a new man. Then, she must pay the new man. To Nicko, Enez had committed a crime and broke the pimp law. She had told Stacey she kept money from him and all about his life.

The next morning, he came to the room. "Pack your things. I'm moving you out of this hotel. Be ready when I come back," he said angrily. Enez packed her things as she was told. When he arrived, she walked to the car with her luggage, and he did not say a word to her. He gave her money for a cheap motel room and food on the Black Horse Pike. Nicko did not eat breakfast or dinner with her, and she slept alone for several days. The only time she saw Nicko was to give him his money. Finally, one day he sat in her room and repeated everything she had said to Stacey. Enez sat on the bed, surprised, but she could not deny a word of the truth.

For a black girl to earn money in Atlantic City was difficult unless she was stealing it. Enez was not really into stealing; she would much rather con a man. It was really time for Enez to move on to another city. She had burned Atlantic City. The money was slow. Stacey and Nicko were no longer staying at the expensive hotel. All of them moved to a hotel near the beach on the cheaper side of Atlantic City.

It was a sunny morning when Enez heard the chain on the door move. "Who is it?" she called out from the bathroom.

"It's Nicko," the voice replied.

Enez walked to the door to see Stacey with Nicko. "Good morning," she said nonchalantly.

Stacey looked at Enez and asked, "Nicko, is it alright if I go outside for a moment?"

"Yeah, go ahead." Nicko looked at Enez with lust in his eyes. She knew that look from his light brown eyes. It meant only one thing, and that was that he wanted to get inside of her body.

"Take off your panties," he said hurriedly. "She'll be back soon." It had been several days since Enez had her man, and she did as he asked for those few moments together with him.

"Enez, I need you to pack your clothes. We are moving to another hotel. I want you with me." He sat in a chair near the door. Stacey knocked, and he allowed her inside as Enez packed her clothes. She quietly gave him a small roll of money and whispered in his ear, "I know this is not what you expect from me." He nodded his head.

Nicko paid for two cheap rooms near the beach. Stacey and Nicko walked to their rooms, leaving Enez to walk alone. She opened the door and fell upon the bed. Enez closed her eyes and almost fell asleep. She heard voices passing her room, so she jumped to her feet and walked to the bathroom to shower. The warm water fell on her naked body as she lathered in Caress soap. Suddenly, the water became cold, and she quickly rinsed the soap from her body. Just as she wrapped the towel around her nakedness, she heard a knock on the door. "Who is it?" she asked.

Nicko answered, "It's me, open the door." She did not hesitate for fear of his temper.

"Woman you sure look lovely in that pink towel," he said, walking towards her to kiss her on the lips. She turned her head, pretending she did not know he wanted to kiss her. He looked at her with a twinkle in his eye. Nicko patted her on her butt when she passed him to get to her suitcases on the bed. As she applied lotion to her body, Nicko said, "I need you to get some day work, so get ready. Here are the keys to the car. I am going to the other room to get some rest. Call me when you get back." She blew a kiss towards him and closed the door.

Day time is family time in Atlantic City, but Enez did as Nicko requested. Fortunately, Enez found a day player. She sat at another casino bar, listening to jazz sounds pour from the amps. Enez ordered her favorite summer drink, gin and tonic with a twist of lime. The bartender was a tall, slim blonde with brown roots and a pretty face. She did not hold much conversation with Enez. Perhaps she was too busy with the old, white gentlemen at the end of the bar.

Moments later, an average height, white man sat next to Enez. The bartender called his name, “Sam, are you having your usual?”

He looked at Enez and said, “Honey, what is the usual?”

Enez turned slightly to answer him, “Gin and tonic with a twist of lime.”

“Tammy, that’s what I’ll have, and give the lady one too. Oh, excuse me. I see you already have one. Would you like another?”

Enez looked down at her drink, “Yes, I would like a fresh one, please. Thank you, Sam.”

Sam looked at Enez through his brown eyes and asked, “Darling, are you a gambler?”

She smiled, “No, Sam, I am not a gambler.”

“How do you know my name?” he asked, laughing.

“I heard the bartender call your name.”

“Oh yeah. Tammy knows me. I’m a regular here in Atlantic City.”

Enez’s favorite song came on the sound system, “Wishing on a Star.” She began to sing the lyrics to the song. Sam sat back and put his arms around Enez. He whispered to her, “This may be our lucky day." When the song ended, Sam said, "Come on, girl. Let's go gamble. He grabbed her hand and led her to the black jack table. Sam sat next to her and told her every move to make on the table. Enez and Sam left the table with $2,500. Sam gave Enez $1,000 to keep for herself.

She spent most of the day with him. They went to dinner and ate oysters and crabs, then they walked on the boardwalk. "You know, I have been with you all day and have not asked you your name. You don't have to tell me. I will call you Lucky Stars," Sam said.

A dose of reality suddenly formed in Enez's heart. She knew their encounter would have to end soon. "Sam, I will have to leave you soon." They stood by the railing, holding hands as they watched the sea birds fly across the waters. Enez thought to herself, "How free they must feel." Perhaps Sam knew she was a working girl, and that's why he never approached her to sleep with him. He just wanted her to have good time. "Sam, it's getting late, and I must pick up my girlfriend from the hotel."

He looked at her, smiled, and kissed her forehead. "I won't hold you any longer, Lucky Stars. I have really enjoyed my day with you. I hope you too have enjoyed your day."

Enez stopped at a phone booth to tell Nicko she was on her way to pick up Stacey. She knew she was running late, and she did not want Nicko to be angry with her. She phoned the hotel room again and again, but Nicko did not answer. Finally, she decided to knock on the hotel door.

As she arrived at the inn, she smelled the ocean water. Enez took deep breathes, hoping she would not find Stacey and Nicko smoking crack. She saw Stacey peek from the window as she pulled the curtain back before opening the door. Nicko laying the on bed, and appeared to be asleep. She looked around and saw his underwear lying on the floor and evidence that they had been smoking crack. Her heart was crushed! Once again, she had walked in to find evidence of Nicko and Stacey having sex or getting high.

As she stood there, she thought about another time in Atlantic City. Nicko had sent Enez to work, and Stacey stayed at the hotel in the one room they shared between them. Enez walked in to find Stacey lying on the bed, naked. Hurt, Enez confronted Nicko, whereupon he slapped and kicked her to the floor. She watched herself being slapped through the images in the mirror. Now, she focused on her day with Sam.

She had just left a man who appeared to care about her feelings, a man she would probably never see again in her life. Now, she was in a room with a white woman from Denver who liked her man and crack cocaine. Enez shook Nicko's foot to get his attention, and he looked at her with one eye. She looked at him and then turned to stare at his underwear. He lifted himself from the bed, naked, and slowly reached for his underwear. Enez walked briskly to her room and waited for Stacey to finish dressing. Enez freshened and packed her clothes. She quietly walked to the car in the parking lot and threw her suitcase in the trunk. When she came back to the room, the phone was ringing.

"Stacey is ready. You got my money?" he asked abruptly.

"No, Nicko. I couldn't hit a lick. You know day time is not good for working girls."

He cleared his throat, "Yeah, well you better have my money before you dot that door again." She waited for him to hang up the receiver.

As Enez stepped out, Stacey walked towards her, and both women got in the car. They rode in silence until Enez left Stacey at one of the casinos. She wanted to keep her thoughts of the day, so Enez rented a nice room at the Comfort Inn and enjoyed her restful night. The next day brought happy moments. She was now alone with her money and thoughts of the lifestyle that she desperately wanted to leave.

One warm night, she met Sam again as she walked the board walk. Their eyes met, and their hands reached out to each other. "Hi, Lucky Stars," he said with a warm smile, and tears ran down her cheeks. "What's the matter?" he asked as he wiped her tears.

"Oh, I'm just so happy to see you, Sam." Over the next week, Sam gave Enez the best time she could have asked for. He wined and dined her in the best restaurants and took her shopping. She felt at peace with Sam, yet she still missed the familiar, old lifestyle.

Sam and Enez were at a casino lounge late one evening. Sam was telling Enez a funny joke when Greg's woman approached Enez. "Hi, can I speak to you for a moment?"

Enez excused herself and walked a few steps with Tina. "Girl, you know that last night you ran off. Guess what? Stacey robbed a man for $5,000 right after you dropped her off."

Enez thought to herself, "Well, so what? I have had more than $5,000 worth of fun with Sam." Enez began to smile as she thought about it.

Tina slipped Nicko's hotel phone and room number in Enez's hands. "Call him, girl," she said with a wink in her eye.

Later that evening, Enez called Nicko's hotel room while Sam slept. Nicko answered, and Enez immediately began talking, "What's up? I heard Stacey made a big sting for ya. Well that's nice. I'm glad you're happy with her."

"Enez, what do you want? Are you ready to come home to daddy? I know you been having big fun with my money. I've seen you walking the board walk with your friend. I want you to come home right now, Enez. You got the car, and I'm ready to leave for Memphis. This girl can't stay here. She robbed a man. I gotta get some more work out of her. You hear me?"

Her heart skipped a beat. He needed her; he wanted her to come back to him. She agreed.

"I want to see you tonight, Enez, okay?" he said affectionately.

"I can't come back tonight, Nicko. I'll call tomorrow." She knew his anger, manipulation, and deceit. Enez was not sure she wanted to return. Several days passed before Enez tried to see Nicko. He was still staying at the hotel, and she decided to call him. Stacey answered the phone, "Hello."

Enez asked, "Is Nicko in?"

Immediately, Nicko answered the phone, "Yeah."

"Hi, Nicko."

"Are you ready?"

Enez hesitated but answered after a moment, "Yes, I'm ready to see you."

"See ya if you get here, Enez," Nicko said, and he gave her the address and directions from the main strip.

It was Sam's last night in Atlantic City, and Enez cherished their time together. Sadly, she packed her clothes, not sure if she would be on her way back to Memphis. Sam gave her $1,500 when he said goodbye.

Her eyes filled with confusion, anger, and hurt as she drove. She knew she was almost four months pregnant since her period had not shown since they left San Francisco. Enez turned the car around several times before she had the courage to park and face her destiny.

She saw Nicko standing in the door from a distance. He recognized the car and looked at her with hatred. Enez entered the room to find Stacy lying on the bed, naked. Shopping bags were scattered about, and Nicko wore new jewelry. When she brought her suitcases in, Nicko dumped all of her new clothes out and told Stacey to get up and pack their clothes in the suitcases he had just emptied. Enez was silent. Nicko told Enez to pick out the clothes she wanted to keep. Enez wanted all her clothes; but there wasn't enough room for many clothes. Enez left some valuable clothing in the hotel room and gave Nicko $300 of the $2,000 she carried in her secret hiding place.

Before morning, they were headed back to Memphis. Stacy and Nicko had been smoking crack, and now they were too tired to drive. Nicko forced Enez to drive, until she started swaying on the highway. He was angry with her and started to hit her, but he changed his mind.

It was Sunday morning, and the only thing on the radio was preachers' sermons. As she was about to turn the radio off, she heard, "***It is better that a man lose his life, than to lose his soul.***" In Matthew, Jesus said to His disciples, "***For what profit is it to a man if he gains the whole world, and loses his own soul.***"

When they arrived in Memphis, things got worse. Nicko finally broke his silence when they arrived at his brother's house to smoke cocaine. It was just enough to tease her appetite. Stacey was becoming angry with Nicko for buying crack for everyone. It had been a while since Enez had gotten high. Stacey pulled Nicko to another room. When he finally returned, he told Enez to get ready to leave. His brother would take her to pick up his children. Nicko gave Enez hotel fare and told her where to get a room.

Enez did as she was told. Daylight was shining through the window when she heard a knock on the door. "Who is it?" she asked.

Nicko said softly, "It's me."

She rushed to open the door. Nicko walked in, and Stacey followed behind. Stacey sluggishly fell onto the empty bed. Next to the bed lay the sleeping children on a pallet. Enez crawled back into the bed in which she had slept. Nicko now occupied the bed, so Enez lay next to him as she listened to him snore. She thought to herself, "Now is a good time to leave." She gently removed herself from the bed and crept to the hotel door, leaving everything she owned behind. She ran to the nearest phone booth located outside a restaurant.

"Hello, Dusty, this is Enez. I am in Memphis and in big trouble. Dusty, I'm almost four months pregnant. Nicko and I arrived last night from Atlantic City. He has this white girl with him in the hotel. I've got to leave Memphis. Will you help me leave?"

"Where are you, Enez?"

She whispered. "I'm at the corner of Elvis Presley Boulevard and Brooks Road. Will you please come and get me?"

"Yes, I'll come. Give me about ten minutes."

Dusty knew her sister was in trouble because she was always the person Enez called to bail her out of a mess. Enez's youngest sister picked her up at the Kettle restaurant near the hotel where she had spent the night.

Over the next few days, Enez lived in a hotel, bought a few changes of clothes, and terminated the pregnancy. Dusty convinced her to move to Orlando, Florida, to start her life over with a new beginning.

* * *

The Prodigal Daughter

Flesh

"***The spirit indeed is willing, but the flesh is weak***" (Matthew 26:41). Deep down, Enez had had enough of her flesh. She wanted something different.

Friday morning, Enez heard a car horn coming from the parking lot of the hotel. She peeped from the golden curtains and saw her sister, waiting patiently. "Okay, I'm ready," she said as she got her luggage. She was ready to leave the room that had been her safe haven, and a tear of joy fell from her cheek. Her excitement grew as she thought of her new beginning and new life.

"Good morning, Dusty," Enez said happily.

Dusty was filled with happiness for her sister, "Are you ready, Enez?"

"Yes, I am as ready as I could ever be, Little Sis."

They were quiet during the ride to the bus terminal, and they walked in to the station together. It was crowded with travelers and people waiting for passengers. Enez paid for her bus fare at the ticket counter. She had already called about the schedule to Orlando, Florida. Soon, departure time arrived, and Enez looked into her sister's brown eyes for comfort and then hugged her goodbye. She did not look back as she walked to the bus. From her window seat, she could only see her sister's shadow as her journey began.

A brown-skinned woman wearing headphones sat next to her when the bus made a stop to pick up more passengers, "Lordy, Lordy. Lordy," the woman said quietly. She glanced at Enez as she pressed the front of her skirt down. "Hi, my name is Delores."

Enez smiled at the woman, "Hello, and mine is Enezi." Enez turned to face the window, hoping for a quiet ride to Orlando.

As the bus pulled out, Delores reached for the cassette player on her lap and started singing, "***Living below in this old sinful world, Hardly a comfort can afford; Striving alone to face temptations sore, Where could I go but to the Lord?***"

Enez turned to stare at the woman and saw that her eyes were closed. Enez's eyes began to fill with tears as she turned back to her window view, and Delores continued to sing, "***Needing a friend to save me in the end, Where could I go but to the Lord?***" Enez slept peacefully until they arrived in Florida. Enez said good bye to her new friend as they retrieved their luggage. She walked toward a row of cabs waiting on arrivals. Her cab driver was a young black man.

Dusty had lived in Orlando back in her earlier days, so she was familiar with the hotels in Orange County. She recommended the Eduardo Suites and gave Enez the address before Enez left Memphis. Now, Enez provided the address to the cab driver.

Enez's heart was burdened with life's storms as she sat in the cab. She needed someone to talk to, and she told the cab driver of her drug habit. Talking about cocaine fully aroused her addiction, and it was not long before she discovered he too had a drug problem. Soon, they were smoking cocaine, and he was picking up customers for her to date. The intensity of the drug kept the search for the first hit going. Finally, the cab driver was ready to stop searching, and he convinced Enez to check into the hotel and get some sleep. She checked in and took a sleeping pill he had given her. After that night, she did not get high with him again, although they became good buddies. He was not a flashy pimp, just a cab driver.

Enez found a job, working in a topless club. She saved her money and bought nice things for herself. She should have been happy, but she was not. Her heart was with Nicko, and she would not let go.

Nicko's sister-in-law, Betty, always knew how to get in touch with Nicko. Enez telephoned Betty in Memphis. "Hey girl, this is Enez. How are you?" Before Betty could reply, Enez asked, "Where is Nicko?"

Betty was silent for a moment, then she answered, "Nicko is in Phoenix, Arizona, with Stacey. Girl, they left the same day you left. You want his phone and room number where he is staying?"

Enez quickly said, “Yea give me his phone number, and I’ll call him later.” The two women said goodbye.

It had been two months since she had spoken with Nicko, and she knew he would not be happy to hear from her. She wanted to let him know of her accomplishments without him. As she dialed the number, she remembered how many times he had hurt her to be with other women and how he had made her leave most of her clothes in Atlantic City. She became increasingly angry as the phone rang. Finally, the desk clerk answered, “Sunshine Hotel, may I help you?”

“Yes, may I have room 211, please?”

“I will ring that room for you.”

Enez took a deep breath. A woman answered the phone, “Hello.”

Enez thought the voice sounded familiar, and she felt the jealousy forming in her heart. Aloud, she softly asked to speak with Nicko.

“Nicko, telephone,” the woman said loudly. She could hear Nicko in the background, asking, “Who is it?”

“I don’t know. Come to the phone.” Enez heard footsteps approaching the phone.

“Yeah,” he said hastily.

“Hi, Nicko,” Enez said with a smile on her face. “How are you?”

He was quiet for a moment. Then, he told the woman who had answered the phone to get him ice from the machine. When he was alone, Nicko began to talk, "Where are you?"

She hesitated to tell him, but she thought, "What the heck? He is on the other side of the nation." She answered, "I'm in Orlando, Florida."

"Hey Enez, I need you to send me something."

For the first time since she had left him in Memphis, Enez felt she could relax and talk to him. "Nicko, I am doing just great here in Orange County. I know you have someone there taking care of your business. You don't need me or my money. I just called to say hi and nothing more," she said after taking a deep breath.

She heard the room door open in the background and the woman's voice, "Nicko, I bought you a root beer. Would you like me to open it now for you?"

"Naw baby, I'll get it later," he answered.

Enez was filled with envy because she wanted to be with him. She knew this was not a good idea as she looked around her. She saw the beautiful suite, her new jewelry and clothes, and she quickly thought, "What am I thinking?" Suddenly, she said, "Nicko I have got go now. Talk to you later." Enez hung up the phone before he could say goodbye.

Enez called Nicko several times over the next few weeks. She was tempted to meet him in Phoenix, and he tried to convince her to come, but she would not go. He called her suite one evening before she left for work, and he sounded very humble, “Hey baby, what’s up with ya?”

“Oh, getting ready for work,” she said as she applied her lipstick, “What’s up with you?”

“Stacy’s in jail in Las Vegas. I sent her and another white girl to Vegas. They were caught trying to use knock out drops on an undercover police. I need you to send me some money.”

Her heart ran cold. The sound of a sharp knock caused her to jump. “Who could that be?” Then, she remembered that she had asked the cab driver to pick her up early. She asked, “Who is it?”

“It’s Benny, baby! Are you dressed?”

She looked at the receiver, and she knew Nicko was waiting for an answer. “Hey Nicko, I gotta get back to you on that. I’ll call you after work.”

Several days passed before Enez talked to Nicko again. This time, he was in Memphis when he called one early Sunday morning. “Hi baby, I left the west coast, and Stacey is still in jail in Las Vegas. I need you to come home to me. I miss you.”

She sat up in bed and thought of how much she missed him and how alone she felt without him. She decided to go to him very suddenly, and she answered quickly, “Yes, I’ll be home on a flight this week. I’ll call you and give you all the flight info so you can pick me up from the airport.”

Before she left Orlando, Enez got a new hair style, manicure and pedicure, new clothes, jewelry, and luggage. She sent herself several thousand dollars through Western Union. Enez was not sure about the situation with Nicko, as she remembered all the times he mistreated her. She would soon learn there was a near-death price for returning to Memphis. She thought he would be happy to see her. How wrong she was.

Just before she left the hotel, Enez phoned Nicko at his brother's house. After two rings, Nicko answered, "Yeah, speak your piece."

"Hi Nicko, my piece is this! I'm arriving in Memphis at 1:15 this afternoon, on Flight 757, American Airlines. You want to check the terminal location because you know these flights may change."

"You better know for sure I will be there." He hung up the phone without saying goodbye.

She was nervous about seeing him again. The last time she had left Nicko, she was running from him, and now she was returning to be his lady, and she expected him to be her knight in shining armor. Her three large suitcases were packed, and she was dressed to kill. Golden streaks highlighted Enez's dark brown hair, and her golden complexion complimented the new make up she wore. She looked classy in her $200 dollar pants suit as she confidently walked through the hotel lobby in her high-heeled pumps to pay her last phone bill. She stepped out with the bell hop and saw a taxi, waiting on a fare. The bell hop walked to the passenger side of the taxi and asked, "Can you take our hotel guest to the airport?" The cab driver nodded his head towards Enez as he got out to place her luggage in the trunk before they drove off.

She finally arrived in Memphis after a short flight. Her heart beat fast, and her thoughts were hazy. Enez could see Nicko among the people waiting for other passengers on from her flight. The evil look in his eyes was one of her first warnings, and his first words to her were, "Where is your luggage, #@*?$?"

She knew he was angry with her, and she became afraid. Nervously, she answered, "My luggage is downstairs."

They walked together and waited for her luggage to arrive. She thought about calling for security because she did not want to go with him. Enez was afraid for her life but ashamed to ask for help. She wanted him to be happy to be with her as she tried to tell herself that everything was okay, but she knew better. She had seen that look in his eyes before, and it had almost been fatal. There was help. She looked around to see a sign that said "SECURITY." She knew she was facing near-death as fear ran through her body, spirit, and soul. The enemy convinced her it was alright, "You are home with him. He is not going to hurt you." Finally her luggage came down the shoot.

Her body shook with fear as they walked through the airport corridors. As they left the terminal, a blue Monte Carlo stopped in front of them. Nicko pulled Enez's arm and escorted her to the car as he signaled the driver to open the trunk. It was Nicko's oldest brother, David. Nicko opened the passenger door for Enez to get in the back seat. She sat quietly as he sat in the front. As the car moved forward, Nicko asked her, "Where is my money?" His voice was insistent as he turned his head towards her.

She stared at him, not knowing what to say. She knew he was deadly serious. She stuttered as she answered, "I don't have any money."

He reached over the front seat and hit her viciously across the face. It happened so quickly, her glasses fell from her face. He jumped over the seat and got in the back with her. "I asked you, where is my money?" She looked into his face and did not see a trace of a smile on his cold features as he waited for her to answer. "Get down on the floor. You better not scream," he demanded. He pushed her to the floor and stomped on her again and again. He said, "You better not get up, or I will kill you."

She obeyed. She looked up at him and begged him to stop only to see him holding his dress shoe in his hand. He delivered numerous blows to her head again and again until she felt liquid streaming down her face. She lay on the floor, begging for her life, as she felt the top of her head and her swollen face. Blood covered her hands. She lay in a semi-conscious state as the blood flowed freely down her face. Nicko continued to hit her, and she heard him say, "You better not pass out, or I'll take you to Mississippi and dump you in the woods where no one will find you." The body that wrapped her spirit remained conscience as she mustered every bit of will power she could.

Nicko continued to ask her for money until she came up with a story, hoping to calm his rage. She begged, "Please Nicko don't hit me again." Tears ran down her face and mixed with the blood running from her head, nose, and mouth. "I have some money at the Western Union downtown," she grasped for breath.

"I will call downtown to see if any money is there."

She wanted to get away from him and did not plan to give him her money after the beating he had just given her. Quickly, she thought to tell him, "A woman has to ask for the information. This is the code to receive money from the Western Union."

As they sat in the back seat, she trembled next to him. Nicko said to his brother, "David, take us over to Tony's house to use the phone so she can call Western Union."

Enez peered through her one good eye and saw David looking at her in the rear view mirror. She lowered her gaze as he drove through the South Memphis streets. As they approached the public housing near the African American College in south Memphis, Nicko told David to get out and knock on the door. When David returned, he said, "Man, no one is answering the door."

Nicko said in a cold voice that frightened Enez, "Tell you what, man. Take me to pick up my son around the corner. I want him to see what I've done to this #@!$*."

Enez sat still as David continued to drive. She stared out the window as they approached another set of public housing. Nicko's twelve-year-old son was in the drive, playing with his friends as the car approached.

"Hey, Little M, go tell your grandmother you're going to ride with your daddy I'll bring you back later." Nicko instructed the boy.

Enez watched the boy go around the corner and return just moments later. He got in the front seat with David and looked at Enez in the back seat as she began to tremble.

"Little M, pass me that joint in the ash tray and push the car lighter in for me," Nicko said as he glanced at Enez. Silently, Little M passed the car lighter. Enez looked at Nicko in horror as he brought down the hot lighter to burn her legs several times before lighting his joint. He called to his son, "Watch me," as a tear fell from her eye. She withheld her scream of pain as Nicko forced her back down on the floorboard of the car.

"David, drive over to Bad Foote's house so she can use the phone." Once again, David did as his brother told him.

When they arrived, Nicko got her suitcase from the trunk of the car and found a dress for her to change into. "Get out and change out of those bloody clothes."

Every part of her body hurt with each move she made as she got out of the car. She raised her eyes to the swaying treetops and said, "Jesus, help me."

She remembered what he had said to her, "You better not run or holler. I'll catch you and kill you. I'll leave you where no one will ever find you." She quietly changed her clothes.

Blood was still on her face as a man and woman walked past them. They knew Enez and Nicko, but they did not stop to hold a conversation.

Nicko said to Enez, "Come on, woman. I want Bobby to see what I've done to you." Then, he spoke to the man, "Bobby, hold up! I want you to see what I've done to this dirty @#$%^."

Bobby and the woman stopped in their tracks as Nicko pushed Enez toward them. She stumbled, almost falling to the ground, and Bobby reached out to help her balance.

"Yeah man, I just wanted you to see," Nicko boasted. "Hold your head up so they can see you."

Enez held her head up to them and peered through her swollen eye. She saw the woman turn her head and walk away, and Bobby followed her. Enez quickly dropped her head as she turned to follow Nicko to his friend's apartment. Nicko knocked on the door, and Enez could hear voices as a tall, pretty woman with wide hips answered the door. "Oh my God! What happened to you?" She grabbed Enez and immediately took her to the bathroom. The woman wiped at her face to stop the bleeding, but it would not stop. The blood was flowing much faster now.

Nicko opened the door and handed the phone to Enez for her to call Western Union. The phone line stayed busy. God had saved her. He had heard her calling, "Jesus help me!"

Nicko decided to ride to the Western Union, but first he stopped at Tony's house. The house was dark as they drove by. Enez was in the car, and she saw the sun setting to the west as she looked from the window. The gray clouds were dark, and the stars twinkled in the sky. David parked the car in an alley near the Western Union.

"Little M, I want you to walk in the Western Union with Enez. Make sure she doesn't call the police." Nicko looked at Enez and coldly said, "Put these glasses and cap on."

She realized this was her only chance to save her life. She did not say a word as she walked into the Western Union with Little M, blood flowing from her face and her legs wobbling as she walked. Several customers looked at her in fear. Just ahead, she saw a sign to the bathroom. Enez and Little M walked to a table, and she said "I'll be right back," as he sat down. She was in excruciating pain with every step she took. In the bathroom, she saw her face in the mirror and cried. Her eyes and head were swollen. As she returned from the bathroom, David sat next to Little M. He said, "Come on, Enez. Get what you came in here to get so we can go."

She walked to the cashier as David stood on one side and Little M on the other. Enez looked at the woman from under her cap and asked, “Ma’am, would you call an ambulance for me, please?”

The woman replied, “I can’t call you an ambulance, but I can give you a quarter, and you can go across the street to use the pay phone.” Behind the cashier was a large window, and Nicko stood outside watching her. Enez told the woman, “I can’t leave this building. Please call me an ambulance.”

“Ma’am, I have to call the police first, and then they’ll call you an ambulance.”

“Call whoever you need to call. I need an ambulance.”

While the woman called the police, Nicko waved to his brother and son to come out. They ran out of the building. Enez’s body was broken, and her heart was shattered. She could not understand how someone you love could be so cruel. She walked to a nearby chair and sat down to wait for the police and ambulance. She passed out soon after the ambulance arrived, and the rest of the night was a hazy blur to her.

The morning sun shone through her hospital window. As she turned her head away from the window, a nurse and a man walked through the door. “Good morning, Ms. Brown,” the nurse said politely.

A man wearing a dark suit and a police badge stepped forward. "Good morning. I am Sergeant Ewing, and I need to ask you some questions. Ms. Brown, you took a very terrible beating last night. Do you know who did this to you?"

She took a deep breath and sighed before saying, "It was my man."

The officer looked at her. "Would you like to file charges? Ms. Brown, are you aware of your injuries?"

She shook her head no in response. A doctor stood near the police officer, and now he said, "Ms. Brown, your skull was fractured. You have 25 stitches on the top of your head, and you lost quite a bit of blood." The doctor stepped out of the room while Sergeant Ewing finished his questioning.

"Now Ms. Brown, would you like to file charges against this man?" He gave her a small mirror.

As she looked at her reflection, she saw the bandages that covered her head and said, "Yes, I would like to file charges."

"Ms. Brown, I will take the report here in the hospital and start the process of filing charges. Do you have a safe place to stay?"

Once again, Enez shook her head no in response to his question.

"I will call a shelter for abused women to pick you up from the hospital. But first I must take pictures of all your injuries."

Enez followed Sgt. Ewing to a small room where he took pictures of the brutal injures all over her body. First, he took several pictures of her face from many angles. Next, he took pictures of the cigarette lighter burns, then the bruises all over her body. Sgt. Ewing walked Enez back to her room and gave her one of the pictures to remind her of the brutal and cruel event that happened to her.

"Ms. Brown, that man needs to be taken to a field and have done to him what he did to you." That sounded like a very good idea to her.

Later that night, the doctors were ready to release Enez since her vital signs were good. Soon, a woman arrived to take her to a domestic violence shelter. Her hair was the color of fire, and her skin was ghostly pale. Her voice was calm. As the woman and Enez rode to the secret shelter, Enez said aloud, "He answered me."

The woman quoted from the Bible, " '***I am not sent but unto the lost sheep of the house of Israel.***' Enez, He is talking about you. God spared you last night only by His Grace and Mercy. Not because you are a righteous woman, but because He loves you. He loves you more than you could ever love yourself."

Rain spattered against the window as Enez sat up and stared out in pain and disgust. She climbed from the bed slowly, walked to the mirror, and stared at her swollen face and head wrapped in bandages. Pain wracked her body as she shook and gasped for air, bending over trying not cry from the pain. She tried to shake off her emotions, but that almost fatal day kept replaying in her mind.

Enez rested physically and emotionally over the next two weeks. Enez phoned her stepfather. She wanted help to find out what was going on within her. She wanted to blame everyone for her unhealthy choices and not take responsibility for choosing the wrong turn in life. She walked to the house phone located in the hallway near her bedroom and dialed her stepfather's phone number. As he answered, Enez paused to catch her breath before she said, "Daddy, what cha doing?"

"Oh not a thing! How about yourself?"

She thought for a moment before asking her next question. "You remember when I was a little girl and we lived on Dunnbent?"

He quickly replied, "Yes I remember. What about it?"

"I am trying very hard to understand what the problem with me is. I remember one day you came home from work, and you hugged and kissed my sister, but you didn't pay any attention to me. I stood there, waiting on my hug and kiss and to sit on your lap, but you never even looked at me. If only you had hugged me that day, I would not feel so unloved now."

Enez heard him clear his throat, "Girl, you must be crazy. I have never done anything to you."

She paused for a moment. "I never said you did anything to me." Before she could say anything else, she heard the phone return to its cradle. Her heart fell to the pit of her stomach as she returned the receiver to its cradle and began to weep.

A hand touched her shoulder to give her the comfort she needed. A soft spoken woman said, "***And he shall turn the heart of the fathers to the children, and the heart of the children to their fathers…***" Enez turned toward the short, slim woman and saw a smile upon her beautiful face. Enez returned the smile and said, "I wanted my stepdaddy to love me."

The woman looked at her, "He loves you in his own way."

Enez held her head down. Suddenly she said, "It was me. I didn't think he loved me because he did not love me the way I wanted him to. He took me in his life and gave me his name, knowing that I had not come from his body."

Another time, her little sister stepped into her life to pull Enez away from the insanity. Or maybe it was to send her away because she was an embarrassment to the family. She called her sister, "Hello, Dusty. This is Enez. How are you?"

"I'm doing just fine," the voice on the other end replied.

Enez felt humble. She was battered; her spirit was shattered; her soul was ready to die. Enez had nothing: no clothes, no money, no self-worth, and no friends.

"Enez, do you want to leave town? I can send to you Washington D.C. Is that far enough for you? I will buy you a one-way bus ticket. Call me tomorrow evening."

"Thank you, Dusty. I will call you."

As she walked back to her room, Enez noticed a scripture placed on the wall near the phone. "***To another the gifts of healing by the same Spirit***" (1 Cor. 12:9). The words she read soaked inside her spirit, and she thought to herself, "The same spirit Who rescued me over two weeks ago is now sending me a gift of healing."

* * *

Prayer

Two days later, Enez left for Washington D.C. Before she left the shelter, an older woman who had left her abusive husband of 15 years prayed with her and gave Enez a religious booklet with an encouraging scripture in it, "***For we trust we have a good conscience, in all things willing to live honestly.***" Enez left Memphis with just a few dollars, some changes of clothes, and hope to find a new life for herself. During the long bus ride, Enez held close to her heart the Savior Who she was longing to know. "***Watch and pray, that ye enter not into temptation***" (Matthew 26:41).

Almost a day later, she arrived at the Washington D.C. bus terminal. Suddenly, she became frightened as she thought to herself, "Have I been wearing a mask?" She realized she was far from home and did not know a single person. She was startled as the bus driver tapped her on the shoulder, "What's wrong, lady? Don't tell me you're lost."

"No, no I'm not lost," Enez smiled.

"Give me your ticket so I can identify your bag."

When the bus driver located her bags, she slowly walked into the building. She had not thought about the answers to her own questions, "Where will I sleep? What will I do now?" "***My yoke is easy, and my burden is light.***" Enez was too overcome with blinding rage to trust His voice. Enez knew getting into a shelter would be easy because of the black eyes and scars that had not quite healed. Enez sat in a chair to think.

Enez glanced at the plump woman who sat next to her. "Hey, my name is Pat," she said. "Are you from around here?"

Enez was silent for a moment. "Well, no, I am not. I'm from Memphis, Tennessee." She thought to herself, "Should I tell her I'm running from an abusive man?"

Pat broke the silence between them, "So, what brings you to D.C.?"

Enez hesitated, "I'm running from an abusive man."

Pat looked into Enez's eyes, "That's why I'm here, for women who are looking for shelter. Here, take this number and call the shelter. Do you have change for the phone?"

Enez reached inside her pocket and found some change. The thoughts of hopelessness that had been in her mind were now gone as she walked quickly to the phone booth and dialed the number to the shelter. Enez said, "My name is Enez, and Pat gave me your number. I'm from Memphis, and I'm a victim of domestic violence."

The woman listened quietly and then said, "Enez, my name is Tammy Faye. I'll come right away to pick you up from the terminal. What are you wearing?"

"Blue jeans and a red t-shirt that says Memphis on the front of it."

Tammy Faye described her car to Enez and instructed her to look for the car on the west side of the building. When they hung up, Enez returned to the area were she had met Pat, but she was nowhere in sight. The reflection of the street lights shone on the wet pavement, and the air smelled like fresh morning dew. Soon, Enez saw a brown Toyota at the corner traffic light as it made a right turn into the terminal.

Tammy Fay called out her name as she stopped the car. Enez breathed a sigh of relief when she saw that Tammy Faye had described herself perfectly. Her face was covered with freckles, and her hair was fire red. She weighed about 120 pounds. Enez noticed her East Coast accent. When they reached the shelter, Tammy Faye comforted Enez with her words, "We are here for you."

Enez was offered food and a shower in the two-story house. After her shower, she was led to a room where another woman was lying on one of the twin beds. A small lamp sitting on a table between the beds lit the room. The woman turned to Enez, "Hi, I'm Vickie," she yawned.

"I'm Enez. Do you mind if we talk tomorrow? I'm really tired and need some rest."

Vickie reached over and turned off the lamp. "OK, good night," she said.

The next morning, the sunlight shone through the blinds. Enez sat on the side of the bed, listening to the birds near the window. Enez was about to walk to the window when a woman came in and announced that she was wanted in the office. "I'll show you where the office is after you get dressed. They like for us to be fully dressed when we come downstairs. Oh by the way, in case you don't remember from last night, I am Vickie."

Enez looked at the woman and remembered the small framed silhouette under the covers. She had not recognized her voice. "Okay, give me about ten minutes," she said as Vickie closed the door behind her.

Enez had not talked to anyone except for Tammy Faye up to that point. Now, as she finished putting her shoes on, Vickie returned. "Yeah, I am ready," Enez said. The two women went downstairs and walked through the kitchen. Vickie knocked on the door of a room behind the kitchen.

"Come in, please."

Enez walked in as Vickie excused herself.

A woman behind the desk looked over her glasses as she extended her hand to Enez. "Have a seat, please," she smiled. "I am Susan, the intake person for the shelter. I need to get some information from you. Tammy Faye said you're from Memphis. Tell me a bit about what happened, if you're comfortable talking about it."

Enez stared at her hands and then lifted her face to find Susan looking into her eyes. "Yes, I can talk about it. I was involved with a pimp for many years, and he was always very abusive towards me. The last time I saw him he beat me really, really bad. I ended up in the hospital and then a shelter. I want a new life, and I thought I could find it if I left Memphis."

Susan wrote notes as Enez spoke. Just as Tammy Faye had told Enez the night before, she said, "We're here for you. You can stay for two months, but we expect you to look for employment and save your money to find a place to live. After you get a job, we'll want you to pay $15 per week for rent. There are daily group meetings, and you'll share in keeping the house clean. Everyone takes turns cooking the meals. There are some women who work days, but they have chores too." Susan came from around her desk and gave Enez a hug. Together, they took a tour of the house.

"The laundry room is to the left of the kitchen, and behind that is the store room. This room is always locked. You'll have to sign out for detergent, soap, and other female products you might need. Through this door is the food pantry. The counselor on duty will take out items for the daily meals. Now I'll give you two sets of towels and bed sheets. You're responsible for keeping them clean. Oh yeah, we'll give you bus tokens to look for a job too. Do you have any questions for me?"

Over the next few weeks, Enez attended support group meetings and looked for a job. One night, a woman shared her testimony of survival from the grips of her violent husband. His Grace and Mercy began the healing process of her broken spirit. God had knitted her human being together again for His glory. God had a plan!

Enez knew all to well the grips of old Satan and his tactics. She tried temporary jobs that did not last long enough to save money. Enez started to become frustrated and anxious. Her two months were coming to an end, and she was becoming desperate. Patience was not one of Enez's virtues, and she soon returned to her old life. Early one morning, she thought to herself, "I need some money." She asked for her weekly bus tokens and proceeded to get dressed for the day. Many beautiful pieces of clothing had been donated to the shelter, and she chose a cream colored skirt and matching blouse with brown high-heeled pumps. Her dark hair was pulled away from her sculptured face, and her lips were shining red. She wore glasses that appeared to give her the innocence she so desired. She was now ready.

Enez walked out of the shelter doors to make her money. She was familiar with the bus route and where the action was for women of the afternoon.

Enez went to one of the most elaborate hotels downtown. As she entered, a nice looking white man waved at her. They had a few drinks in the lounge area before he escorted her to his room. Although Enez had gone back to her old lifestyle, she always returned to the shelter before curfew to maintain the rules and regulations. Many women at the shelter practiced God's Word. In group, Enez heard one woman say, "At all times we must wait on God. There is NOTHING we can do on our own without His Marvelous power. He loves us, we must trust Him, have Faith in what he desires us to do according to His Word."

The house was quiet. Enez and Vickie talked as they lay in their beds, staring at the ceiling. Enez said, "Vickie, I know I'm leaving my Shelter in the midst of the storm. But this is all I know. I keep trying to be the one to control my life."

Vickie cleared her throat, "You know, Enez, an airplane can't fly right without a good pilot. A life cannot fly right without the Good Shepherd. Enez, God talks to us about this. He says, '***I have gone astray like a lost sheep…***'"

They were silent for a moment. Then, Vickie quietly asked, "Enez, what are you gonna do with your life?"

Hoping her answer would satisfy Vickie, Enez said, "I'm going to do what I do and save my money until I can get me a place to live."

"I will always have you in my prayers, friend."

Vickie did not divulge Enez's decision to remain in an ungodly lifestyle. Vickie remained Enez's friend.

Early one morning, Enez went to the kitchen to do her morning chores. She saw a young woman with three children, sitting at the dining room table in the adjourning room. She had not seen them before that day. The woman's skin was a smooth, creamy coffee, and she wore a torn t-shirt and blue jeans. Her feet were bare. Her children sat huddled close to her, as if she might suddenly disappear or as if they wanted to protect her. Enez asked the woman, "Would you like me to give your children some breakfast while you wait?"

The woman looked at her through Betty Davis eyes and answered in a Washingtonian accent, "Yes, I would appreciate that so kindly." Enez heard the woman say to the children, "Go wash your hands. You remember where the other nice lady showed you the bathroom."

Enez returned with plates for each of the children. It was a good hearty breakfast of sausage, eggs, hash browns, and biscuits. Enez went back upstairs to get ready to leave for the day.

Another day, it was time for support group. The children had gone to school, and the women gathered in the living room in comfortable, high back chairs and couches. It was a warm, beige colored room, with nature paintings on the walls. Tammy Faye entered the room and sat in one of the high back chairs. "Alright ladies, you know why we are here this morning. Let's start by going around the room and giving your name. We'll start on the left side of the room." Enez sat in a chair, and when it was her turn, she said, "My name is Enez. I moved here from Memphis, Tennessee."

When the group finished, the new woman, Dianna, stopped Enez in the hallway. "Enez, I never thanked you for feeding my children yesterday. I really appreciated your help. I work for the telephone company in D.C., and I won't be here too many more days. I need a roommate to help me pay the rent."

A few days later, Enez and Dianna moved into a two-bedroom apartment with her children. Enez agreed to sleep in the living room on a hideaway bed. The living arrangements were great. Dianna worked days, and Enez hustled the streets at night.

Early one winter morning, Enez got a phone call from one of the counselors at the shelter. "Hello," Enez said sleepily.

"Enez, I saw you last night near Thomas Circle. Are you still in your old behavior?" Bobbie, the counselor from the shelter asked with concern. "Jesus is waiting on you to make the right choice. You have been blessed. I know you do not see it. I have been there, Enez, and I know how hard it is to give up old behaviors that have worked for you. God can and He will make a new creature of you, Enez, if you give him a try."

Enez broke the silence, "I know I still want to run something, but I've run right into the enemy on the streets of Washington D.C. Bobbie, when I save enough money to get my own place, I'll stop hustling the streets."

Bobbie's calm voice was very sincere, "Enez, I will always have you in my prayers. I know God has a better plan for you. Call me, Enez. Do you still have the number at the shelter?"

Enez nodded and replied, "Yes, I do have the number," as the women said their goodbyes.

Enez was called the Renegade from the South because she did not have a pimp. Her money stayed in her pocket, and she walked the streets alone. God's special Angels must have been watching over her.

Just before the stars covered the nightly sky, she got dressed for the evening. Her legs were covered with silky, black panty hose, and her red mini dress slipped over her shapely body. Red and black high heeled pumps gave her the height she did not inherit. Her brown long hair bounced with curls, and she wore eyeglasses to give the impression of innocence.

As Enez arrived at the club, one of her closest male friends waited for her inside. She sat down next to her friend.

"Hey Enez, you are looking lovely as always. Girl, I know you are going to knock them out tonight," He nodded with approval.

"Yeah, I really hope so, Sammy. I need to get my own place real soon," she replied, sipping on the beverage Sammy had ordered for her. He knew Enez liked to drink Gin and Tonic, with a twist of lime.

She heard the ice clink in Sammy's glass as she stared out the window. "You wanna hear your song tonight?" he asked.

Enez glanced across the street at the tall building. It looked different at night. She did not answer as her thoughts were on other matters. She moved her body to the music playing from the jukebox. It was Anita Baker, singing "You Better Watch Your Step."

Enez had a policy to never work around black hookers because she thought they were nothing but trouble. To look at her, a person would not know whether she was a business woman or a hooker. She was dressed in an outfit that a secretary might wear, with just enough make up to highlight her natural beauty. She did not believe in looking like a hooker, since that was sure to produce a call to the police. That would be a turn-off to the high-paying men, and hotel management would become the wiser. Enez repainted her thick lips with glossy red lipstick. She looked at her watch and said, "Well, it's time for me to get on my hustle. I won't come back to the club tonight. Sammy, you have a good night."

"You too, baby. Be careful."

Outside, a man stood across the street, staring at her before he called her name. She glanced at him as he said, "Aren't you Nicko's woman?"

Her heart began to race, and fear moved her legs faster than before. She thought to herself, "Who is this man? How does he know my name in connection with Nicko?" She felt him following her towards the hotel. Suddenly, Enez heard Sammy's voice calling her name. She turned to see Sammy behind the man. Enez stopped, and so did the man behind her.

Sammy approached them both quickly. "Hey man, do you think you know this woman?" He was 6 foot 2 inches tall and weighed 250 pounds, whereas the stranger was about 5 feet 2 inches and maybe weighed 160 pounds.

He answered quickly, "Yeah, I know her from Memphis. She was with my partner. I just wanna know if she is looking for a pimp."

Sammy warned the man not to approach Enez again. "This is not Memphis, and you don't want trouble from D.C. players." He walked away saying, "Don't forget, Dingo baby." Then, he stood in the shadows as he watched Enez enter the hotel lounge.

She frequented this hotel lounge two nights a week. Tonight, she ordered a Coke on ice. A man sat next to her while she enjoyed the music played by the pianist. She sat quietly, sipping on her Coke. She thought about requesting a jazz tune from the pianist as the man said to her in a southern droll, "Hey, I am Pat. Short for Patrick." He looked at her glass, "What are you drinking?"

She looked at her glass before answering, "Oh, I'm just drinking Coke on ice."

Pat signaled to the waitress, "Sally, I'd like to order another scotch and water and another Coke and ice for the lady, please." Their conversation began with his business in Washington. Enez noticed a wedding ring but did not mention it or any children, as she knew that would kill any money making propositions she had in mind. The waitress returned with their drinks, and he asked her to run a tab.

They continued drinking, and soon his flesh began to take over his mind. Enez knew she was in control at that point. He suggested cocktails in his room, and Enez accepted the offer. Before he could take his clothes off, he fell asleep, and his wallet was available for Enez. They never discussed money, but she had watched him as he paid for their drinks and tipped the waitress. She knew she had a "Duck." Enez opened his wallet to find several $100 bills and quickly removed them before she quietly left the room. Although the night was still young, she decided to flag a taxi back to Maryland.

It was a winter walk to the neighborhood store when the driver in a dark green Cadillac parked in front of the store. Their brown eyes met as he got out of the car, and she noticed he was a nice looking man. He was a tall man with a pleasant smile. “Hey baby,” he said in a baritone voice as he opened the door to the store for Enez. She picked up her items and noticed the man at the cashier’s counter as she stood next in line. The man turned and told the cashier to add her items to his purchase. He turned back to pay the cashier and said, “No thank you, I won’t need a bag” as the cashier attempted to put his soda in a bag. “I am sure she will need a bag, though.” The cashier put Enez’s items in a bag and Enez thanked the man and the cashier.

They stood outside together. “Pretty lady, what’s your name?” he asked her.

She recognized him and knew he was not a pimp. He was a drug dealer. They started dating soon after. He often came downtown to Peggy’s Place and watched her work, but he never asked Enez for money. They took trips to Atlantic City almost every weekend to relax.

There was something strange about this man. He had a secret life other than his life with Enez. Enez frequently received calls from a man who threatened to kill her if she did not leave Harry alone. At first, she thought the man was playing games, but it became serious when the man called her Atlantic City hotel room one evening before Harry arrived. Enez mentioned the phone calls when Harry arrived. The phone continued to ring, and Enez answered, “Hello.”

The voice on the other end was muffled, "I'm in the parking lot, and you need to tell my man to come out now, or there's going to be some trouble." The phone went dead. Harry made a phone call and told the person to stop calling.

Finally, over dinner, Harry admitted to Enez he had a wife and a two-year-old daughter.

Enez asked, "What about the male phone calls?"

Harry took her hand and explained, "Her brother may be in on this caper to scare you."

"Harry, I can't continue this relationship with you. Somebody could get hurt! After this weekend, let's call it quits. I've had a wonderful time being with you." Although he was not happy, he accepted her reaction to his married life, and they did not see each other again.

It was past ten o'clock one night when Enez entered one of the finest Hilton Hotels. The lounge was quiet tonight. The bartender was talking to a customer when Enez sat on the bar stool and crossed her legs. As she looked in the mirror behind the bar, she saw the hotel's limousine driver signal to her. She walked to him, and he said, "I saw you getting out of the cab, and I wanted to talk to you."

She was not convinced of his honesty. "Talk to me about what?"

"Look, I know you're a hooker and a classy one to be a black chick. I've seen you on M street."

"So, what do you want with me?"

He looked at her with a smile, "You ain't one of those thieving hookers are you? I get some really good paying men, and I don't want no woman who is going to steal."

Enez agreed with him, and they became business partners. Some nights, she rode the subway to downtown D.C.. Other times, he drove her around to pick up customers. One cool winter's night, there was a chill from the waters of the Potomac River. As they rode through the spotlights from Thomas Circle; she spotted a familiar face standing next to a statue. It was Nicko's first cousin, Oscar.

Two weeks before, Nicko called Enez collect from Los Angeles. She had given his sister-in-law her phone number. She accepted the call. "What's up, Enez? I'm not going to hold you long. I need you to send me some money. Baby, I don't have nobody. The white girl is in jail, and I am round here snatching little old ladies' pocketbooks."

Enez did not want to hear anymore. "Yes, I will send you something Western Union tomorrow, but please don't call me anymore." Enez said bitterly. He agreed with a laugh as they said their goodbyes. The next day, she sent him money and did not accept any more collect calls from him.

Now, Enez noticed Oscar wearing diamonds from his neck to hands. The lights from the streets and cars gave them their sparkling glow. She had the driver stop the limo, and Oscar was surprised when he saw her. They exchanged numbers.

It was a slow night, and Enez decided to have the limo driver take her back to Maryland. Her room mate was still up, watching TV. Enez sat on the side of Dianna's bed to talk to her about the coincidence that night. "Dianna, guess what? I saw Nicko's cousin standing in the middle of Thomas Circle tonight. My friend, Bruce, the limo driver stopped the car in traffic and we exchanged phone numbers."

Dianna's mother was from the south, and she instilled religious scriptures in Dianna's childhood development. Dianna looked at her and quoted, "***But put ye on the Lord Jesus Christ, and make not provision for the flesh, to fulfilleth lust there of***" (Romans 13:14).

Enez communicated with Oscar over the next several days. One night after hustling all night, Enez found herself in the car with Oscar, crossing the 14th Street bridge into Virginia. His eyes focused straight ahead as Enez's words slurred from the alcohol she had drunk at the hotel earlier that night. "I'm ready to have a man in my life and move out of my shared apartment."

Oscar pulled up and parked in the garage of a modern weekly rate hotel. He spoke softly as he told Enez to pack her clothes and move into the suite with him and his other women. Enez chose Oscar to be her man as she gave him the money she had made earlier that day. The night passed quickly. She had made the choice to leave the freedom of her life to a life of human slavery. She looked at the Potomac River's waters, watching the freedom of each wave, wishing she had not made the choice in her drunken state of mind. Neither of them wanted anything more from each other but to live a worldly life. She gave him her money, and he took care of her. Her rent was paid, she ate at the finest restaurants, and she had money for shopping trips. There was never a dull moment with Oscar and his other women.

Vickie Lee staggered into the hotel suite one dreary night. Her blonde hair fell into her eyes as she slurred harsh words to the redheaded woman seated at the edge of the bed. The women were like a tag team. They chose the same pimp and followed him. The redhead, Monica, stared at Vickie Lee. "I don't care what you're talking about, Vickie Lee. I was leaving your drunk $%^& in the street."

Vickie Lee staggered back and stood with her legs spread wide. Her small hands reached inside her bosom and pulled out a roll of money. "I know Daddy will like this trap tonight. Where is Daddy anyway?" she asked drunkenly.

Monica said sharply, "He went with Snow to get another room for her alone."

Vickie Lee tried to slam a chair on the floor when Oscar suddenly walked in to the room. Her temper was at a boiling point as she turned to him. "Where is Snow, Oscar?"

"Where is my money, Vickie Lee?"

Vickie pulled up her blouse, walked over to Oscar, and handed him five crisp one hundred bills.

Vickie Lee was one of Oscar's top thievery women. Oscar looked at Vickie Lee and said, "Don't look like you robbed anybody tonight."

Monica whispered, "Naw, she was too drunk."

Oscar turned to stare coldly at Monica, "Lately, your money isn't exceeding two hundred a night."

"Hey ladies, I'm feeling pretty good this morning. Let's go out and eat breakfast," he said with a smile on his face as his mood shifted. He walked out with Enez, Monica, and Vickie Lee trailing behind him. Suddenly, he stopped two doors down and told the women to meet him in the lobby. As the women waited, Snow and Oscar exited the elevator.

Oscar drove a foreign car. He did not like to show off to the police, especially with him being a black man with three white women. Vickie Lee sat in the front with Oscar as they all piled into the car. She was in a disgusting, drunken mood, and they all wanted to keep the scene peaceful.

Oscar bought Enez a round trip ticket to Memphis for her to visit her daughter for her birthday. Enez trusted Oscar, and he was good to her. He never called her derogatory names or hit her.

Oscar sent Enez, Monica, Vickie Lee, and Snow to New York on a train. From there, they traveled to Atlantic City to work their hustle. Oscar started having problems with his girls as they started becoming jealous of each other and drifting away from Oscar. He started out with three white women, but eventually only Snow and Enez remained. Snow was a pretty, natural blond headed girl from Florida. Oscar sent Enez to Atlantic City to set up living quarters for the women to live and work. Atlantic City was Enez's city – she knew the city well.

As night fell, darkness covered figures in shadows, and the high-roll gamblers crowded the casinos. Where the daytime tourists had stood on the boardwalk, happily watching seagulls and the ocean waters earlier in the day became darkly ominous spots where men and women walked with drunken steps.

Enez's steps were confident as if she was royalty. This was her city. Her tapered haircut with blonde streaks fell on her face and bounced with every movement of her silky black dress. Her legs were covered with sheer black stockings and black pumps. She entered a crowded casino and heard bells ringing, voices shouting, and lights shining. The waitresses carried drinks to gamblers, and men tipped them while the women watched with envy. As she walked through the casino, Enez noticed the blackjack tables and stood next to a gambler to watch. After the dealer won the hand, she decided to enter the lounge.

A local band was on stage. The lead singer, a young woman, sounded very much like Minnie Riperton as she sang Riperton's hit song, "Lov'in You." Enez sat at the bar to watch the show when she heard a deep voiced man ordering a drink. Enez turned to see a slim white man sitting next to her.

She watched the bartender as he paid for his drink and noticed the man received change for a hundred dollar bill. Enez turned towards the show, pretending to pay attention to the stage. She felt his presence behind her.

"Can I refresh your drink ma'am?" the bartender asked her in a soft voice.

"Yes, I'd like that very much."

The man seated next to her spoke politely, "Can I pay for your drink?"

"Yes, thank you," she replied.

The bartender said, "That will be $5.25 please," as she placed Enez's drink in front of her. The man took a 20 dollar bill from his previous change and gave it to the bartender. "You can bring me another round, Susan, and keep the change," he said with a half smile on his face.

"Are you enjoying the show? The singer sure can sing," he said as he cleared his throat.

The bartender returned with his order, "Thank you, sir. Is there anything else I can get for you?"

"No, no, not at this time, but thanks for asking." On the stage, the guitar player announced a 30-minute break. The man continued their conversation, "I'm so sorry, I didn't properly introduce myself. I'm Frank, and you sure are a beautiful woman! Have you ever gambled before? I like to blackjack," he grinned.

"No, I don't know how to play," Enez said with confused look on her face.

"Tell you what, miss. Oh, by the way, what's your name?"

"Veronica, but you can call me Verne," Enez lied with a bright smile.

"Okay Verne, let's go to the table. I'll put the money down, and you just play. I'll tell you what to do."

They walked on to the casino floor and stood by a table that had just begun playing. When the dealer lost, Frank signaled Enez to sit down, and they played until they won $3,500. Frank split half the money with Enez, and then they walked to another blackjack table.

As he continued gambling, she whispered in his ear, "I have to go to the little girl's room. I'll be right back." Enez left the casino to go to her hotel. She never saw Frank again.

A few nights later, she got lucky again. This time, she met a man who trusted her with his ATM card and PIN number. He was a lonely man who wanted a companion. He wined and dined her for two days. Finally, Enez grew tired of him and decided to empty his bank account before she moved to another section of Atlantic City.

Two weeks later, Oscar and Snow arrived in Atlantic City. On Snow's first night in town, Oscar bragged that she had earned $1,000 in an hour. Enez, Oscar, and Snow lived in rundown hotels on the Blackhorse Pike for four weeks. Eventually, the women became familiar faces to the police and local casinos, and it was time to give the city a break.

Oscar came to Enez's hotel and laid across the bed as he stared up at the ceiling. His eyes drifted around the room until they connected with hers in the mirror. "Well, Enez," Oscar said quietly, "looks like it's time for us to move back to Alexandria, Virginia. This time, I think I'll rent a one-bedroom duplex. You can have the bedroom, and I'll sleep with Snow in the living room."

"Oscar, it sounds like you've already got this planned."

Oscar sat on the edge of the bed and rubbed his forehead, "Yeah, we just came here for a minute. I want to continue to get down in D.C. Pack up all your things because we're leaving in the morning." He walked towards the door to leave and paused, "I'm going out for lunch. Do you wanna go, or do you want me to bring you something back?"

She smiled and asked for a Philly steak.

Oscar knew just the deli Enez liked to eat subs from. He smiled at her, "Okay baby, I'll get that for you," he said as he closed the door behind him.

Later, the stars blinked as she walked the boardwalk. She smelled rain in the air and thought, "This is my last night, working the casino." She smiled and nodded towards the man standing at the door as he said, "You look like a winner tonight, lady. Good luck!"

Enez walked into the lounge and ordered red wine from the bar. The hour went by slowly, and she began to wish she could be back in Washington D.C. with her old roommate. She wished she had not been so impulsive. Finally, a man sat next to her and ordered a drink and food. She looked at the oysters he had ordered and thought how nice they would taste with red wine. Her mind was not on earning any money tonight. She had had her fun with Oscar, and now she was ready to move on with her life. The sound of voices filled the lounge as patrons talked and laughed.

She thought to herself, "I have a few hundred dollars tucked away. I can give Oscar a couple of hundred dollars and have a good time on my last night here." She signaled the waitress and ordered oysters on the half shell and another glass of red wine. The man that had sat next to her was gone. She sat daydreaming, when a deep voice interrupted her thoughts. She jumped back in surprise as a man said, "Hey, baby." His blue eyes traveled down to her crossed legs as he pulled out his wallet to order a drink. Enez noticed he had a lot of money crammed in his wallet. "How are ya doin, little fine lady? My name is Jimmy." He smiled from beneath his cowboy hat as Enez extended her hand out to him. She studied him closely with an expert eye.

"You mind if I sit down next to ya?" He did not wait for her reply. Enez was attracted to his blue eyes as he sat down. "What's your name, honey?" he asked.

"Just call me Honey," she said, pulling her skirt down.

He cocked his head sideways as he looked at her, "Your skin complexion sure is pretty like honey." Enez could not believe it; this man was trying to hit on her! "I reckon you've been told that before, huh?"

They talked for another thirty minutes before Enez excused herself to go to the bathroom. She decided not to return because her intuition warned her about him. "It is better to be safe than sorry," she thought to herself. As Enez walked out of the casino from the rear, she noticed the night had cooled down and she wrapped her jacket around her body as she walked down the boardwalk.

Enez was not looking for work tonight. She just wanted enjoyment, but that is not what she found. She heard a man yell, "Over here, Officer! He's over here!" She saw a white man lying on the ground, holding his chest and moaning. She looked around at the crowd, and no one seemed to be concerned about the man clinging to life. She had never seen death before, and she did not want to see this one, so she hurriedly ran through the front of the casino in just enough time to catch the Jitney, a small bus that shuttled tourists to all the casinos.

Enez saw a colorful sign for the Castle Casino. She had not been to it before because it was off the boardwalk. The bus stopped at the casino, and she walked to the entrance. She saw running escalators, huge chandeliers on the ceilings, and red, carpeted floors. As she walked, she heard bells ringing from the slot machines and people smoking, drinking, and gambling. As she approached the rear of the gambling floor, she saw a lounge.

The room was dimly lit by candles on the tables, and soft jazz played in the background. She found a table and crossed her legs as she sat down. She took a deep breath as the waitress approached with a pleasant smile, "Good evening, may I get you something to drink?"

"Yes, I will have a Coke, please." Enez thought to herself, "I've had my limit and I surely don't want to go back to the hotel drunk with a lie." She looked at her watch and thought, "Another hour, and I will be okay."

She relaxed to the sound of the music as she sipped her drink. "It's funny," she thought, "how I wanna break away from a man who treats me with kindness. I'm about to have my own place, and I want to break out on him." She stared down at her now empty glass and thought, "All the good stuff is gone from the glass, just like this relationship with Oscar."

As she left the casino, she flagged a taxi to return to the hotel. Oscar was not there when she arrived. She got several hundred dollar bills from her secret stash to have in case he came to her room before going to sleep, but she did not hear his knock until the next morning. Oscar unlocked the door to find Enez getting dressed in the bathroom.

"Good morning," Enez said with a bright smile.

He smiled back at her and asked, "Is everything packed and ready to go?"

"Yes, I'm all ready to go."

Oscar did not realize their arrangement was coming to an abrupt end. "Okay, I'll put the luggage in the trunk, and you take the keys to the hotel office. We'll stop and get breakfast before we hit the highway."

The Italian woman at the front desk recognized Enez and smiled, "Good morning, Enez," she said with a heavy accent.

"Good morning to you too," Enez winked at the woman. "I'm turning in the keys for the two rooms I rented."

"Oh, you're leaving us, huh? Are you going back to D.C.?"

Enez ignored the question. "Do I owe you for any phone calls?"

"All phone calls are paid up. That man paid for all the calls."

"Okay Mary, I will see you next time I'm in town." Enez walked out to the waiting car. Snow was asleep in the back seat as Enez slid into the front.

Oscar stopped at a White Castles diner for breakfast just before they reached the New Jersey Turnpike. They reached D.C. almost four hours later.

When they arrived, Enez, Oscar, and Snow rented a one-bedroom duplex. Oscar kept his bankroll in his sock. Enez relaxed about her investment when she saw all the money Oscar pulled from his sock. She tried not to worry about the choice she had made to be with Oscar. The next few weeks passed quickly.

One day, Enez walked slowly towards L Street and decided to check on her old stomping ground, Peggy's Place. When she arrived, she saw the restaurant had not changed. It was still small, with pimps, hookers, and wanna-be's hanging around. A young man dropped a few coins into the juke box, and the sounds of Marvin Gaye's "What's Going On" filled the place. The man danced over to a bar stool and turned with a smile to Enez.

Enez ignored him as she signaled for the waitress. "What can I get you, honey?" the waitress asked as she chewed on her gum.

"I'll have a cognac and a side order of Coke, please," she replied with a half smile.

The man ran his eyes over Enez's tight-fitting, cashmere dress, then looked at her legs until she blushed and smiled at him. He approached Enez's table with a smile as he asked for her name. Enez knew the pimp law: she had not left Oscar, so she was silent. The man grabbed the back of a chair and sat down as he studied her closely with his light brown eyes.

"I already have a man," she answered him.

He looked at her coldly and smiled, "Well, you must not be happy if you're sitting here and not getting your man's money."

She sat, hoping he would go away. She looked toward the end of the bar and noticed Deena walking to one of the bar stools.

"Hey baby, if you're ever looking for a real pimp, look up Duke," he whispered in her ear as he got up from his chair.

Enez walked over to the end of the bar where Deena sat. "Hey, Deena."

Deena looked like a replica of Angela Bassett. Deena turned as she exhaled a cloud of cigarette smoke from her nostrils, "Hello, my friend. Sit down and have drink with me."

Enez looked at her watch and decided it was getting late. She needed to earn some money. "Deena as always, it's good to see you, but I'm going to pass on that drink."

Deena nodded her head in agreement, "Hope we can get together soon."

"I'll keep that in mind."

Back at the duplex, Enez paced the living room floors, waiting on Oscar to return. "I got money saved and I want out of this relationship," she repeated to herself over and over. "He will understand. I don't want to be here anymore. Besides, he is Nicko's cousin. He doesn't have anything tied up with me."

Enez heard a car door shut and peeped from the small window in the kitchen. It was Oscar, and he was alone. "Perfect," she thought to herself. Oscar dropped into a red velvet chair when he came into the living room.

Enez said, "Oscar, I have something I need to talk with you about."

He turned to look at her and saw the lifeless expression she wore on her face. He had a clue that he was not about to hear good news. "Yeah, baby."

She sat across from him in a matching chair. "Oscar, I'm not happy being here anymore. I want out," she said nervously. Enez knew Oscar was not like Nicko.

He looked at her for answers, but he only asked one question, "Where can I take you?"

"I called Dianna. She said I can come back to her place to stay."

"Whenever you want to leave, Enez," he said with a smile.

"I'm already packed, Oscar."

Oscar never looked annoyed as he drove Enez to Dianna's apartment. That was the last time Enez saw Oscar in D.C. She knocked on the door, and

Dianna welcomed her with open arms so that she would not be homeless.

That night after dinner, Dianna and Enez had a long conversation while the children slept. Dianna once again spoke her mother's everlasting words from the Bible, "***Man that is born of a woman is of few days, and full of trouble***" (Job14:1).

A few days passed, and Enez once again found herself working the downtown streets of D.C. She met a man at Peggy's Place. He was tall and handsome, and she found him to be very interesting. He made her laugh, he called her sweet names, and he paid a lot of attention to her.

He smiled at her, "I know you're not sitting here by yourself, not a pretty lady like you. Where is your man?"

Enez had seen him in the bar before, but he had always left quickly and had not paid any attention to her. Now, he sat down next to her. She looked at him with astonishment and said, "I didn't ask you to sit down with me."

He smiled, "Oh, but your eyes asked me. What's your name?"

Before she could tell him, a waitress asked, "What can I get for you two?"

Enez ordered a cognac and Coke. The man replied, "Oh I don't need anything right now."

Enez returned to their conversation, "Oh, my name is Enez. What's yours?"

"My name is Carl. I am from D.C."

The waitress returned with Enez's order. As Enez reached for her money, Carl gave the waitress the amount. They laughed and talked together for several hours. He was very handsome, and Enez was attracted to him. It would be a few days before she would see him again.

The D.C. winter snow fell, and the streets were filled with pimps, prostitutes, drug addicts, dealers, and men looking to fulfill their sexual desires. The white hookers dressed in mink coats covering their half naked, freezing bodies. The black hookers stood near Thomas Circle, walking to stay warm, while their pimps watched their half naked money (women) without coats.

Enez walked in the bar wearing a black, full-length leather coat to match her high-heeled boots and leather mini-skirt. Her brown leopard sweater accentuated her shapely breasts and waist. Deena sat by a window, watching the snow fall.

"What's up, girl?" Deena asked Enez happily.

"You know, the same old, same old."

Deena smiled as she blew a cloud of smoke, "Sit down with me. I haven't talk to you in a while. I saw you talking with Carl a few nights ago. He's bad news, Enez. Carl and his woman smoke crack like two old broke cars. I just thought I'd tell you. You know, we renegades gotta watch each others back."

Enez looked out the window to see Carl and a woman entering the bar. She had not seen Carl since the bar, and he nodded his head in greeting as he passed her. She walked to the bar with her empty glass, “Peggy, will you refresh my drink, please? I’ll pick it up on my way back from the ladies room.”

As Enez walked past Carl, he grabbed her arm and twisted her body to face him. Her eyes dropped to his strong hands as his companion sat motionless on her bar stool. Carl said, “You appeared to be busy with Deena when I walked in. I didn’t want to interrupt you.”

He moved his grasp to her hand, and she slipped it away as she gently whispered in his ear, “I can’t see you anymore.”

Carl laughed quietly and turned away from her on his bar stool.

When Enez returned from the ladies room, Carl was leaving the bar with a sideways glance at Deena. Perhaps he knew Deena had told Enez about his drug habit. The bartender placed Enez’s drink on the table, and Deena continued their conversation. “Enez, I know two businessmen in town who wanted a date tonight. I asked Sharon to meet me here earlier, but she hasn’t shown up, so why don’t you join me?”

Enez asked quickly, “How much are they paying?”

Deena smiled at her, "One hundred fifty dollars a piece. Girl, all they want is less than an hour of fun. They're my regulars. Look, if you're interested, we need to get a cab now."

At the corner traffic light, Deena flagged a cab for them. The cab driver was a Jamaican man with a strong accent. "Where are you going, ladies?"

"To Georgetown on M Street," Deena replied.

Enez sat by the window and watched the tire tracks as they were quickly covered by huge snow flakes. She was mesmerized by the sound of the windshield wipers as she thought about the purity of the snow and hoped her life could be pure also. She was thinking about her daughter when Deena's voice interrupted her thoughts to give instructions to the taxi driver. Deena paid the taxi driver when they stopped. They pulled knitted caps over their heads as they walked to a nearby Greek restaurant where Deena met her clients before going to their hotel rooms.

Two men were sitting at the bar when Deena and Enez walked into the restaurant. Deena approached the bald headed man, and he spoke to her in a Greek accent, "Hello, Nina."

Enez laughed to herself. The bald headed man reminded her of Telly Savalas from the 1970's detective show, Kojak. Any moment now, she expected him to say, "Who loves ya, baby?" since that was one of Kojak's famous lines on the show. The men escorted Deena and Enez to a table.

The sound of tinkling, metallic coins coming from the stage at the center of the restaurant caught Enez's attention, where she saw women dressed in sheer, green and purple harem pants. Precisely placed beads covered their pants, and the women wore scarves over their hips. The fabric swished back and forth as they moved their hips from side to side, dancing in their bare feet. Their outfits were completed by matching veils covering their faces and colored coins inserted in their belly buttons. The music and language were unfamiliar to Enez's ears.

The other man, who had been quiet since their arrival, now asked Enez her name.

"Oh, I'm sorry, baby. I am Dee, and you are?" Her mind was still on the belly dancers. Perhaps the beautiful costumes they wore reminded her of her own dancing years.

The man placed his arms on the table and answered, "My name is Jim."

Enez extended her hand and said, "Nice to meet you, Jim."

"Would you like something to eat, Dee?" he asked her as he picked up a menu from the table.

"No thanks, I'm not hungry. I'd just like to order a drink."

Jim finished looking over the menu and decided he would not order anything to eat either as a smiling waitress walked towards the table. Enez still did not know the bald man's name until the waitress called his name, “Mr. Buddy, what are you eating tonight?”

Buddy stared down at the menu without answering. Deena spoke up immediately. “Vera, why don’t you give us our special: lamb and steamed veggies.”

Buddy agreed, “Yes, that sounds good, Vera.” Jim asked for another glass of red wine, and Enez asked for a Coke on ice. She knew she had had enough alcohol. For the next hour, they watched the dancers perform, as they talked, ate, and drank.

Enez soon became overwhelmed by the men’s conduct. She had no idea what would come next. Jim placed two one hundred dollar bills in Enez’s palm as he held her hand. After another hour had passed, Buddy looked at the women and asked, “Are you ready for a taxi?” Enez thought he meant for them to leave the restaurant and finish the night in their hotel room.

Deena responded, “Are you ready for a taxi?”

He smiled, “Baby, I’ve had a great time tonight, but I have an early meeting, and I need some rest.” He waved to the waitress and asked her to call a taxi. As the cab arrived, Buddy slipped something into Deena‘s hand. She smiled and kissed him on the cheek.

They walked outside into the blistering cold and snow, and each pair got into two awaiting taxi cabs. Buddy gave the driver of the women’s cab a fifty dollar bill and said goodbye to them. Enez never saw Jim again after that night.

"Enez, are you going back to Maryland tonight?" Deena asked while she refreshed her lipstick.

"Yes, I am. It looks like we're going to have some heavy snow, and I want to be at home to enjoy it."

"You've never seen snow like this before in Memphis?" Deena looked surprised.

"No, Deena. We don't have knee-deep snow in Memphis."

"Well, girl, you're in for a treat. Do you have snow boots?"

"Snow boots, never heard of them," Enez replied.

"Then we'd better have the driver take me home first. I'll give you my extra pair," Deena laughed.

Deena lived near Rhode Island Avenue, which was not far from the shelter where Enez had once lived. As they neared, Enez thought about her purpose for moving to D.C. She remembered how spiritually and physically broken-hearted she had been. Suddenly, Deena interrupted her thoughts as she instructed the driver to turn in the driveway and wait for her to return. Enez waited in the back seat until Deena returned with a boot box. She gave the box to Enez and said, "Good night."

As they drove off, Enez reminded the driver that she lived in Prince George County. He nodded his head in acknowledgement. Finally, she arrived home after 25 minutes of careful driving. Everyone in the house was asleep, and she quietly went to bed and fell asleep.

For several days, she watched the snow fall as it covered the parked cars. School was cancelled, Enez watched them while their mother worked. Thinking about her own daughter brought tears to her eyes. She held her daughter's picture to her chest and whispered, "I'm so sorry, honey, that my life is so messed up. Maybe one day I will get it together." She tucked the picture back inside her wallet and began preparing lunch for the children. Later, Enez watched the news. The news reported the streets were clearing, and schools would open the next day.

When everyone left for school and work the next day, Enez thought about searching for day-time work in D.C. She looked at her savings and decided to prepare for work. Her eyes drift around the closet as she picked out some warm clothing. She chose a beige sweater and dark brown corduroy pants and boots. After she applied her lip gloss, she put on her beige cotton hat and all-weather coat on. Enez took the subway to D.C.

She stopped at a restaurant on L Street for a cup of hot coca and heard a horn blow in her direction as she left the restaurant. Enez turned to see a man in a brown Lincoln Continental, rolling his window down. She smiled at him as she kept walking. Her instinct told her he was a hustler as she heard him open his car door and call out to her in a deep voice, "Baby, I just wanna talk to ya. You're looking good to me. Let me take ya to brunch."

She stopped walking and turned to face him. He wore big diamond rings and a fancy suit. His hair was relaxed and curled, and his caramel brown complexion was flawless. Enez liked what she saw and decided to let him take her to brunch. She stood still as he approached her, "Hey, baby, how about it? Let me take your fine self to brunch."

"I don't just get in any man's car."

"That's right," he said with a smile. "So let's walk down the street to Charlie's Restaurant. They serve a mean brunch." Enez agreed. "If I was a betting man, I would say you don't have one," he said as they walked to Charlie's.

She looked at him curiously and asked, "Have one what?"

The hostess appeared before he could answer her. "Sir, would you like a table for two, smoking or non-smoking?"

"Yes, in a cozy corner please. Non–smoking is fine." They followed the hostess to a table, and he pulled out the chair for Enez after he helped her with her coat.

"Hmm," she thought, "he is a gentleman."

The hostess said, "Your waitress will be with you in a moment. Here is your menu."

Enez pretended to look at the menu. She had eaten at this restaurant many times and knew the menu. The man said to her, “I apologize, I didn’t tell you my name. My mother named me Arthur, but I picked up the name Sugar as a teenager. And who are you?”

“My name is Enez,” she replied.

The waitress now stood beside him asking, “Are you ready to order?”

Sugar looked into her face as Enez ordered, “I’d like to have the Spanish omelet with dry toast and a glass of water with lemon slices.”

“That sounds good, Enez. I believe I’ll have the same thing.” He looked at the waitress and said, “That was easy, wasn’t it?” The waitress half smiled and took their menus.

Sugar sat across from Enez and looked into her eyes. “You know, they say your eyes are windows to your heart.” He took her hand and began telling her about himself. “I’m from Englewood, California. I left Cali a year ago and moved to D.C.”

The waitress returned with their beverages and placed condiments on the table. Sugar looked annoyed at the waitress, as if she had interrupted his train of thought. When she walked away, he turned back to Enez. “As I was saying, so there is no misunderstanding, I really need to explain myself to you. I am a pimp, looking for a good black woman. Are you a good woman, Enez?” He now turned his attention to his glass of water and squeezed a lemon slice into it; anticipating her answer.

As she placed her napkin on her lap, Sugar followed her movement with his eyes. "I'd like to ask you a personal question. Would you please be honest with me?" She asked in a soft voice. "Do you have other women?"

The waitress arrived with their order before Sugar could answer. "Is there anything else I can get you?" Sugar looked at Enez before he replied, "No, we are good right now." He turned his attention back to Enez and calmly said, "Yes, Enez, I have another woman. I told you I am a pimp. Now does that answer your question?" He had her attention now, mostly because he was honest with her. Sugar finished his meal while Enez played with hers. "Baby, would you like to get a carry out?" he asked her.

"No, I have some business to take care of," she said, as she pushed herself away from the table.

"Is there anywhere I can take you?"

"No, I plan on staying downtown for awhile."

He looked into her eyes as he studied her. Maybe he knew she was a hooker. "Enez, do you mind taking my phone number?"

She knew exactly what he meant. Enez was far from being a green horn to the street game. "Yes, I'll take your number, Sugar."

"I really want to hear from you, baby," he said as he put his scarf around his neck. He took a ten dollar bill from his wallet and picked up the bill from the table. They walked to the cashier, where he paid the bill and then walked out together. Sugar gave Enez a napkin with his phone number written on it, "I am sure I will see you again. You will make sure of that, won't you?"

Three days later, she decided to call Sugar. He answered the phone. "May I speak with Sugar, please?" she asked although she knew it was him who had answered the phone.

"Yeah, this is Sugar. Is this that sexy woman I met downtown three days ago?" he asked with excitement in his voice.

"Yeah, Sugar it's me."

"I was beginning to give up on you calling me. Enez, I saw you downtown the other night on the track. I assumed you didn't see me. Are you ready to come see me? I want to see you again, Enez."

Her nervousness disappeared as she began to relax. "I'm glad to hear you want to see me, Sugar. I want to see you too."

"Where do you live? Can I pick you up?"

She hesitated a moment before answering him, "I have a roommate with children. I've always respected her and the children by not inviting people that I really don't know to our home. I hope you understand." He was silent over the phone lines. “I can meet you tonight around seven o’clock downtown on L Street at Peggy’s Place.”

“Yeah, that sounds good, Enez. I will see ya then.”

Later that night, she walked into the smoke-filled room to see Sugar waiting at a table near the front. He immediately rose from his seat, took her arm, and escorted her from the building. Enez walked with him as they crossed the street to the parking lot of an office building where Sugar had parked his car. He unlocked her door and opened it for her before he walked around to the other side and placed his hat and coat in the back. Inside the car, he turned the heater on, and the car immediately began to warm up. Enez removed her hat, coat, and scarf and then crossed her legs. She wore black sheer stockings and red knee-high heeled boots. She pressed down her red leather skirt as they rode in silence, listening to the jazz music coming from the radio.

Finally, he spoke in his deep voice, “Are you comfortable, baby?” For the first time since they got in the car, Enez noticed his attire. He wore a double breasted navy blue suit, matching shirt, tie, and alligator shoes. He smelled of Gray Flannel Cologne. Sugar parked his car in front of a building that she was familiar with, but she had never been inside.

They walked through the lobby and into the elevator, where he pushed the button for the 12th floor. Sugar put his arms around her waist as the elevator doors opened and they walked down the hall. Sugar stood in front of a door to unlock it and then stepped back to allow Enez inside first. She stepped inside the suite and saw a kitchen to her right and a beautifully furnished living room straight ahead. The extra thick brown carpet covered her boots as she walked through the rooms. Enez sat down on the couch, looking around and noticed the French doors. "Sugar, what is behind the French doors?" she asked.

"That's my bedroom, baby," he replied as he walked towards the doors to open them. "I am going to get comfortable. Make yourself a drink if you'd like."

She watched him go to the bedroom and noticed that he left the door open. Enez sat quietly. When he returned, Sugar walked over to the bar and mixed himself a drink. "Baby, I see you didn't mix yourself a drink. Would you like one?"

"Yes, Sugar, I'd like a drink," she replied as she walked towards him with her hips swaying side to side. She sat on the bar stool and watched him mix her drink.

Sugar walked over to the couch and sat down. He placed his drink on the glass cocktail table and signaled Enez to join him. He stared at her with lust in his eyes. Enez was a very attractive woman, and he knew she would be an asset to him. "Listen, baby, how would you like to travel to California with me? I believe you would do well there." Sugar sat back on the couch and waited for her to answer.

"I have never been to California."

"I didn't ask you if you had been there before, baby. I asked if you would like to go there with me and make some money." Before she could reply, he apologized for his rudeness. He shrugged his shoulders, and muscles moved under his silk mahogany pajama shirt. "I know you are ready for a man and a place of your own."

She studied his handsome face. "Sugar, I'm not sure what I want to do right now," she replied softly.

He stared at her for a long time before he spoke, "Baby, I know I haven't made a mistake, and you know it too. I know you calling me tonight was not a waste of my time or yours. You are a mature woman, and I know you know what you want. So don't toy with yourself," he said, half amused.

Enez reached across the couch and laid her hand on top of his. She looked into his eyes and asked, "When do we leave?"

"Just as soon as you can pack your things." Her eyes followed him as he walked to the stereo. She heard the sounds of Barry White as she tossed her head back on the couch, and Sugar dimmed the lights. He laid his head on her lap and said, "Baby, you remember I told you I have another woman. Her name is Shannon, and she works the hooker track near Thomas Circle. Shannon came with me from Englewood. I hope you are not a jealous woman." Enez moaned lightly and placed her hands on his now naked chest. He placed his hand over hers, "I really want you with me, Enez." Suddenly, Sugar sat up on the couch and looked at his watch. "Listen, I am going to shower and change clothes. We need to go back downtown so you can take care of my business."

When she decided to choose Sugar, she had taken for granted he would sleep with her that evening. It was going to be a wonderful change, moving to California, she thought to herself. The evening flew by as Enez worked the hotel lounge. By midnight, she had earned several hundred dollars. She looked at her watch and remembered that she was to met Sugar at 12:30 on the corner of L and 12th street.

The winds were high, and her scarf was wrapped around her face as she walked quickly to be on time. She saw his headlights blink at her just as she crossed the street. She slid into the back seat of his car, for there was another man occupying the front. Sugar took quick glances at her in his rearview mirror as he cruised through Washington's downtown streets.

"Man, I have been looking for this woman most of the evening. I know she ain't got jealous on me. I am trying to leave for Cali in the morning. You know it's time for me to get back on the west coast," Sugar said anxiously.

"Hey, man, isn't that your woman over there?" the slim passenger asked.

"Thanks, Billy." Sugar slammed on the brakes and pulled next to the woman, who immediately jumped in the backseat as Sugar drove off. No one spoke for a moment. Then, Shannon took a large drink from a Coke bottle. The contents smelled of whisky. Sugar glanced at her in the rearview mirror. "Look, man, I need to take care of my business with these women. I will get back with you later, Billy. I'm going to take you back to your Cadillac." Sugar said, while turning corners and speeding through green traffic lights.

After he dropped Billy off, Sugar said, "Enez, sit in the front with me."

Shannon said, "Sugar I need to talk to you," as she sipped from her bottle.

"Yeah, yeah, I know you do, don't you?" Sugar replied with contempt in his voice. He slipped in a tape, and Marvin Gaye's silky voice filtered through the sound system with "What's Going On" As they cruised to a hotel parking lot, Sugar turned down the music and said to Enez, "I'll come back in a minute. Let me take care of business. Come on, Shannon, You said you needed to talk to me."

Shannon staggered behind Sugar as they left the car. Enez followed them with her eyes until they entered the elevator in the hotel lobby. Soon, Sugar returned to the car, and he appeared agitated. He glanced at his watch and noticed that it was long after midnight. Silently, he drove towards his house. He turned to stare at Enez when they stopped at a traffic light. He smiled at her, "I'm taking you home with me tonight. Baby, I want to leave D.C. tomorrow afternoon for Cali. In the morning, you need to make arrangements to get your clothes from the apartment." When the traffic light changed, he pulled off and turned up the volume on the car stereo. As they passed a Waffle House, he asked her, "Are you hungry? I am going to order breakfast." Without waiting for an answer, he parked the car. "Come on, Enez, I'm hungry."

After breakfast, Enez and Sugar went to his house. It was just as they had left it hours earlier. Sugar handed her a towel from the closet as he said, "You'll find everything you need under the bathroom sink."

Enez hung her coat in the hall closet and walked into the bathroom to prepare her bath. She found Caress soap and nice smelling lotions under the sink. After her bath, she found a gray silky gown placed across the bed in his bedroom. She picked it up and felt the newness of the fabric as she slipped the gown over her head. Sugar looked at her and signaled her to join him in the bed. She curled under him as they slept till the break of dawn.

The sound of the telephone ringing awakened Enez. Sugar sat back on the bed and listened to the voice that came over the receiver. "Sugar, I thought you were coming back to my place last night. I've been waiting on you."

He made himself comfortable as he put his pillow behind his head. "Woman, I didn't tell you that. I told you to get some rest. We are leaving this afternoon for Cali. I hope you packed your clothes while you've been waiting for me." He watched

Enez as she got up from the bed. Then, he signaled for her to come back to him. "Listen, Shannon, I want you to have your clothes packed before I get there. I'll be there by noon, so have yourself ready. Do you hear me?" Sugar hung up the phone without saying goodbye.

"Enez, you need to call your ex-roommate and let her know you're moving out today out of courtesy. Do you owe her any rent or anything?"

"No, no, we are tight on that end," Enez replied as she dialed the phone to call Dianna.

"Hello," Dianna answered.

"Dianna, I need to make this short. I'm going to come by the house to pack my clothes because I'm headed to California this afternoon."

The two women were silent for a few seconds before Dianna broke the silence. "Well, Enez, you are grown. Today, I am off from work. I have a doctor's appointment. I think I'm pregnant. My appointment is not until after noon. Are you sure you'll be here by noon?"

"Yes, I will be there at noon." The two women said their good-byes, and then Enez placed the receiver on its cradle. Enez managed a small smile as she returned to Sugar.

The phone rang again, and Sugar answered, "Hello. Yeah what's up, man?" Sugar's eyes became wide. "You say what?!" he exclaimed. "Cadillac Tony's woman, China Doll, was killed last night? Man, what happened?" he asked. "She tried to rob the man, and he grabbed her by her hair and drug her down the street in his car window!? Man! She was the best money maker Cadillac had with him." Sugar was silent for a moment before he continued to repeat what the caller said, "They found her behind an abandoned apartment building with her neck broken and blood flowing from her mouth. Who found her, Slick?" Sugar asked. "Man, that's L.B.'s woman. You say she saw China Doll fooling with the man and him pulling off with her hanging from the window?"

Enez got up from the couch when Sugar snapped his fingers at her and pointed towards the bedroom. "Hey, man, me and my women are leaving for Cali today. So, I'll holla back at you later." Sugar hung up the phone and joined Enez in the bedroom. "That's bad news for Cadillac Tony. But look, baby, we need to strike out of here now. First, we'll stop and pick up your clothes, and then we'll get Shannon," he said as he packed a few items into his garment bag and suitcases. Sugar did not pack all of his things. Perhaps he would return to D.C.

The sound of laughter came from Dianna's apartment as Enez used her key to open the door. "Yeah, I am going to the doctor today. Girl, I really wasn't trying to have anymore children, but you know if you don't use protection this will happen. Well anyway, my ex-roommate just walked in, so I'll catch up with you later," Dianna said as she hung up the phone. "Enez, I packed your things for you so we could have more time to talk Do you really want to leave with this stranger?" she asked Enez.

Enez looked at her and returned her compassionate smile. "Yes I want to leave with him. Don't worry, if I am not satisfied, believe me, I know how to leave."

"Yeah," Dianna said softly, "but that ain't going to be worth a cent to you, Enez, traveling with him."

Enez heard a car horn blowing in front of the apartment. She walked to the window and pushed the curtain back slightly. "I must leave now, Dianna. Thank you for your help and concern for me. I will call you when we reach Cali." Enez said as she walked towards the door, not looking back.

Sugar opened the trunk of the car for Enez to put her suitcases in before she slipped into the front seat. When they arrived at Shannon's motel, Sugar stopped to study Enez closely. Finally, he spoke, "I'm going up to the room to get Shannon. I'll return momentarily." Soon, Shannon and Sugar appeared with her luggage. Sugar opened the trunk for Shannon to place her suitcase inside. The frown Shannon had worn as she walked to the car was now a smile as Sugar asked Enez to change seating arrangements with Shannon.

Enez looked at Shannon, "Sure baby, whatever you like."

After everyone was seated in their seats Sugar began to make a U-turn in the direction of downtown D.C. Sugar parked his car in front of a large, run-down convenient store and spoke politely to the elderly man sweeping the sidewalk as he entered the store. There were several men standing outside the store, and Enez recognized one of them as he glanced at her through the back window of the car. The last time she had seen this face was when she left him at Peggy's Place. Carl walked over to the car and knocked lightly on the window.

For a brief moment, her heart skipped a beat as she saw Sugar standing behind Carl. "Hey, man, what are you doing standing at my car?" Sugar asked demandingly.

Carl turned to see Sugar and replied, "Man, she was with me, and she owes me some money." Sugar looked at Enez, and she nodded her head as she responded to Carl's accusation.

"Carl, man, she is my woman. She doesn't owe you anything." Sugar walked to his car, and Carl left. Sugar handled the Lincoln car as if it were a toy. Its smooth glide through I-66 traffic caused Enez to fall into a deep sleep. When she woke up, she heard the humming voice of Lamont Dozier singing "Trying to hold on to my woman." Her heart instantly fell as she thought of her days with Nicko and wondered if he was still in L.A, where she last spoke with him. Enez soon forgot about Nicko when Sugar said, "Let's stop and get something to eat and a hotel room for the night." She looked at her watch and realized she had been asleep for several hours.

While they waited for a table at an Italian restaurant, Sugar suggested, "I imagine you haven't seen your folks in a while. I'm going to stop in Memphis so you can visit them, okay?"

Enez looked at him with a heart warming smile and kissed him on his cheeks. "Thank you, Sugar, for thinking of my feelings," she said.

The next morning, Sugar phoned Enez's room. "Hello," she said.

"Hey baby, it's time to get up from your sleepy head."

"Oh Sugar, I've been up for awhile now," she said as she opened the drawer of the night stand. There was an open Bible in the drawer, and her eyes fell upon a scripture. She read Isaiah 59:10, "***We grope for the wall like the blind, and we grope as if we had no eyes; we stumble at noonday as in the night; we are in desolate places as dead men.***"

Sugar was now on the other end saying, "Are you still there, Enez?"

She nodded her head as if he could see her. "Yeah, yeah, I'm still here, Sugar. I'll be down in just a minute." Enez walked down the stairs quickly with her overnight case. The trunk was open, and Sugar stood nearby as Enez placed her case in the trunk. She turned to see Sugar standing close by her side. His eyes seemed to undress her as he slowly looked over her entire body. He closed the trunk, and they walked separately to the car doors. Enez noticed Shannon sitting in the back seat. Sugar nodded his head, giving Enez permission to sit next to him. She felt Shannon's eyes following her.

Before they got on the interstate, they stopped at a Waffle House. The group was silent and only spoke to the waitress to place their breakfast order. After breakfast, the two women waited for Sugar in the car as he paid for their breakfast. Shannon spoke arrogantly, "Well, looks like my man has more taste than what he generally displays in black women."

Not bothering to respond to Shannon, Enez pulled down the sun visor to refresh her lipstick. Sugar walked swiftly back to the car opening the front door. He adjusted his rear view mirror, started the Lincoln's engine, and placed the gear in reverse. They were now headed for Memphis.

Shannon wanted to converse with Enez, so she decided to ask Enez questions. "Do you have a daughter or son in Memphis?"

Quickly, Enez answered, hoping Shannon would not ask her any more questions. "I have a daughter, and her name is Amara."

"Does your family live there too?"

"Yes, my family lives in Memphis. I was born and raised in the south," Enez answered.

They had been on the interstate for several hours, and Enez had not asked Sugar any questions. Now she looked at him, and soft, warm words were on the tip of her lips. He glanced at her and whispered, "We'll talk later, baby."

They arrived in Memphis early in the evening. Enez called her sister from a phone booth. "Hey Dusty, this is your sister. I'm here in Memphis and would like to see Amara." There was a moment of silence while Amara came to the phone.

"Hey, are you coming over to Dusty's house?" Amara asked in her soft voice.

"Yeah baby, I'm on my way to see you. I'll be there in a minute.".

The sky was dark, and the stars twinkled as Enez looked through the car window. Her heart began to beat faster, and she was afraid. Enez knew she had not been a very good mother to her daughter. Her legs became weaker with each step she took towards the back door. She could hear the sounds of children laughing and playing inside as she knocked. A child answered, "Who is it?" Enez peeped through the window and saw Amara standing in front of the door with her hands upon her hips.

"It's me, Amara, your momma." Enez's sister helped Amara with the door. As she walked in, Enez saw a beautiful child, standing before her, waiting with a warm reception. Enez picked up her daughter and twirled her around and around. Amara's sandy brown pony tails twirled about her head like helicopter propellers. She was still going around and around when her feet hit the floor, and they both fell out on the floor laughing.

Soon, Enez heard the familiar horn blowing in the driveway and knew that Sugar had arrived to pick her up. She turned to find Amara standing behind her. She looked into Amara's brown eyes and hugged her small body to her while she kissed her cheeks. "I know you don't understand, and believe me I don't either, but I have to go now. I'll come back to be with you someday." They held hands until Enez reached the back door, where she hugged and kissed Amara one last time. She walked out the door and did not look back.

Sugar studied Enez as she got into the car. Perhaps he thought from the look in her eyes that he should not have brought her to see Amara. "Are you okay baby?" he asked. She nodded her head in response, for the lump in heart throat caused her not to be able to speak. "Baby, let's get a bite to eat, and we'll go to the hotel room," he said as he continued to stare at her.

That night, she tossed and turned in her bed throughout the night. Finally, Sugar reached out and held her as she started to cry. Enez sat up in bed and began to talk to Sugar. His heart softened, and she fell into his intimate caress as he wiped her eyes and whispered, "Baby, it's alright, I understand." He held her small chin in his hand and stroked her hair, "I need you to come with me as we planned. Now let me get some sleep I have a long drive ahead of me." He flattened his pillow, and they both fell asleep.

The next fourteen hours passed slowly for Sugar. His bankroll was dwindling, and nothing was coming in. Sugar decided to stop and check in to a motel in Amarillo. After he had gotten the motel keys he told Shannon and Enez, "Get a shower and get out here to get me some money." The women walked to their rooms with their overnight luggage.

Enez was not familiar with the area. She knew this was Sugar's territory, and she had better do what he said. She stood in the shower with the hot water racing down her back as a movie of her life played in her mind. She remembered what an older woman had once said to her, "***Their feet run to evil…***" She thought, "Yes, mine did. "***The way of peace they know not; and there is no judgment in their goings***." Her night in Amarillo was short. She quickly took care of Sugar's business and returned to the motel.

The next morning, Sugar knocked on Enez's motel door. She was already dressed and ready to leave. He sat on the bed and asked, "Where is my money, baby? What time did you get in this morning?"

She gave him several hundred dollars, "I came in just after 2 am."

Nine hours later, they were in Phoenix, Arizona. It was very warm, and the grains of sand stirred in the midst of the hard blowing wind. Beautiful green cactus plants lined the manicured landscapes. The scenery was familiar to Sugar and Shannon, and they excitedly showed Enez where they had lived on the west coast.

She sat next to Sugar in a lounge chair, sipping champagne from a tall stemmed glass on the balcony of a fine motel. The orange rays of the sun appeared to draw closer to her as the skies darkened. Several palm trees stood tall and faced her with their big green leaves. She smiled, savoring the moment. This place was really something else, she thought to herself. As she turned to go back into the room, Sugar twisted her around in his arms and caressed her slowly and gently, and she groaned and moaned for him softly.

"Let's take a shower together," he whispered in her ear. Silently, she followed him. He held her tightly in his arms as the warm water fell upon their bodies. Enez was beginning to feel something she had not felt with a man for a long time. She called his name, "Sugar…," she started to say she loved him, but the words would not pass her lips. He gently pushed her body against the shower walls, and they made passionate love to each other.

After the shower, Sugar wiped the steamed mirror and glanced at his face. He swore as he stared at his face. "I need to shave." He shook his head in wonder, "This is something I never allow – an unshaven face." Enez wrapped a towel around her body as she passed him to enter the bedroom. "Listen, baby. I want you to look in my suitcase and bring me my toiletries." As she gave him his items, he smiled at her, "Get ready to be a very busy woman tonight." She walked away, nodding her head in agreement.

Enez was putting on the last touch of lipstick when she heard Sugar talking to Shannon. "I know you're ready. I'm coming to your room in a few seconds." He quickly placed the phone on its cradle and then walked to the mirror to admire himself as he placed his brim on his head. He winked at Enez and gave her the car keys, "Go to the car, and I'll meet you downstairs."

Sugar drove slowly on the way back to the hooker track and parked the car in front of a restaurant. "Shannon, I want you to show Enez the hot spots. Enez, I know you know how to work these streets. Ladies, bring daddy some real money home tonight." He got out of the car and walked inside the restaurant.

It was not long before Enez separated from Shannon. After walking a few blocks, she saw a Plaza Hotel. She walked inside with her hips swaying from side to side as she approached a bar stool. Soon, a gentleman approached and struck up a conversation. "How are you, young lady? Can I buy you a drink?" he asked. He looked like he had already had too many himself.

"Yes, I'd like a Long Island iced tea, thank you." Enez looked at him to size him up and noticed he was wearing a diamond ring and necklace. The bartender came back with her order. Their conversation continued through another round of drinks. Finally, the man whispered in her ear, "Come to my room. I got something for ya." She looked at him with curiosity as he slipped a one hundred dollar bill in the palm of her hand. Enez knew she really needed to get Sugar's money, but she hesitated for a moment before whispering in his ear, "Let's go up for a night cap, baby."

Upstairs, the man fell into a deep sleep before he even touched Enez. She immediately went to his wallet and stole several hundred dollars while he slept. She slipped out of his room and took the elevator to the garage, then found herself on the street. Her heart raced as she looked for the restaurant where she last saw Sugar. Finally, she reached the restaurant, but his car was gone. She saw a taxi and flagged for him to stop. Sitting in the back seat, she told the driver the name of the motel and street it was located on. The driver was familiar with the city, and in minutes she was in her room.

Before she took her clothes off to shower and relax, she removed the money from her bra. Enez counted almost one thousand dollars. She thought to herself, “My baby will be happy with me this morning.”

The knock on the door caused Enez to awaken from a heavy sleep. She sat up in the bed as though she had been dreaming. Someone knocked again. She peeped from the curtains to find Sugar standing at the door. As she walked to open the door, she realized the latch was on the door. Sugar entered the room.

“How long have you been here, Enez? I saw you when you jumped in the taxi. I know you got daddy something real nice this morning, or you wouldn’t be here. Am I right about it?”

She reached inside the pillow case and removed the bank roll she had stolen from the man at the bar. Sugar hesitated for a moment and asked curiously, “How much is this?”

She lay back on the headboard of the bed and said proudly, “Nearly a thousand.”

Sugar began to count the money. “Yeah, baby, you got us a nice sting tonight.” He walked over to his suitcase where he hid the money before he checked his watch. “Baby, get yourself some rest. I’ll see you later on this morning.” He walked towards the door and reminded her to double lock the door before he kissed her good night. She closed the door after him and went to bed.

It was Sunday morning. Enez sat up in bed and turned on the television with the remote control. A well dressed black man was standing behind a pulpit, reading. He said, “***Behold the Lord’s hand is not shortened that it cannot save.***” Quickly, she flipped the channels as she thought to herself, “Is the Lord trying to save me this morning? Hmmmm, I am not ready to be saved.” She turned the television off and went to the bathroom. The telephone rang, and she stumbled to the nightstand to answer it.

“Good morning, Enez. In about an hour, we’re going to breakfast. I will see ya in a minute.”

“Yeah, yeah see ya in minute,” She returned the phone to its cradle.

An hour later, Enez sat outside on the balcony, waiting for Sugar. She heard him turn the key inside the lock. She looked back to find him standing by his suitcase. “You ready, baby?” he asked.

She nodded her head, “Yes, I’m ready.”

They got in the car without Shannon and drove through the quiet streets. There was very little traffic and few people stirred about. Sugar was quiet, and he appeared to be agitated. Perhaps this was why Shannon was not with them, Enez thought. He finally began to sing with Lamont Dozier. "From the corner of the streets I found her…I tamed the wild life around her…" As he stopped the car for the red traffic light, he looked at Enez and continued to sing, "Enez, don't ever go away, my bouquet. Rose, Rose…." Just as smooth as the song he sang, he parked the car in front of a very nice restaurant. A hostess met them inside the restaurant. "Good morning. How many in your party, sir?"

Sugar smiled at the tall, slim blond woman, "Two in non smoking, please."

She returned the smile, "Follow me, please." They approached a small booth by a window with a beautiful scenic view. The hostess asked, "Is this good for you, Sir?"

"Yes, yes, this is fine," Sugar replied.

"Here are your menus. Your waitress will be with you in just a moment."

Enez stared out the window. "Baby, what are you eating this morning?" Sugar asked her as he looked at his menu. She answered him, still staring at the beauty outside. "An egg omelet with sausage, mushrooms, tomatoes and cheese sounds good, and some dry toast."

His eyes met hers, "Listen, baby. I want to leave for California in a couple of days. We will live in Anaheim. I have a half brother that lives in L.A. and a son."

A Hispanic waitress who spoke very good English finally came to their table to take their order. "Are you ready to order, Sir," she asked.

"Yes, the young lady would like an omelet with sausage, mushrooms, tomatoes and cheese. Oh yeah, and a slice of dry toast. I believe I will have the same, and an order of pancakes with a tall glass of orange juice. Baby, what you are drinking this morning?"

Enez said quickly, "A glass of water will do fine, baby."

Sugar gave the menus to the waitress. "I believe that will be all for us. Thank you." The waitress smiled at Enez and walked away. "As I was saying, baby, I know you will do real well in Anaheim. I have a nice place in Orange County, near Disneyland. You and I will live there together. I need to send Shannon back to Denver for some family business." She sat at the table very quietly. Sugar excused himself to go to the bathroom. While he was away, the waitress returned with their food order. There was not any discussion during breakfast.

Afterwards, Sugar drove around the city before he pulled up in front of a house. The yard was well manicured, and the house looked like something from a Spanish historian magazine. "I will be right back, baby." She nodded as she watched him walk down a cobble stoned path to the front door. A small framed woman answered the door, and Sugar went inside. It was not long before he returned to the car. As he pulled onto the freeway, he handed Enez a big bag of weed. "Put this in your purse until we reach the hotel." She suddenly realized this was the reason for his visit to the house.

Soon they reached the hotel, and Sugar said, "Go to your room. I will be with you later." It was a few hours later before Sugar returned. The phone rang as they were relaxing, and she heard Sugar say, "What's up man? Oh yeah, she saw a picture of me…when is she getting out of jail, man? Yeah, yeah, I'll be in Anaheim in a few days. Look here, man, I'll get back to you later."

Enez walked out to the balcony, stood near the railing, and took a deep breath. "Oh," she exclaimed in surprise, and then blushed as she glanced into Sugar's eyes.

"It's nice out here isn't it? The air is warm. Are you happy, baby?"

She stared at him in amazement that someone cared about her happiness. "Sugar you know, for the first time in a long time, I am happy. The man I thought I loved for many years was very violent towards me." She chose to ignore the fact that her new man was a pimp.

"Baby, I know you are a good woman, and you want a good man to be good to you. Let me tell you, I don't need a jealous woman working for me."

They looked into each other eyes briefly, then turned to see the stars twinkle in the sky. The phone began to ring again, and Sugar walked inside to answer it. Enez overheard him say, "Are you ready right now?" He sounded agitated with the caller. She walked in the room as he took his house shoes off and put on his dress shoes. "Baby, here is twenty dollars. If you get hungry, order yourself something to eat. I will be back later, alright? And leave the latch off the door." She walked with him to the door and closed it behind him.

After taking a hot shower and shampooing her hair, Enez began to relax. She ordered food from room service and watched TV the rest of the night. The next morning, Enez found Sugar lying next to her as he promised. He was sound asleep. She quietly got out of the bed and walked out to the balcony. Enez breathed in the fresh morning dew. As she sat on the iron cushioned chair, the wind blew through her brown silky gown causing her nipples to harden and her body to shiver. Perhaps he missed the warmth of her body next to him as he slept as she heard Sugar say, "Baby, come back to bed and keep me warm." He turned towards her as she walked in. "Oh! What a beautiful sight to see you. Come here, girl."

She smiled at him and jumped on top of him. He grabbed her and held her tight in his arms. He patted her on her butt and tossed her to his side. "Listen, I want you to get some day time work in today. The money is good here in the day time. I am going to call Shannon and get her up." He called Shannon and said, "Get ready for work." He sat on the edge of the bed, stood up, and stretched before he went into the bathroom to take a hot shower and shave. His well sculptured body was wrapped in a bath towel around his waist when he entered the bedroom. Sugar selected a suit to put on from the many he had hanging in the hotel closet. Enez watched him as he picked out a baby blue silk pants suit and laid it across the bed. He walked back to the closet and removed a pair of baby blue leather sandals from his traveling shoe rack. He dropped his towel as he applied lotion and cologne all over his body. “Enez, come apply lotion on my back for me, baby.” Enez was turned on by his lotion and cologne, but she knew this was not the time to make love to him. Quickly, she disregarded the thought and applied the lotion on him before she disappeared into the bathroom.

When she returned, he was fully dressed as he gathered his wallet and keys. “I am going to Shannon’s room. Enez, be ready when I call you.” She knew he meant to be ready in at least 30 minutes. He closed the door after himself.

Working day time meant working the streets. She knew in order to work the streets, she had to dress the part. She pulled out a beige mini skirt suit and leopard print spike heeled shoes from the closet. She completed her outfit with a pair of dark brown fish net stockings and a blonde Tina Turner wig that she occasionally wore to work the streets. She applied lotion to her body with a fine oil and perfume and then put on her make up with care. Enez finished dressing a few seconds before Sugar called her to come down to the car. After a last look in the mirror, Enez opened the dresser drawer for a box of condoms. She placed a packet inside her purse and proceeded downstairs to the car.

The day time work was just as good as the night. It was not long before Enez attracted her first date for $100. She worked the streets for several hours. Later, Sugar pulled up next to Enez. He rolled his window down and asked, "What does my bank roll look like?" Enez pulled out a fat bankroll from her bra as he said, "Get in the car, Enez." He then pulled up next to Shannon. "What's up, Shannon?" he asked. She walked over to his window and whispered in his ear. Sugar stared at her for a moment. "Well, I guess you need more time," he said as he sped off. Sugar took Enez back to the hotel room, and it was the next morning before she saw either Sugar or Shannon.

She ran from the shower to answer the phone. "Good morning, baby. Did you get a good night's sleep?" she heard Sugar ask. "Start packing your clothes and mine. I will be over in a few minutes to help you." He did not wait for her response. Enez knew from the sound in his voice that Sugar was ready to make his move to Cali. She began humming a tune Frankie Beverly wrote, "The Rollin' Hills of California." When Sugar arrived, she looked into his face and saw a sparkle in his eyes as he smiled. Sugar grabbed her, holding her tight in his arms. Her breast pressed against his chest while she felt the rhythm of his heart beat. He slightly pushed her back to look into her eyes and said, "Baby, let's make a move from here."

The drive was very pleasant. Shannon slept most of the way. When they arrived in Anaheim, Sugar drove to his place. The streets were lined with palm trees. Men and women were skate boarding in the hot sun and wearing almost nothing. A man stood at the balcony of the apartment as Sugar unlocked the door to enter. The man grabbed Sugar to give him a brotherly welcome. "Hey man what's up? Glad you're home. Who is this lovely lady you have with you?"

Sugar walked over to the couch and lit a joint. He pointed to the man and then to the chair to sit down. "Ronnie, you know Shannon."

"Yeah, yeah, you know I know Shannon, man." Ronnie said while reaching for the joint.

"This is Enez from Memphis. And that's all you need to know about my woman." The room was filled with a cloud of weed smoke now. Sugar passed Shannon a rolled up joint as he sat back on the couch and listened to the sounds of the people talking below outside. Suddenly, the phone rang. "Is that you, Connie?" he asked as he sat towards the edge of the couch. "What time are they releasing you, Connie? Yea, yea, I'll be there. You just make sure you are ready to be there for me."

Ronnie asked Sugar about his telephone conversation. Sugar answered, "Man, she is a broad that saw a picture of me and chose me over a picture. Man,. I am gonna see if she is real." Sugar sat back on the couch. "Shannon and Enez, go to the car and get our luggage. You broads need to get you some rest; you got some work to do."

Sugar took his time driving. He finally reached the hooker track. The women got out of the car as they said good night to Sugar. The area was not new to Shannon, but it was definitely new to Enez. Her short legs kept in stride with Shannon's long shapely ones. The busy California streets filtered the scene of the night life, with beaming car headlights and women looking for men to satisfy their needs.

A late model car approached Shannon and Enez. The driver was an older white guy with a gray beard. The smell from his cologne gave the air a special aroma. This aroma attracted Enez. She knew his cologne was very expensive. She and Shannon bent over to talk to the man through his passenger window. "Do you wanna party, ladies? You two look different than those other women. You look clean. I'll pay real good. I got a hotel room just across the street."

"What's real good?" Shannon asked.

"Oh what about 150 dollars a piece."

"And what do you want for it?"

"A party."

Both women agreed and got in his car. The man did as he promised, and the two women did as they were paid to do. The next few nights went very well for the women, and Sugar was happy with the money that they brought in.

The phone call came just as Sugar was walking towards the door. Enez answered the phone. "Hello."

"Yes, is Sugar there?"

"Hold on a minute." Enez gave the phone to Sugar as he walked towards her. He said, "Yeah, this is Sugar. I will be there in 30 minutes. Don't you move." Enez heard him muttering to himself, "I'll teach her not to play with a pimp."

For the next few days, Sugar put up with Connie, an old drunk hooker. Enez overheard him mention to his other pimp friends that she claimed to be a good thief but he had not seen it yet. She was not worth him losing two good women. Sugar got rid of Connie faster than a speeding bullet.

One Friday night, a drunk Connie was on the hooker track. Connie had once been very attractive, but now her small eyes and long nose diminished the slim black girl's beauty. Some nights, Sugar did what pimps called spot pimping, checking on his women. Shannon and Enez had already seen Sugar driving slowing down the Boulevard, but Connie did not see Sugar creep up on her. She was running her mouth off to some man and raising her dress up to show her nakedness underneath. Sugar grabbed her by her neck. Before she could say a word, he slapped her and said, "Come on, you go with me." After that night, Connie was never seen with Sugar again, but Enez saw her on the hooker track other nights.

One warm night, Enez was working on the streets of Anaheim. The money was slow coming, and she knew she had to bring her share home. There was a white man in a white truck, riding around most of the early night. Enez heard some girls talk of a man who was riding around with handcuffs attached to his rear view mirror. They said he was not the police.

Just as she stood near the drive of the hotel parking lot, she saw a parked white truck. The white man in the truck blew his horn. Enez smiled at him as he waved her over. She looked for the handcuffs in the rearview mirror as she walked toward the truck, but she did not see them. He was a slim white man with a clean shaven face. He asked her for a date, and she said yes before she saw his handcuffs. The man told her she was under arrest and to get in the truck. Enez did not ask for a badge. She got in the truck with this presumptuous police officer. As he entered the backside of a dark ally, the man said, "I won't take you to jail if you have sex with me." Enez agreed. "Come sit close to me so you won't start any funny business. She sat next to him, and he placed her hand in his lap. He parked the truck behind a vacant building and made her get out. He handcuffed her to the steering wheel, put on a condom, and proceeded to rape her. When he finished with her, he took her to the spot where he had first picked her up. Just as the other rapes she had been through, Enez buried this one also, deep within her inner self.

* * *

His Grace and Mercy

Sugar became mentally and physically abusive towards Shannon and Enez. Shannon and Enez were smoking weed heavily, and Sugar began smoking crack. In his past life, he had a drug problem, and now it had come back to haunt him. He was not only smoking weed, he also laced it with crack.

After several weeks in Anaheim, Sugar was finally ready to send Shannon to Denver for a visit to her relatives. Enez agreed, since she understood what it was like to miss family. One night, Enez overheard Shannon telling someone she was several months pregnant and needed to come home to have the baby. Enez could not keep the information from Sugar. "Sugar, I need to talk to you alone," Enez said urgently. He followed her outside. She stared up at the stars, and her heart skipped a beat when Sugar touched her elbow.

"What's going on, Enez?" he asked with concern in his voice.

"I overheard Shannon talking on the phone, and believe me I was not eavesdropping. She said she's pregnant, and that's her reason for going home. Is she pregnant?"

He answered defensively, "And so what if she is? What does that have to do with your business with me?"

She thought back to her experiences with Nicko and his wife with their child and how defenseless she had felt. She was quiet as she looked down the street. She knew Sugar was not her boyfriend. He was her pimp, and leaving was not going to be easy. Sugar walked inside to grab his jacket as he closed the door behind him. She wanted to run after him, but her legs would not move. Later that night, she lay awake in bed, looking into the darkness. She thought to herself, "I can't stay with him like this anymore. He's smoking crack, and Shannon's going home to have a baby. I gotta get out now."

The next night could not have been a better time for her. The air smelled of rain, and a few stars shone brightly in the sky. Enez walked the Boulevard in her blue jean pants and high heeled shoes, but she did not work the streets this night. She worked her favorite scene, the hotel lounge. There was a convention in town, and most of the visitors were staying near the Disneyland hotel. Enez walked into the lounge and made herself comfortable at the bar, where the bartender took her drink order. As she ordered another drink, two men sat next to her. Their business meeting was cut short when one of the men received a telephone call. The other man stayed to finish his night cap. Enez looked at him from the mirror behind the bar, and their eyes met.

"I couldn't help but stare at you. I'm sorry, but you have such a beautiful smile," he said.

"Well, thank you. I noticed you staring at me. I was beginning to wonder if there was something unusual about me I hadn't noticed. My name is DeDe. And yours?"

"My mom named me Tom," he replied with a smile. "Are you from around here?"

"No, as a matter of fact, I'm not. I'm here visiting a friend."

"Can I buy you another drink?"

"Yes, only if you'll have another with me." After thirty minutes, Tom asked her if she had a room at the hotel for them to have another night cap. She replied, "No, but we can certainly get one, can't we?"

"Yea, DeDe, I don't think my roommate would appreciate me waking him up. So, let's get a room."

Enez and Tom walked outside and took a cab to a nearby inn. Tom paid for a room while Enez waited in the lobby. When they got to the room, Tom opened his wallet to give her $100. She saw several other hundred dollar bills in his wallet. Enez took off her clothes while she watched Tom remove his. Before he finished stripping, Tom had passed out on the bed. She shook him and blew in his ear, but he did not move. Enez tiptoed towards his wallet and took every bill he had before she ran down the back stairs to flag a cab. As she got into the cab, she was surprised to see drunken Connie in the back seat. Enez told the cab driver to get rid of the other passenger and take her to a nice motel, for which she paid him handsomely.

When Enez unlocked the door to her room, she fell across the bed and counted fifteen hundred dollar bills. She knew this was her ticket out of

California and away from Sugar. Enez called Sugar at the hotel. He answered, "Hello."

"Sugar, I didn't call to do no talking. I just want out, baby. I wanna come get my clothes. Is that alright with you?"

"Yea, yea. That's alright with me, Enez, if that's what you really want to do. I ain't gonna hold you back if you wanna leave me, but I thought you was really diggin' me. I sho was diggin' you. So when do you plan on coming by? I'll have Shannon pack all your clothes, and they'll be waiting for you at the door."

"Okay, Sugar. I'll call you in an hour," her voice shook.

He may have heard the shakiness in her voice, "Don't be afraid of me, baby. Be afraid of yourself, cause you are confused right now."

Enez held the receiver in her hand as she thought to herself, "I have to finish this as I had planned. If I were to stay, he would never treat me the same again. To him, I have no reason to leave. But for me, I do."

Enez's heart beat wildly as her taxi arrived because she was frightened. She did not want Sugar to hurt her, so she called the police for assistance. When the police arrived, she was escorted to Sugar's room. Her luggage was waiting for her at the door. Quickly, she grabbed her things and did not look back on her journey with Sugar.

"Take me to the airport, please," she told the taxi driver. She removed her luggage from the trunk when they arrived at the airport and walked to the ticket counter to purchase a ticket back to D.C. "I would like to purchase a one-way ticket to Washington D.C., please."

A caramel skinned woman answered her, "The only flight we have leaving at this time departs in an hour and arrives in Maryland."

"I'll take that flight, please."

"This flight has luggage restrictions. You can only take one carry-on and a regular."

Enez looked down at her several pieces of luggage. "Is there any way I can send this luggage on another flight?"

"You can send your luggage on a FedEx flight," the clerk recommended.

Enez sent her luggage on a FedEx flight to Memphis instead of D.C. She decided to call her sister in Memphis to let her know of her plans. "Hi, Dusty. I can't talk long. I need you to pick up my luggage tomorrow."

Dusty was silent for a moment before she said, "Okay, I'll take care of it for you."

Enez next called her friend, Deena, to pick her up at the Maryland airport. "Hi, Deena. I need you to pick me up at the airport in Maryland. I'll meet you at the baggage claim."

"Girl, I can't wait to see you! I'm glad you're safe and coming back this way. I'll be there. Look for me in Charles' light blue Caddy."

Enez suddenly noticed a woman nearby, reading from a flyer. "***Then shalt thou delight thyself in the Lord: I will cause thee to ride upon the high places of the earth. Their thoughts are thoughts of iniquity; wasting and destruction are in their Paths.***"

"Enez, Enez! Are you still there?" Deena asked nervously.

"Yeah, yeah. I'm here, Deena. A woman just passed by, reading some words from a flyer, and it caught my attention. Anyway I heard what you said. I look forward to landing back in D.C., but I gotta go. I don't want to miss my flight."

The flight to Maryland was long, but not long enough for Enez to gather her thoughts about the future. When she arrived, Deena picked her up at the airport, as scheduled. "Enez, what happened to you and Sugar?" Deena asked curiously.

"Sugar's other woman was pregnant, trying to go home to have her baby, and he started smoking. I can't support a pimp and a habit. Girl, I'm glad to be away from all the pimp and hooker drama."

Winter was in the air in Washington D.C. The trees were bare, and their branches stretched lifelessly towards the car parked in Deena's graveled driveway. Once inside, Enez looked around in surprise. She saw brand new televisions, stereos, clothes, and kitchen appliances. Deena went to the couch to join her male friend. "Enez, this is Michael. Michael, this is Enez. Girl, why are you standing like a statue?"

Enez shrugged her shoulders and walked towards the kitchen. As she returned to the living room, she overheard Deena and Michael talking about people who wanted the merchandise that surrounded them. Enez excused herself without asking any questions.

Later, Deena and Enez got dressed to work the streets. An hour later, they had $600.00, and Deena wanted to call it a night. Enez still had the money from Cali, and she was not hurting for more, so she agreed. "Yeah, let's call it a night," she yawned.

Enez took a shower before going to bed. In Deena's bedroom, she saw her male friend counting money on the bed. He looked up at Enez as he stood up to leave the room. As Deena walked him to the door, Enez heard him say, "Call me if you need some more."

"Some more of what?" Enez wondered. She heard Deena climbing the stairs before she entered the room. Dena walked to her bedroom dresser and opened the top drawer. She placed a cocaine pipe on the dresser and next to it laid a mirror with three crack rocks upon it. Deena turned to see Enez watching her every move. She asked, "Do you want to get high?"

Enez's belly began to ache, and her mouth watered. She was afraid to get high because of her disease of addiction, but Enez was defeated by the disease and readily got high with Deena. The disease had been asleep for a year, but now it opened it's ugly eyes. Deena and Enez bought a great supply of crack that night. The next morning, Enez lay across Deena's bed, feeling depressed and ashamed. As the days passed, Enez and Deena continued to make money and kept getting high.

The Christmas holiday was fast approaching, and Enez wanted to go to Memphis to visit her family. She looked from the kitchen window to see snow in the in the sky as she thought of the days ahead. Nat King Cole sang over the radio, "Chestnuts roasting on an open fire…" She held a cup of warm cocoa as she entered the living room, where Deena sat on the couch. Enez looked at the beautiful Christmas tree and gifts underneath it. "Deena, I plan to visit my relatives for Christmas. I need you to show me how to use the credit card scheme."

Deena walked to the china table and reached inside the bottom drawer. "This is a new card. We can go shopping on this card now. Do you really want me to teach to you?"

Enez responded quickly, "Yes let's go."

They returned from their shopping spree with the car full of gifts. Enez proudly wrapped the expensive gifts for her relatives, and a few days later, she bought a round trip plane ticket to Memphis.

Enez arrived in Memphis on Christmas Eve. She flagged a taxi outside the baggage claim terminal. The driver stared at her through his rearview mirror as she gave him the address to her grandmother's house. She stared back into his deep black eyes, and her heart skipped a beat before she looked away. She looked out her window during the ride to her grandmother's house to let him know she was not interested. When they arrived, the taxi driver helped her with her luggage and gifts. As she entered the kitchen, her grandmother embraced her like a burning fire, and Enez was consumed in her flames. She was so happy to see Enez.

Enez found a pamphlet on the dresser as she unpacked. She picked it up and read, "***They have made them crooked Paths: whosoever goeth therein shall not know peace.***" She slowly walked to the twin bed and sat down as she thought to herself, "There isn't any peace in my life. Only sin after sin after sin." After a while, she returned to the kitchen, where she found her grandmother baking cakes and pies for Christmas dinner. "Can I help you?," Enez asked, like a child wanting to learn how to bake.

"Yes, you can apply oil and flour to the cake pans. Make sure you don't put too much flour in the cake pans." The kitchen was quiet except for the humming of the mixer until her grandmother said, "Honey, God can fix anything."

Enez stood quietly by her grandmother's side. She finally broke the silence, "I'm tired. I'd like to take a nap." It was not until the next day, she opened her eyes to see her daughter, and she smiled and hugged her. "Hi, baby! How is my big girl?"

Amara jumped on the bed and sat next to Enez. "Are you here to stay with me, Momma?" she asked.

Enez looked into Amara's beautiful brown eyes and said, "I am always with you." She pointed to her head and heart.

"Momma, you can't see me in there." Amara touched her mother's chest. "Come on, Momma, get up." Amara grabbed her mother's hand and pulled her toward the door.

"Okay, baby. I'm coming."

As they entered the family room, Enez heard her mother's voice before she saw her sitting in a chair near the fire place. "Hi, Momma. How are you?" Enez asked as she sat on the couch with her grandmother and daughter.

"Hi, Enez. How are you?"

The room was no longer quiet after Enez's step-grandfather turned on the television to watch the evening news. Enez thought about her grandfather, who died when she was eighteen. She loved her grandfather, and he loved her. She remembered how much he had loved Amara too. Now, her grandmother was married to a man she had known since childhood. Enez was happy to see her grandmother living a middle class life. Soon, Enez's sister and one-year-old nephew pulled up in the driveway. Enez opened the door to help her sister. "Merry Christmas, Dusty," she said with a smile and a hug. On this Christmas day, the house was filled with laughter, conversation, love, and the aroma of good food. The family did not leave Enez's grandmother's house until late in the evening. Enez knew the joy and peace she felt now was only temporary.

"Well, Enez, we must go now," her mother said as she got Amara's coat.

"Please let me put your coat on for you, Amara." Enez wrapped Amara in her love as she looked into her eyes and whispered, "I love you. Don't you ever forget it."

Amara looked into Enez's eyes with her hazel eyes and hugged her mother for dear life. It was Enez's turn to study Amara, and she wondered if she really wanted to return to D.C. She looked down at the floor thinking, "Tomorrow, I will leave for my return to D.C., and it may be a long time before I see my daughter again."

The next morning, a taxi arrived at Enez's grandmother's house to drive her to the airport. She was silent during the drive. Enez walked swiftly through the terminal as she thought about the wonderful visit with her family and how she would have preferred to stay in Memphis with them. She soon dismissed that thought and knew it was time to get back to business.

Deena picked Enez up at the airport with some not so good news. "Enez, I'm having problems with my landlord. I have two weeks to find somewhere to live, so I can't take you back to my place."

"I have enough money for a hotel room. Drop me off at the downtown Sheraton."

Deena looked at her in surprise. "Oh, you have money for a room? Well, you can pay me for a room tonight, then."

Enez rubbed her forehead, "Deena, haven't I always paid you to stay in your place? Anyways, I need to pack the rest of my clothes, but first I need some time to myself."

At the hotel, Enez walked to the elevators with the bellhop. As the elevator doors opened, she saw her reflection in the mirrors inside the elevator. She turned away as she noticed the thickness around her waist and pushed the button for the 5th floor. She looked at the key card to remind herself of her room number: 516. The elevator doors opened, and she walked with the bell hop to her room. Inside the room, the bell hop placed her luggage on the luggage rack and folded her spread back. Enez stood near the dresser watching him and gave him a tip as he left. She threw her tired body on the queen sized bed to find rest.

The room was dark now, and her body ached with hunger. She noticed she still had on her traveling clothes as she pulled the covers back and got up from the bed. "Oh my," she thought as she looked at her watch, "I must have been very tired." Enez knew she needed to earn some money, but she did not want to show her eagerness at the hotel where she would live.

She pressed her head against the headboard and stared at the blank television screen as she reached for the remote control. Her stomach rumbled as she flipped through the channels. She noticed the room service menu across the room and thought, "I need to make some money tonight, but I'm going to stay in and rest. Besides I'm hungry." She looked over the menu and decided on a steak dinner. After she ate, she fell into a deep sleep once again.

Over the next few days, Enez continued to earn money on the streets. She then took notice of the fact that she had not had a period since she had left Cali. Enez decided to return to Memphis. She bought a one-way plane ticket. Her life would once again take more turns and twists.

* * *

Starting All Over Again

She was longing for Him. She needed to be wrapped in her Savior's arms, protected from the evils of this world. The One strangers talked about while she lived the wilds of the world. The One she refused to serve.

Her flight to Memphis departed from Washington D.C. on schedule that early Tuesday morning. Enez was on her way back home, with a different attitude about her life.

A few days after she arrived, Enez called her great aunt, her grandmother's sister; one of the few relatives with whom she had not burned her bridges. She walked to a nearby phone with confidence and ease. She had been living with an old classmate, and now it was time to move on. "Hello," she said taking a deep breath.

"Nez, is that you?"

"Yes, it's me, Auntie," she answered back quickly. "How are you?"

Her Auntie replied in a strong voice, "I am doing just fine."

"Auntie I've moved back to Memphis and been staying with some friends for a few days. I need a secure place to stay."

Her aunt quickly replied, "Yes, Enez, you can come live with me for a few weeks. When would you like to come?"

Tears fell from her eyes as she asked, "Is it alright if I come today, Auntie?"

"Yes, sweetie, you can move in today. Do you need a ride?"

"Yes, if you don't mind, I sure do need a ride. I am staying at 5419 Court Ave."

"Enez, can you be ready in an hour?"

"Yes, Ma'am, I can be ready in an hour. I'll be ready." She leapt for joy as she walked quickly back to the apartment to pack her clothes.

The Prodigal Daughter

The clouds moved behind the shining sun as she walked out to her Auntie's baby blue 1984 Cadillac. Enez saw her beautiful smile as she approached the car. She heard the trunk lock pop and quickly opened the trunk to place her luggage inside. Her classmate stood next to her, wishing her well as a tear dropped from her cheek. Both women turned away so they would not see each other's faces. Enez got in the car, full of excitement and nervousness. They rode quietly until they reached a red brick two-story house on Brown Ave.

The house stood several feet behind a wrought iron fence. The driveway led to the back of the house, where her Auntie parked her car. Enez took a deep breath before she began to remove her luggage from the trunk. Inside the house, she placed her luggage on the marble floor.

Her aunt called out from a doorway, "Come on, let me show you your room."

Enez walked through a large kitchen and then down a hallway that led to a beautifully decorated guest bedroom. The comfortable colors calmed the quiet storm within her spirit as she sat in a chair next to a window with a pleasant view of magnolia trees. "I just want to sit here a moment and look at the beautiful spring time scenery."

Dinner was served in the dining room. The aroma coming from the kitchen beguiled the fact that her great aunt was not the world's greatest cook. Enez remembered her aunt's rules as she came to the dining room. Her aunt was a Seventh

Day Adventist, so she did not eat pork. She did not allow pork to be cooked in her pots or even enter her house. On Friday after sun down, reading the Bible was the only activity allowed. On Saturday evening, all regular activities would resume.

They sat across from each other at the table. Enez said, "Auntie, in California manicurist shops are on every corner. I've noticed there aren't many manicurist shops in Memphis. This could be a profitable profession for me. I've been thinking about enrolling in cosmetology school, but I seem to have a major problem. I'm pregnant, and I don't know if I want to keep the baby." Enez looked at her Auntie as she waited for her to answer.

"It appears you enjoyed your meal," she smiled at Enez.

Enez nodded, "Yes, the meal was delicious."

The women got up from the table and cleared the dishes. Before retiring to bed, Enez heard her Auntie call for her from the family room.

"Enez, have a seat. I need to talk to you." Enez sat next to her. "It's wonderful that you want to attend school for a career to become a manicurist. I'm glad you want to do something positive with your life. I'll not make a comment on your pregnancy. This is a decision you have to make on your own because you will have to live with your choices, not me."

Enez rose to her feet and bent over to kiss her Auntie on the cheek. She held her Auntie's hand

and said, "I'm tired, and I need to get some sleep. I have a long day ahead of me tomorrow."

The next few weeks were unbearable for Enez with her pregnancy. She woke up almost every morning to find herself leaning over the toilet with nausea.

One morning Enez talked with her Auntie about finding a place of her own. After breakfast, her Auntie drove her to a house. As they pulled into the driveway, a short stocky woman in a house dress appeared from inside the house. "Hi, Ms. Edwards," the woman said in a southern voice.

"Hi, Fannie. This is my niece I called you about this morning." Her Auntie had not mentioned that she had already spoken to this woman. "Look, I don't have much time to chat today, so I'd like you to show her the place and give me a receipt for the rental."

The woman spoke to Enez, "Hi baby, they call me Ms. Fannie, and some call me Momma. I have several foster children who live with me until homes are found for them. Now, let me show you where you will live."

Enez walked with Ms. Fannie up the concrete walkway, while her Auntie waited in the car. Ms. Fannie opened the door, and Enez was surprised to find a small room with a divided wall.

"Enez, I have a male renter on the other side of this room. His entrance is on the other side of the house. He is a very nice older gentleman." Enez looked at Ms. Fannie with a smile, and Ms. Fannie returned hers. "You have your own bathroom, but no kitchen. If you like, you can eat with us. I hope you will like it here." Ms. Fannie closed and locked the door before they returned to the car.

Enez got in the car and nodded in approval of her new living quarters. It appeared that it would not have mattered, as her aunt had already written a check for the rent, and Ms. Fannie had already prepared a receipt.

As a month went by, Enez's baby grew inside her womb, and she continued to go to cosmetology school. Enez was not very comfortable at Ms. Fannie's boarding house because the foster children who were temporarily placed there ran away from home, and the police were called several times. Her sister was not pleased with Enez's living arrangements, so they began to look for an affordable apartment.

A knock on the door awakened Enez from her afternoon nap. "Who is it?" she yelled from her bed.

"It's me. Open the door. I got some good news for you," Dusty called out. "Girl, put your clothes on! I want to take you to see this apartment in Midtown," she said when Enez let her in.

When they arrived, Enez exclaimed, "Oh this is beautiful!"

Her sister smiled as they walked towards the apartment building. A young blonde woman met them at the foot of the steps. "Hi Dusty, you said you would come back with your sister. And you must be Enez?" The woman removed her hands from her blue jean pants pocket and reached out to shake Enez's hand. "Glad to meet you, Enez."

Enez extended her hand to the woman.

"Your sister told me you're looking for an affordable one-bedroom apartment. I believe I have just what you're looking for. By the way, I'm Lorie. Jim, my husband, and I are the owners of these two buildings." She pointed to the two brick buildings ahead of them as she walked. "Jim also keeps everything working around here, and that includes me."

When they reached the apartment, Enez walked inside and immediately saw potential. The floors were hardwood and waxed to a shiny sheen. To the left, the wall was lined with a steam heater, and to the right was a window air conditioner and what appeared to be a closet. She walked through the French doors to the bedroom and then noticed a bathroom to the left and the kitchen to the right.

"This is our one-bedroom apartment, and it rents for $280 monthly," Lori said, walking into the kitchen. "The kitchen appliances are new, and Jim finished painting just yesterday." Enez opened the cabinets and felt the texture of the kitchen counter. She fell in love with the apartment. "Enez, we require first month's rent and deposit same as rent."

Enez turned on her heels and said, "Yes, I will take it. When can I move in?"

The walk back to the front of the building was much quicker than before. The women went inside Lori's office to sign the lease and write a check for the apartment. "Enez, I am sure you will be delighted with your new apartment. Here is our office number. If you have any problems, be sure to call us. If we are not in the office, leave a message. Now here is your key. You are all set to go."

Dusty and Enez talked excitedly as they drove back to Enez's place. "Thank you so much, Dusty, for helping me find an affordable place."

Dusty shook her head as she waved at Enez, "I got a bed and couch I'm no longer using. We can move those things on top of my car tomorrow morning." Before Dusty and Enez separated, they agreed on a time for moving the next morning. Enez needed to tell Ms. Fannie she was moving the next day. Her walk to the front door was as brisk as the spring wind. The door was open, and Enez looked inside to see Ms. Fannie sitting at the dining room table, shelling peas and watching television. Before Enez could knock on the door, Ms. Fannie invited her in, "Come on in."

"Hi, Ms. Fannie," Enez said in an excited tone.

"What are you so exited about today, Enez? I saw you leaving with your sister. Everything must be alright with you." Enez sat down near Ms. Fannie. "What's on your mind, Enez?" Ms. Fannie asked. The television played a commercial about Tide laundry detergent, and a woman on TV said, "It will get Georgia red clay out of your clothes."

Ms. Fannie laughed as though the woman had just said a joke.

"Ms. Fannie, I'm moving tomorrow to a one-bedroom apartment."

"Well, Sugar, you know I'll miss you. If you ever need a friend, you got one right here in me." She reached out her hands to Enez, and Enez fell into her arms as she hugged her.

"Thank you so much for trusting me to stay on your property. I'll miss you, too. I'll return your key in the morning."

Early the next morning, Dusty came by to pick her up. Enez put her luggage in the trunk and then walked to Ms. Fannie's door, where Ms. Fannie stood waiting for her. She walked out to the porch as Enez gave her the key and a big hug. Enez walked away, only looking back to smile at Ms. Fannie before she got inside the car.

For the next few weeks, Enez enjoyed decorating her new apartment, attending school, and having more visits with her daughter. Her morning nausea slowly came to an end. Her life seemed to have turned for the best. Until one day, she got a phone call.

It was a Saturday morning, and she was sleeping in. The telephone rang, and she eagerly answered, not anticipating to hear the voice of the person on the other end. "Hello," she said. The voice on the other end frightened her, as her heart fell to the pit of her stomach. "How did Nicko get my phone number?" she wondered. She listened quietly.

"Hi Enez, this is Big Daddy." Enez had heard he was in jail. She was still silent and afraid. "I am in jail. I sold some dummy crack to an undercover cop, and I had a warrant for parole violation and assault and battery against you. Now, baby, you know that was a long time ago, and I want you to drop the charges against me. Baby, you know you should not have been play'in with me about my money. You get on that phone tomorrow and drop the charges. Tell them you changed your mind. You hear me?" he asked in a demanding voice. Instantly, she was moved by his controlling nature.

A recorded voice broke into her thoughts. "You have one minute before you are disconnected." Then, she heard another familiar voice that had been silent during Nicko's conversation. It was Nicko's sister-in-law, Betty. Now Enez remembered that she had seen Betty in the mall one afternoon and had given her the phone number. Before Enez could say a word to either Betty or Nicko, the call was disconnected.

Nicko called Enez several days in a row. Sometimes, she would not accept his collect calls. He would have to have someone else pay for his calls. When Enez did talk to him, he promised her he would never hit her again, and he was through smoking crack. After several attempts, he won her heart.

It was several days before Nicko's court appearance for the charge of assault and battery. Enez attempted to contact law enforcement to drop the charge. She learned that the state would pick up the charges after she dropped them, so she became very nervous and afraid of Nicko's reaction to the news. Finally, three days before his court appearance, Enez reached an officer of the state.

A woman answered the phone, "Hello, State Office. This is Mrs. Miller. May I help you?"

"Yes, Ma'am. My name is Enez Brown, and I want to drop a charge for assault and battery against Nicko Nelson."

After a moment of silence, Enez heard a man talk on the line, "Yes, Ms. Brown, I have the case. I am Lieutenant Jones, and I have a written request from another office that you would like to drop the charge against Mr. Nelson. Are you sure this is what you want to do, Ms. Brown? I have seen the pictures the reporting officer took of you in the hospital. Are you sure you want to drop the charges?"

Enez did not hesitate to answer, "Yes, I want to drop the charges."

"Okay, Ms. Brown. If you will meet me on Mr. Nelson's court date, which is this Thursday at 9 a.m., you can sign the papers, and the charges will be dropped."

"Thank you." Enez did not contact Nicko before his court appearance. It was Thursday morning, and her stomach was very nervous as she dressed to meet the law officer.

Grey clouds covered a sky that was filled with sunshine the day before. She held her umbrella handle tightly as she waited for the city bus. She moved away from the curb as the bus approached so she would not get splashed by the rain. Enez boarded the bus and walked to a seat near the front. The movement of the windshield wipers began to hypnotize her as she was lost in thought.

At the courthouse, the hall was filled with men and women who appeared to be lawyers. They wore suits as they carried their briefcases and papers. Some had a parade of people following them. Enez stood near one of the many elevator doors in the lobby, waiting on one to arrive. She pushed the button for the 5th floor when she entered the elevator. She wanted to turn around and run, but she was afraid. As she stepped off the elevator, Enez searched for the court room. Just to her left was the room that would take her back to a time in her history that she thought she had put to rest. Now, she would open it once again.

Enez peeped inside the court room to find no one inside. She found a seat in a back row near the door. Her hands were sweating, and her stomach was upset. She stood to walk out of the court room when a tall, bald headed man in a blue suit asked her, "Are you Ms. Brown?"

"Yes, I am Ms. Brown."

He motioned her to come with him. "Ms. Brown, I am Bobby Taylor with the department. Please follow me to the lobby area. I need you to sign your waiver to not prosecute Mr. Nicko Nelson." Enez nodded her head in an agreement.

A bailiff appeared in the hall saying, "Anyone with business in Division 5 needs to come in and have a seat." Enez moved from her seat and followed Mr. Taylor. As she entered the courtroom, she saw Nicko watching the door. His angry light brown eyes fixed upon her face, and she was paralyzed with fear. She heard him whisper towards her, "Drop the charges." Enez trembled as she sat in the last row of the court room.

After hearing several other cases, Nicko's case was finally brought before the judge. Mr. Taylor proceeded to talk to the judge, informing him Enez Brown, the plaintiff, had dropped the charges. The judge dismissed the case. Relieved, Enez left the court room. A city bus arrived as soon as she exited the building. As the gray clouds moved, the sun peered through them. Her thoughts were now on the life growing within her body.

Nicko continued to call Enez from the Shelby County jail after his court date. He was still serving time for parole violation and a drug charge. In the meantime, Enez decided to terminate her pregnancy. A Friday morning after testing and a counsel visit to the abortion clinic, Enez was ready for the procedure.

The Prodigal Daughter

Her body was numb as she sat in the back of the taxi. This was not the first time she would terminate an unwanted pregnancy. She entered the clinic, which looked like a huge two story house. Enez walked to the receptionist's desk. "Hi, my name is Enez, and I have a 9 o'clock appointment for a procedure."

A woman in a white nurse's jacket stopped by the desk while Enez waited on a response from the receptionist. "Yes, we have you scheduled. Your blood work has come back from the lab."

The receptionist looked over Enez's paperwork, "The doctor checked your lab work, and it appears you may be more weeks pregnant than you think," the receptionist whispered in a calm voice.

Enez knew it was true, but she was determined to terminate the pregnancy now that Nicko would be coming home soon. "No, no. I am sure my last period was three months ago."

The receptionist said, "I will be right back, Ms. Enez. You can have a seat, and the doctor will be with you soon."

Enez talked with Dr. Lowe and convinced her that she had only missed three cycles. Enez paid $250 to the receptionist, and she was taken to a room upstairs. Her walk down the corridor was long and filled with nervousness. The nurse opened a door to a room filled with medical equipment. "I need you to undress from the waist down and wrap your bottom with this covering. Are there questions before the doctor comes?" the nurse smiled to put her at ease. "I will be here with you during your procedure." Enez nodded her head, glad for the support. The comforting nurse left the room while Enez undressed.

Enez waited with anticipation. Soon, someone knocked on the door. Before Enez could respond, Dr. Lowe and the nurse entered the room.

"Okay, Enez, I need you to scoot all the way back and place your feet in the stirrups. Make sure you bring your bottom to the edge. Nurse Western will assist me with the procedure. Do you have any questions?" Dr. Lowe placed her face mask on, and Enez could only see her baby blue eyes. "I am going to deaden your cervix area. Nurse Western is going to give you a gas to put you to sleep during the procedure. Enez, you are going to feel some pulling." Enez nodded her head and experienced a deep sleep immediately.

She awoke from the medication in a room with other women who had made the same decision she had. Her throat was dry, and her insides felt empty. "Nurse, may I please have some water?" she asked. After Enez fully recovered from the medication, the nurse gave her a prescription for pain and more information about the aftermath of the procedure. Enez left in a taxi.

A few days later, Enez stood in the bathroom looking in the mirror when she suddenly felt a big cramp in her abdomen. The pain was unbearable, and she began to cry out to God. "God, please forgive me for this awful thing I have done." The phone rang, and she heard her neighbor's voice as she answered, "Hello," weeping in pain.

"Enez, this is Brenda. Is something wrong?"

"Yes, Brenda. I am having severe cramps. I am going to call the clinic. I will call you back." Enez called the emergency number for the clinic. "Hello, I had a pregnancy termination a few days ago in your clinic. I'm having severe cramps, and my body is releasing some items."

The woman on the other end asked in a concerned voice, "Honey, what is your name?"

"My name is Enez Brown."

"Ms. Brown, can you arrive at the clinic in the morning so the doctor can examine you?"

"Yes, I can be there first thing in the morning."

The next morning, the doctor examined her and released her with a D&C procedure.

Her life was once again spinning out of control. Her school funds were depleted. Enez began to search for what was missing from her life. She continued school, but she also continued to talk with Nicko occasionally from jail.

One day, as she waited on her bus, an older woman sat next to her. The orange, brown, and red autumn leaves rustled past them. A calm wind moved Enez's hair as she combed her fingers through it. The older woman said, "I love this time of the year, don't you?"

Enez nodded her head in agreement. The woman said, "You know in Matthew 4:4, it says '***It is written, Man shall not live by bread alone, but by every word that proceedeth out of the mouth of God.***' In Genesis, God said He created all of this beauty we see around us. And that is His Word. Honey, what church do you belong to?"

Enez looked at the woman strangely and answered, "I don't go to any church." Enez looked ashamed.

"Young woman, it is good to go to church and learn about Jesus. Do you have family?"

"Yes I have family here in Memphis."

"Are you close to your family?"

"No, not that close."

"Have you done some things in your life that they haven't forgiven?"

"Maybe."

Both women looked down the street to see the bus coming closer. "Baby, get in Church. The Church can help you." As the bus stopped, the woman got up and looked at Enez. "I am praying for you."

Enez sat in her seat as the bus doors closed. She thought about the stranger telling her to attend church and that she would pray for her. She stared out the window, thinking how much she wanted to know Him, how she longed to live with Him and He in her. “My life has been nothing but a living hell. I really want to make a change for the better,” she thought. She pulled the cord to ring the bell for the bus to stop.

Each day, Enez thought more and more about making a change. She did not want to revert back to her old behavior for money. Her rent was due, and she had no food in the house. Enez remembered what the older woman at the bus stop had told her about the church and getting help.

Early one morning, Enez jumped from her bed and found the telephone book open to the yellow pages. She found listings of churches titled Baptist, Lutheran, Catholic, Methodist, AME, CME. She called several without getting an answer. Finally, her index figure fell upon listings for Churches of Christ. She traveled the page with her heart, and her eyes fell on Highland Street Church of Christ. Enez dialed the number, and a man answered the phone, “Hello,” he said politely.

“Hello, my name is Enez Brown. May I speak with the minister, please?”

“The minister is not here right now. Is there something I can do for you?”

Her heart beat in despair as she began to tell him her troubles. “I am in cosmetology training to become a manicurist, and I need help with my rent. Someone told me a church would help me.”

“Do you belong to any church organization?” he asked her calmly.

With all honesty and shame, she answered him, "No, I am not in any religious organization."

"Where do you live?"

Enez answered quickly, hoping she had found financial help, "Poplar and McLean Avenue in Midtown"

He chuckled and said, "You are near Vance Avenue Church of Christ. Brother Nokomis Yeldell is the minister there. Here, let me find the number for you. You know, becoming a member of the church is a great start to helping you spiritually. Now you write this number down. Little lady, you need to start going to church." He gave her the phone number to Vance Avenue Church of Christ before he said, "God Bless you."

Enez dialed the number as soon as she hung up. The phone rang three times before a man with a strong baritone voice answered, "Hello. Vance Avenue Church of Christ."

"Hello, my name is Enez Brown, and I need help to pay my rent."

After a few seconds of silence, the man asked, "Ms. Brown, are you in church?"

Once again, Enez answered honestly through her shame. "No, I am not in a church."

"Ms. Brown, my name is Nokomis Yeldell. I am the minister here at Vance Avenue. I'd like to invite you to our Sunday morning Bible class and worship service this Sunday. Do you have transportation?"

"No, I do not have transportation, but I do want to attend services on Sunday."

"Ms. Brown, I will have the bus driver pick you up at 8 am."

Enez agreed and thanked the minister before she said goodbye. She sat quietly on the couch, her heart filled with joy.

Enez remembered reading somewhere, "***Blessed are the poor in spirit; for theirs is the Kingdom of heaven. Blessed are they that mourn: for they shall be comforted. Blessed are they which do hunger and thirst after righteousness: for they shall be filled.***" She smiled to herself as she thought, "Now His promises will become hers."

The weekend passed without any conversation with Nicko. With a calm spirit and a willingness to change her life, Enez attended church services. She heard the Word, believed the gospel, repented of her sins, confessed with her mouth Jesus Christ is the Son of God, and was baptized in the Name of Jesus at Vance Avenue Church of Christ.

A sister in Christ said, "The Angels were having a good time in heaven on this day. You have turned towards the Light to be with our Savior."

For several weeks, Enez studied Biblical stories that were like a mirror to her own life. She learned in scripture, Jesus gave the people what they needed, and so had her brothers and sisters at Vance Avenue Church of Christ. The Church helped her pay rent that month and showed Enez a love that had been unknown to her.

There were silent evenings when Enez was not aware of the enemy's tactics, but she had been warned about his cunning. Sister LaVaughn said in one phone conversation, "Now, you know the enemy is not comfortable with you leaving his dark and gloom. You are still a babe in Christ. Do not forget to take the first step a newborn babe takes in receiving Christ. Before we can understand the Savior, we must study His Word and pray daily. The Lord says, '***Man shall not live by bread alone: but by every Word that proceedeth out of the mouth of God.***' Enez, we must have spiritual food to feed the spirit and guard us from the ways of the enemy. You have followed the plan of salvation, but don't leave your doors open for the enemy to attack you. Remember he attacks through the flesh. Let me read to you another scripture that reminds us what part of us is weak and confirms the enemy's attack. Matthew 26:41 says, '***Watch and pray, that you enter not into temptation: the spirit indeed is willing, but the flesh is weak.***'"

Sister LaVaughn continued, and Enez listened with all of her heart, "Enez, it's not enough to attend midweek Bible Study, Sunday school, and worship. You must walk in the Light, for He is the Light. I hope that I have said something to you to help you to stay with the Lord. If you ever need to talk, I am here for you. God said in Hebrews 10:25 '***not to neglect the assembly of ourselves and to encourage one another***.' Call me, Enez."

Enez took a deep breath and said, "Thank you so much, Sister LaVaughn. I hope you have a good night."

"Thank you, Enez. Remember, I love you, and I am here for you. Good night."

Enez attended Bible studies and worship services every week. Finally, Enez allowed Christian women into her life to help direct her in a positive path as her life in Christ unfolded positively.

* * *

The Prodigal Daughter

1987

Autumn of 1987, all things became new for Enez. She started a new relationship with her daughter, daddy, and a new job. Nicko still called her, and Enez continued to accept his collect phone calls, hoping to convince him to become a Christian. Her mother was not yet comfortable with her, and Enez understood why.

One Friday night, Enez decided it was time for her to connect with her daughter. She dialed her mother's phone number, and she picked up after several rings. "Hello," her mother's voice was filled with uneasiness. Fear came upon Enez's spirit, and she wanted to hang up the phone, but courage took over her fear. "Hi, Momma," she said with a dry throat.

Enez heard her mother exhale through the phone, "Hi Enez."

"I need to ask you a question. Do you have a moment?" Enez waited nervously for an answer.

"Yes, I have a moment," her mother replied.

"I'd like to know if Amara could spend some weekend nights with me."

"Yes, Enez. I believe that's a good idea. Next weekend is good."

Enez breathed a sigh of relief as she thanked her mother, and they said their good byes. Enez spent quality time with her daughter over the next few weekends.

One Friday while she waited for her sister to bring Amara, Enez decided to call her daddy. She had not connected with him in two years. A few days earlier, she had asked his sister for his phone number. She had tried to call him but failed to get an answer on the phone. She tried again, and this time the phone rang twice before his husky voice answered.

"Hello," he said in a cheerful voice.

"Hi, daddy. How are you?" Enez asked in her cheerful voice.

"I am doing good. I can hear from your voice that you are wearing a beautiful smile. Sounds like you are happy to me, Enez," he chuckled. "And what can I do you for, Enez? So, in other words, to what do I owe this pleasurable call?"

Enez cleared the lump in her throat as she thought of the last time she had spoken to her daddy. "Well, daddy, I called to hear your voice. I didn't want anything, just to hear your voice."

"Enez, I'll be home in two weeks for Christmas holiday."

Enez was surprised to hear him say he would be home for Christmas. He usually worked the Christmas holiday for overtime at his job. "Oh! That will be great," she said happily.

"Okay, Enez, I am going let you go now. I'll see you soon, okay?"

Enez turned the television on to watch her favorite night-time talk show, Arsenio Hall, as she waited for Dusty to arrive with Amara. Enez had planned a fun-filled weekend with her daughter. On Sunday, when Dusty arrived to take Amara home, Enez immediately got dressed for church.

Enez looked forward to seeing her daddy for the first time in two years, until one night, she got a phone call from her mother. She had just entered her bedroom when the phone rang. Her mother's voice on the other end caught her by surprise. "Enez, Marvin was found dead in his apartment." There was silence between them. "I just thought I would call and tell you."

Enez sat on her bed with the phone clutched in her hands before she fell to the floor and crawled to a corner of the room with tears blinding her. She screamed, yet no sound came from her mouth. The phone rang again, and she staggered to answer it as tears gushed from her eyes and the screams formed in her mind. A woman's voice asked if she would accept a collect call from jail.

"Hey, baby. What's the matter, baby?"

Enez stopped crying long enough to tell Nicko that her mother had just called to inform her that her daddy was found dead in his apartment.

"Enez, I am so sorry to hear that. Believe me, baby, I know how you feel," Nicko continued to talk until they heard the recording, telling him one minute was left, and then they were abruptly cut off.

Alone, she thought about the reconciliation with her father. She began to pray, "Lord, I never got a chance to tell him face-to-face how very sorry I was to cause so much pain and grief. I never got a chance to hug him, or tell him how much I appreciated him for being my daddy. I know he loved me in his own way. We made plans to visit one another for the first time in two years on Christmas of 1987. Lord, he died on December 8, 1987, before I got a chance to tell him I love him."

The skies were grey, and rain poured from the clouds the day Enez, her sister, brother-in-law, and aunt went to Nashville to her daddy's apartment. One of her daddy's co-workers, Earl, met them at the airport. He worked for American Airlines and lived in the same apartment complex. When they arrived at the apartment, Enez saw the blood-stained carpet where he had been found. She could not believe he was gone, gone forever. As she sat on the couch, she looked down to where he once laid. She rubbed her hand across the blood stain, hoping this was all a dream and that he would walk through the door. Finally, she walked to the kitchen as if in a trance. Earl stood near the kitchen sink, talking to her daddy's sister. Enez overheard him saying, "I went to the store early yesterday morning, and I noticed his car in the parking lot. I was away until the late afternoon. When I got back, I saw Marv's car still in the parking lot, but I knew he was supposed to be at work. You know, he has never called in sick or late for his shift. I knocked on the door but didn't get an answer. So, I went to the resident manger's office and asked her to open his door. And of course, Sis, you know the rest. When the resident manager opened the door, there my buddy lay on the living room floor, face down."

Enez asked, "How long had he been lying there?"

Earl stared into Enez's eyes as he answered her, "Baby, he had been dead for several hours, the paramedics said. Blood was coming from his nose, so he had been there for a while. You know your daddy had high blood pressure problems. He was still smoking cigarettes and drinking a little bit."

Enez opened the refrigerator and saw food someone with high blood should not eat. She walked into his bedroom to find it as he had always kept it in the past. His work pants hung from the top of the bedroom door. His jewelry, wallet, and loose change were placed on the dresser, and his bed was unmade. Enez's sister and brother-in-law went to the closet and reappeared with several cloth purple and gold bags, filled with Marvin's saved coins. Enez sat quietly on his bed, longing to have seen him one more time. Perhaps he died happy, knowing that his oldest daughter seemed to be getting her life together. This thought brought a smile to her lips. As she smiled, her aunt walked in, "Enez, we are going to the morgue where they have Marvin." Enez got up from the bed as she remembered their last conversation. She had not noticed his car earlier, but now as they walked to Earl's Cadillac, she saw her daddy's grey and black rag top Lincoln Continental. Dusty unlocked the car. Inserted into the cassette player was a cassette by The Whispers, "It Get Better With Time." She turned the ignition switch, and the car filled with the sounds of the last song he probably heard in the car before his death. It was the title song. Her knees were weak as she got out of the car. Enez struggled physically and emotionally to stay strong as she went through a grieving process she had never experienced before.

The afternoon approached quickly. The sun peered through the clouds as they arrived at the morgue. An Asian woman met Dusty, Enez's brother-in-law, and her aunt at the entrance of the building. She explained it was not good for them to see his body as she discussed the purpose for signing for an autopsy procedure. Enez's mind was still in a trance. Before nightfall, Enez and her aunt were on a flight back to Memphis without her sister and brother-in-law. A few more days passed before Dusty returned to Memphis to make funeral arrangements.

For the first time in two years, Enez saw her daddy. He lay cold and stiff, resting in a grey coffin with a matching suit. She trembled as she walked to see him for the last time. She touched his forehead and lay her lips against his cheeks as she said farewell to the only daddy she had ever known. She walked calmly to the church pew as she focused on their last conversation and remembered the sound of his laughter. As the procession left for the burial, Enez thought about the day Dusty, their mother, and she had made plans at the cemetery for his burial.

"Enez, you pick a site for daddy to lay at rest," her sister had said. The cemetery owner drove them to a site that sat on a hill. There were several vacant spots as they walked the grounds until they had found a perfect spot. Enez stopped and said to her sister and mother, "Daddy would love this spot. It sits on a hill." They all agreed. Now, as the funeral car parked, she sat in the car to compose herself. The pall bearers carried him to the spot she had picked out. Enez cried goodbye.

* * *

Waiting at the Gate

Enez read a letter the Apostle Paul wrote to the Ephesians in the Bible: "***Among whom all also we had conservation in times past in the lust of our flesh, fulfilling the desires of the flesh, and of the mind; and we were by nature the children of wrath, even as others***" (Ephesians 2:3).

Enez started visiting Nicko in jail and accepting more of his phone calls after her daddy's death. She read the warnings in her Bible Study, but Enez would not listen to what God was saying to her in scripture, "***For wide is the gate, and broad is the way, that leadeth to destruction.***"

A few days after her 27th birthday, Nicko returned to her from jail. "***They come to you in sheep's clothing, but inwardly they are ravening wolves.***" She failed to heed another warning she read in her Bible. It was early Friday morning, and she had just arrived home from the night shift at her waitress job. She heard a knock at the door, and she peeped from the living room window. There stood Nicko and his son on the porch. She opened the door and allowed him inside. Unlike the person she had left years prior, he now looked a hot mess. His hair was stringy, and he wore old raggedy tennis shoes, jailhouse blue jeans, and a coat that someone must have given him.

"Hi, baby," he said. "I didn't know I was getting out of jail today until early this morning. You know I had to go see my son first, and he wanted to follow me. One of my friends drove us over here.

But look here, I need you to give me some money. I gotta pay this man for driving me around, and I will be back later. You don't have to go to work until later this evening, right? So get you some rest, and I will be back later." He held her close to his body as she reached inside her purse and gave him $50, the tip money she had earned on her work shift. He quickly put the money in his pocket, kissed her bye, and walked out the front door.

Nicko did not return before Enez left for work in a cab. She did not hear from him until the next day. An hour after she arrived home, the phone rang. "Hello," she said calmly.

"I am on my way home. See ya in a minute." Then the phone went silent.

Enez placed the phone receiver on its cradle and held her head in her hand. She said out loud, "Lord, what have I done?" After her hot bath; she lay on her bed and fell into a deep sleep. She thought she was dreaming when she heard her name called. Enez sat up quickly in her bed just as she heard her name being called again from outside the bedroom window. She saw Nicko walking towards the back door as she peered out the window. Enez slipped her house shoes on her feet and opened the door to let him in.

"Enez, I don't smell any breakfast cooking. I just knew you would have fixed your man some breakfast this morning," Nicko said as he walked through the house, suspiciously looking around.

Nicko followed her into the living room and sat next to her on the couch as he turned on the television. "Girl, you know it's not breakfast I want from you this morning. Come closer to me and give me what you know you wanna give me, girl." Enez slowly drew closer to him and gave him what they both wanted.

Before noon that day, Enez was back in love with Nicko. Her life with Nicko continued exactly where it had left off a few years earlier. She gave him a key to her apartment and, once again, a key to her heart.

It was a rainy afternoon, and Enez had a scheduled day off from work. She planned to spend a quiet evening with Nicko, but Nicko had other plans in mind for their quiet evening. She heard him talking on the phone, but she could not hear the conversation. When he got off the phone, he said, "Baby, give me that $50 dollars I told you put up for us. I called for a package, and the man will be here soon." He picked up her purse and looked through it for the money. "Where is my money?" he asked, looking anxiously.

"Nicko, it's in my coat pocket," Enez replied nervously. She thought to herself, "Nicko has started smoking crack again." Her heart beat fast, and her stomach was upset. She wanted to cry because she knew he had lied to her. He had promised her we would not smoke crack anymore and not hit her again. "Nicko, you lied to me. You told me you were through with hitting the crack pipe."

He looked at her as she gave him the money. “Yeah I did. I didn’t lie to you, baby. I am lacing it with some weed,” he said with a half smile on his face.

Minutes later, Nicko walked to the kitchen to answer the knock at the back door. He looked through the window and opened the door. Enez sat in the living room while Nicko bought the package. She heard a man say, “Hey, man, I’ll be out late tonight. Give me call if you need anything else.” Nicko walked quickly back to the living room as Enez sat on the couch, trying to ignore him and watch television. As she rose from the couch, Nicko pulled her down towards him. He reached out to her with a marijuana cigarette laced with crack, “Try it.”

“No, Nicko. I don’t want to try it,” she said.

“I want you to try it, Enez. It’s like hitting the pipe.”

She reached for it and took two pulls, “I don’t like the way it makes me feel.” She gave it back to Nicko, and he finished it. Enez did not use crack again for several weeks.

It was the season for the flu virus, and Enez struggled with the virus as she made it to work each day. Finally, on Thursday she could no longer fight the virus. She called her shift manger to call in sick, “Hello, may I speak to Kathy, please?” she asked in a whisper.

“Yes, this Kathy. May I help you?”

"Kathy, this is Enez. I am very, very sick with a bad flu virus, and I won't make it in tonight."

"Don't worry, Enez. I will have Debra cover for you tonight. Just let me know how you are feeling tomorrow."

"Yes, I'll call you tomorrow," Enez hung up the phone and fell into a deep sleep. Later, she woke up to voices coming from the kitchen. Nicko had come home, and he had two women with him. She lay in bed watching Nicko escort the women to the living room to sit on her couch. He walked past her to the bathroom. Enez found the strength to stand in the door as he shaved. She asked, "Why do you have these women in my apartment?"

He looked at her and said, "One of those women is my woman, Vickie."

Enez began sweating under her wool pajamas. The smell of vapor rub and cold medicine came from her pores as she stumbled back to the bed. She heard the water running in the other room while Nicko bathed and then a woman's voice, "It smells like a hospital in here. I'm ready to go, Nicko." Nicko dressed and left with the woman, both of them laughing contentedly. Tears fell from Enez's eyes as she cried into her pillow. The next morning, her body felt weak, but her mind was strong. She packed all of Nicko's clothes and placed them on the back porch. Later, she heard a car outside her bedroom window and heard Nicko talking to someone. Enez peered from the window and saw the woman who had been sitting on her couch.

"Yeah, Vickie, she don't know I was coming to get my clothes anyway," she heard Nicko say. He left her key on the kitchen counter, leaving the door wide open. Enez blew a sigh of relief. "Perhaps he is out of my life again," she thought to herself. Enez felt free once again.

Nicko and Vickie lived in his house on Leatherwood, but Enez's lust for him and her penchance to smoke crack overpowered her as he visited her more and more often. One morning, Enez decided to pay Nicko a visit. A neighbor drove her to the house on Leatherwood. The back door was unlocked, and Enez walked to the guest bedroom, where she found Nicko and Vickie in bed with her children. Enez screamed at the dark skinned woman, "Why are you in the bed with my man? Don't you have one of your own?" Enez shouted.

Nicko and the woman backed up against the headboard before Nicko looked at Enez, "Get out of my house before I hurt you," he said. Enez looked at Nicko with malice in her heart. She walked out, feeling worse than she did had she not come at all.

In the meantime, Dusty was collecting on their father's insurance. Dusty assured Enez she would include her in the inheritance, paying off her bills and giving her a down payment for a car.

Spring was just around the corner and so was Nicko. It was an early Tuesday morning before sunrise. Nicko came to the restaurant where Enez worked. She wiped down the counter as Nicko placed his hand on top of hers. She jerked her hand back, "What do you want?"

"I need to talk to you."

"I am listening."

Nicko paused, "Baby, let me come to your apartment later. I don't feel comfortable talking here. Let me pick you up from work so you won't have to ride the bus."

She agreed so she would not have to wait for the bus. Nicko arrived just before Enez finished her shift, and they walked outside together. In the car, Enez saw the same drug dealer who was at her house several weeks ago sitting in the driver's seat. Enez began to pull back, but Nicko pushed her forward as he opened the door and told her to get in the car. She did not want to cause a scene, so she got in the car with her heart racing in her chest. She knew something was not right. When they arrived at the apartment, Nicko told Enez to give him her money. She did as she was told. Nicko gave the man the money in exchange for a package.

"Hey man, that's why Vickie left you. You smoke like an old truck, but you still my man," the drug dealer said. Enez's body trembled, and she was afraid.

Inside the house, Enez sat on the couch. "Nicko, you said you wanted to talk to me. I thought that's what you wanted."

"I do, baby," he said as he pulled out his lighter and crack pipe. Enez watched Nicko place the crack rock on the pipe, and her belly began to turn. She asked for a hit of it. Soon, Nicko said, "Give me the rest of my money."

Enez walked to the bedroom in a trance and opened her purse to give him nearly one hundred dollars. He immediately called the drug dealer.

She had not noticed the sun set, and she had not slept. The high from the crack was gone, and Enez went into a depression. She lay down on the bed while she listened to Nicko try to reach the dealer for more crack on credit. She could not sleep because of the trembling in her body, and her mind craved more crack. She was physically tired. Enez slowly felt her eyelids closing, and her heart beat was very fast as her legs shook underneath the blanket. Finally, Enez fell into a deep sleep. When she woke up, Nicko was gone, and it was time for her to get ready for work. She was full of disappointment and sorrow as she walked to the bus stop. She saw the headlights of the bus approaching, and then the bus driver opened the door. He was familiar with Enez.

"Hello Enez," he said as Enez dropped her fare into the machine.

Enez smiled as she boarded the bus. She noticed a woman in a nurse's uniform and two young men sitting near the back door as she moved to the middle section of the bus. Her ten-minute ride to work seemed like only two minutes and then it was time to get off the bus. As she stepped closer to the hotel/restaurant, Enez remembered that it was just that morning that she had made a choice to allow Nicko to con her into picking her up from work. The restaurant was very crowded as Enez opened the glass doors to enter.

"How are you, Enez?" the baritone voice asked from a table near the rear window. She walked slowly to his table and stood beside him. "I saw you walking towards the door with your head held down. You looked sad, Enez."

She did not want to tell her favorite customer that she had sank for an afternoon of drugging. She returned a smile and answered, "Oh, I'm just tired, Redd."

Redd looked at her as though he only half believed her. He responded with care, "Baby, you know you can talk to me. I know who you left with this morning." He looked inside his coffee cup as she turned to walk away without responding to him.

After she said hello to everyone at the counter, she walked into the kitchen to fill out her time sheet and clock in. Her heart was heavy as she opened the kitchen door to see Redd staring at her. "Maybe he knows," she thought to herself. Two empty coffee pots were behind the counter, and she grabbed a pot with her head held high as she prepared fresh coffee. The coffee finished brewing as she finished wiping the counter.

"Enez, bring me a cup of that fresh brewed coffee please," Redd said in a polite voice.

She was not ready to hear Redd preach at her but he was surely her favorite customer. Perhaps he was the responsive daddy she missed growing up as a child. After filling a young woman's coffee cup, she walked towards Redd and poured him a cup.

"There is NOTHING we can do good without the Lord our Savior. Be careful, Enez '***They forgot God their Savior, which had done great things in Egypt.***' Enez, don't you forget what God has brought you through," Redd said as her stirred cream and sugar into his coffee.

Enez looked around and noticed that the restaurant was becoming empty. "I'll come back later, Redd. I need to help clean the tables for my shift."

As the calm night went on, she almost forgot the emptiness she had experienced earlier.

Just as Enez had done before, she distanced herself from God and her family. Occasionally, Enez allowed Nicko in her bed, and he continued to see Vickie on Leatherwood and smoke cocaine.

Enez's sister called her one quiet evening. "Hello, Enez. I have the money I promised you, but first I am going to pay all of your bills. Tell me who you owe and how much."

Enez looked in her dresser drawer to find the statements to tell Dusty all the places and amounts she owed money to.

"Okay Enez, next week I'll write you a check for $2000 to do whatever you want to do. See ya later, Sis."

Enez whispered, "See ya later, and thank you, Dusty."

She spent the weekend with Nicko. He lay in her bed as though he knew money would soon arrive in her hands. He walked her to the bus stop at night and was there when she arrived in the morning.

On Monday morning, Enez was awakened by the ringing of the telephone. She removed Nicko's arm to answer it. "Hello."

"Good morning, sleepy head."

Enez sat up in the bed, "Good morning."

There was a pause before either sister said anything. Enez sat on the edge of the bed to put her feet in her house shoes before she walked into the living room for privacy.

"Enez, can you meet me downtown today at my job? I have a check for you."

Enez whispered, "Yes, what's a good time for you?"

"I am looking at noon time."

"Okay, I'll see you then." Enez did not return to bed with Nicko. He stared at her when she walked into the bedroom.

"Who was that on the phone?" he asked.

She smiled at him, "You are so nosy! Baby, I have to meet my sister downtown. I'll come back soon."

Nicko grabbed her by her hips and pulled her down towards him. "And why are you going to meet your sister, Enez?"

She looked at him, wanting to be honest with him but feeling afraid. "She needs to talk to me," Enez answered as she pulled away from him so he could not look into her lying eyes.

Enez soaked in the bath tub as she tried to relax. She heard Nicko talking to someone, so she asked, "Who are you talking to, Nicko? Is someone in the apartment?"

The room was very quiet. Then, she heard his footsteps coming near the door. He opened it while she lay naked in the tub. "My brother is picking me up. He can take you to see your sister. Now tell me what she wants with you again, and this time don't lie to me." He looked at her with his demanding brown eyes.

She turned her head in his direction, and this time she told the truth. "My sister is giving me some money." She turned to finish bathing, not saying another word.

It was late evening before Enez arrived home. She was talking on the phone when she heard a knock at the door. She pulled the curtain back to see Nicko standing there with his brother and another man. "Girl, can I call you back later?" she spoke into the phone before she quickly placed the phone on the cradle. She opened the door to allow them inside. Nicko walked in first, then his brother, and finally the other man.

"Come here, baby, let me holler at you." Nicko, Tony, and the man followed Enez through the bedroom to the living room. Tony and the man sat down on the couch, while Nicko and Enez went back to the kitchen. "Where is the money?" Nicko asked.

Enez looked at Nicko and saw that his pupils were enlarged, and his face was covered with perspiration. Her heart began to beat fast as she grasped for words under her breath. "Nicko, I only picked up a check from her, and I haven't cashed it yet."

He grabbed her arm and hissed at her, "Where is it?"

She walked to the bedroom to get her purse. Tony blocked the doorway. Enez grabbed her purse, and Nicko stood directly behind her. As she pulled out a check written for $2000, Nicko grabbed it and walked to the living room to show the man.

"Hey man, I told you my woman got your money. Look, she didn't get a chance to cash it today. I'll have your money in the morning. I'm going to stay her with her to make sure she takes care of my business. My brother will pick us up in the morning," Nicko sat on the couch, looking very confident.

The man looked at the check and said, “Man, don’t you mess me around about my money. I will see ya in the morning.”

The three men walked out to the parking lot. Enez had the urge to lock the door behind them, but Nicko still had the check in his hand. Enez sat on her bed, feeling very confused and frightened. Nicko came back inside and gave Enez the check. She placed it back inside her purse as she thought to herself, “Fortunately, I don’t have to work tonight.”

Nicko sat in the living room, smoking weed. Enez lay in her bed with her purse underneath the pillow. She finally fell into a deep sleep. The next morning Enez was awakened by Nicko and his brother’s car horn. She rushed to the bathroom to freshen up before going to the bank. Enez deposited the check into her account and withdrew several hundreds dollars from it. Nicko and his brother waited for her some distance from the bank, parked in an alley.

“You get the money?” Nicko asked eagerly.

“Yeah, I got three hundred dollars,” she replied nervously.

“Give it to me so I can pay this man his money.” Enez reached in her purse and gave him an envelope with the money. “I’m going to drop you off at the apartment and catch up with you later,” he said as he removed the money from the envelope. Enez stared from the car window to see a bird flying high in the sky with the freedom she remembered she once owned. “It won’t be long before I come back, baby!" he whispered as she opened the back door of the car. Enez nodded her head in relief that he was gone.

Nicko did not return to Enez for several days. She noticed that she felt at peace while he was gone. Until one night, she heard a knock at the back door as she watched a movie on her night off from work. She hesitated, hoping it was not Nicko. She walked quietly to her bedroom and slightly pulled the curtain back to see Nicko standing at the door, knocking again and again. She wanted to just disappear. It was too late. He had spotted her at the window. "Open the door, girl," he said anxiously.

She opened the door to allow him inside, and he rushed to the bathroom without closing the door behind him. Enez walked back to the living room and sat on the couch, staring blankly at the screen. She continued to stare into space as Nicko took off his clothes in the bedroom. He called her name as he rustled the bedspread. "Enez, Enez come here." She pretended not to hear him. He called her again, but with authority in his voice. "Enez, get in this room right now. Didn't you hear me?" Once again she pretended not to hear him. From the corner of her eye, she saw him get up from the bed and walk closer to her. As she began to get up from the couch, he slapped her down. "When I call you, don't pretend you don't hear me." He grabbed her wrist and pulled her to the bedroom. "Come on and give me what I want now." She removed her clothes and unwillingly had sex with him. When he finished, he fell asleep and Enez returned to the living room with tears falling from her eyes. Enez stared down into the deep black pits of her soul and cried out, "Lord, why me?" She lay awake on the couch for hours.

The next morning, she opened her eyes to see the sun gleaming through the living room windows. She heard Nicko rattling about in the kitchen, complaining that there was no food in the house as he slammed the cabinet doors shut. She lay still as she remembered the events of last night. Grief fell over her spirit as a cloud covered the sun. Nicko walked into the living room, smiling. "I was going to cook some breakfast, but you don't have any food."

She looked at him as though a stranger had entered her home, unlike the man who had forced her to have sex with him just a few hours ago. "Oh, I haven't gone to the store. I eat at work, so I just don't grocery shop much."

"Enez, give me some money, and I'll go to the store and get some food."

She answered from the bathroom as she locked the door, "I don't have any more money, Nicko. I gave you all I could get until the check clears."

Nicko was silent in the next room. When she came out, she saw Nicko searching through the contents of her purse.

"Nicko, I told you I don't have any money."

"So, what are you going to do about eating?" he asked.

"Nicko, I'm not hungry. I can wait until later," she answered as she pulled the used linen from the bed.

"So, hmmm. What am I to do about eating?" She shrugged her shoulders and quickly moved to the other side of the bed. Nicko said, "I'm going to call Tony and tell him to pick me up, so I can get my hustle on."

Excitement ran through Enez's spirit because Amara was spending the night with her. Nicko had not come back since the day he called Tony to pick him up. Enez took a city bus to the grocery store and bought Amara's favorite foods.

She jumped to the window when she heard the sound of a car at the back door to see Amara exiting the car. Her light brown pony tails peeked from under her wool hat. Her coat came just above her knees, and her legs were covered in blue jeans. She held her overnight case and baby doll tightly to keep from dropping them on the ground. Enez waved to her from the window, and Amara smiled. Enez rushed to open the back door. The steam heater blew its whistle as mother and daughter walked into the living room, and Enez removed Amara's coat. Amara's brown eyes behind her thick glasses pierced Enez's heart. She took Amara's hand and led her to the couch.

Dusty stood at the door. "Enez, I'll pick Amara up tomorrow before you leave for work. As a matter of fact, I can drop you off at work, if you don't mind being a little early."

"Bye, Dusty," Amara said.

"Bye, baby. I'll pick you up tomorrow evening, okay?"

Amara nodded her head while she combed her baby doll's hair. Enez said good bye to Dusty and saw the tail lights of her car disappear into the night.

Amara put her baby doll down on the couch as she followed Enez to the bathroom. "Momma, I want something sweet to eat," she said as she moved her hips from side to side.

"Okay, baby. I got just what you like."

Later that night, Enez could hear the strong winds knocking the branches against the bedroom window. Enez watched her daughter sleeping peacefully. She felt like she was dreaming and did not ever want to wake up. As she thought of the free life she could have with God and her family, Enez finally fell into a peaceful sleep.

The whistle from the steam heater reminded Enez that it was winter. She sat on the side of her bed, slipped her house shoes on, and walked to the living room where she found Amara laying on the couch watching Saturday morning cartoons.

"Good morning, Amara," Enez said as she bent over to kiss her cheeks. "Are you ready to eat breakfast?" Enez looked at the clock on the living room wall.

"Yes, Mommy, I'm ready to eat. What are we having? Can I help you cook?" Amara asked as she stood up to follow Enez from the bathroom to the kitchen.

"Yes, baby, you can help me cook. Okay, let's see what we have here! How about scrambled eggs, bacon, grits and toast?" Enez turned to look at Amara.

"Yeah, Mommy! And I'd like cheese in my eggs. Do you have any cheese, Mommy?" she asked in her childlike voice.

"Yes, baby, I got cheese." Enez replied as she turned from the refrigerator, holding slices of American cheese.

Breakfast was almost over when the phone rang. "Mommy, the phone is ringing," Amara said.

"I know baby, but today Mommy just wants to talk to you, okay?" she said with a warm smile on her face. Deep in her heart, she was almost sure the caller was Nicko, and she did not want to talk to him.

The day was filled with games, laughter, television watching, sleep, and more sleep. The night sky fell upon them, and soon Enez's time with her daughter was coming to an end. "Mommy, I don't want to go. Do I have to go back and live with my grandmother?" Amara asked with tears in her eyes. "I love my grandmother, but I want you."

Enez looked at Amara with a blank face. "Come here, baby, let me talk to you. It's not that I don't want you here with me. I love you. Until I have a better job and can really take care of you, it is best that you stay with your grandmother a little while longer. We can spend our weekends together. Okay?"

Amara did not have a happy face until Enez began to tickle her belly. She squirmed all over the floor. When Enez stood, Amara began tickling her mother.

As Enez put on her lipstick, the phone rang. Enez answered the phone, thinking it might be Dusty.

"Hi, it's me. I'm on my way to pick up Amara," Dusty said.

"Okay, we're ready." Soon, Dusty arrived and blew her car horn at the back door.

Enez could not take her eyes off the child she had given life to not so many years ago. Amara's perfect innocence reminded Enez of her own childhood. Amara looked down at the floor. "Hey, little girl, you remember what we talked about." Amara's eyes were now fixed upon her mother as she smiled. Enez closed the car door and waved at the car until the tail lights were no longer visible. She entered the restaurant, feeling worthy and complete.

It was an unusual Saturday night. Things had quieted down, and Enez was relaxing her feet when a group of men walked inside the restaurant at about four in the morning. They moved two tables together to give themselves enough room. Enez got up from her comfortable position and walked over to their table. One man's cigar hung from his mouth as he said, "We want some breakfast this morning. Is Ms. Roberta in the kitchen?"

Enez answered, "Yes, she is here tonight."

The man winked at Enez, "Go tell Ms. Roberta that Johnny is out here, and I want her to take my order. You can get these other fellows' orders. I'm sure you'll do well," he said as he blew a cloud of smoke.

"Are you men ready to order?"

An oversized man said, "Give us a minute, baby, but I tell you what…bring eight coffee cups and a pot of fresh coffee with eight glasses of water. You can take our order when you come back."

Enez stuffed her ordering book back in her waitress apron and swayed her hips to the kitchen to give Ms. Roberta the message. Then, she went behind the counter to prepare their drink order.

Ms. Roberta was a short, older woman with an overbite and huge lips. She raced from the kitchen as she exclaimed in her Southern accent, "Heya boys! And what do you want, Johnny?" She looked over the crowd of men as he answered, "You know, Momma, I want you to prepare those eggs like you did the other night and some of that sausage and gravy."

She looked at him, "And you couldn't tell my waitress?"

The men laughed as Enez placed a water glass and coffee cup in front of each man and poured their coffee. “Okay are we ready? Sounds like somebody already got their order taken, especially.” She quickly returned with their orders and placed platters grits, bacon, sausage, scrambled eggs, hash browns, biscuits and dry toast as the men talked and laughed.

One man said to the dark-skinned man she had stood next to earlier, “Yeah, man, you rolled those dice hard tonight. Little Shorty lost all his money and sent his woman back to get more and lost it too. That man wasn’t having any luck at the crap table!”

After the meal and another round of coffee, Enez placed the receipt for each person on the table. “Hey baby, you can just put all those receipts in front of that tall man over there,” a man wearing diamond rings and a tilted hat pointed at the dark skinned man. “Baby, his name is Black, and he is paying the tab tonight.”

Black winked at Enez and gave her a hundred dollar bill, “Keep the change,” he told her.

“You better watch out! Black likes him a short red-boned woman,” another man said.

Enez walked to the counter to put the money in the register when Black ambled over and asked Enez for her phone number. Without hesitating, she wrote her number down on a napkin. He smiled at her and placed the napkin in his wallet as he said good night.

The morning sun's reflection bounced off the windows as Enez cleared the dishes and restocked for the next shift. Nicko walked in and sat at the counter, trying to get Enez's attention, but she ignored him. Instead, she walked to the front desk to give the manager her shift bank and proceeded out the door to a waiting cab parked near the front entrance. She did not look back. Enez went straight to her apartment and did not hear from Nicko for several days.

Enez felt at peace for several weeks. She resumed attending worship services and spending more time with her daughter. Enez's sister did as she promised. Dusty gave her a $800 check as a down payment on a car.

The sunlight shone through her bedroom window as she reached over to make a phone call. "Hi Debra. I'll make this short. Do you have time to take me car shopping on Covington Pike?"

The woman responded, "Yeah, I'll take you. What time would you like to go?"

"I can be ready in an hour."

Enez slipped on her house shoes and rushed to iron her pants and shirt. Then, she ran a hot bath. Before long, Debra was outside blowing her car horn. "Okay Debra! Let me grab my purse, and I'll be right out," she called out.

The rays from the spring sun shone brightly through the front window of Debra's 1987 green Monte Carlo as she drove on the interstate to

Covington Pike. They sat in silence as Al Green sang his hit song, "Let's Stay Together." Enez thought about Nicko as Al Green belted out, "…whether times are good or bad…let's stay together." Her eyes lit up as they drove up to the Toyota car dealership. Debra parked the car, and they walked to the office to find a salesman.

A blonde haired man approached them with a reassuring smile. "Good afternoon, ladies. Which one of these new cars attracts you?" Enez looked around in amazement at the beautiful vehicles in the showroom. "My name is Tony Raye, and I'm here to put you in a car of your dreams that you can afford."

Enez had a refreshing smile on her face as she said, "I am Enez Brown," and extended her hand out to him. "I am looking to buy a car."

He gestured for Enez and Debra to follow him as they walked to a cubicle with a desk, file cabinets, and a telephone. "Have a seat, ladies." He sat in his chair and turned to remove papers from a file tray as he asked questions to verify Enez's identity and credit eligibility. "Yes, yes! Ms. Brown, I believe we can put you in a car today. Do you have your down payment?"

Enez looked in her purse, "Yes, I have $800."

"Okay! Let's walk out to the car lot. I have a 1987 two-door Toyota Corolla FX, with automatic transmission and 10,000 miles on it. I believe I can put you in that car today. It takes about two weeks before the papers are final, though."

Mr. Raye, Debra, and Enez passed several cars as they walked through the lot. Finally, Mr. Raye stopped next to a black car. Enez rushed to look inside the vehicle as he gave her the key to open the door. She slid onto the black cloth seats and looked around as she noticed the stereo cassette player, electric windows and tinted windows. She started the ignition and asked, “Can I take a test drive, Mr. Raye?”

He walked to the other side of the car, and Enez unlocked the door and moved forward as Debra slipped into the back seat. They went for a short test drive, and Enez decided she wanted to purchase the car. Debra and Enez entered Mr. Raye’s office to fill out temporary release papers. Finally, it was time for Enez to drive off with her car.

Enez was sitting on the top of the world. She had a new car, was spending time with her daughter, and had a job. But Enez was not attending worship services. She always used the excuse that she did not get off work until seven in the morning, and she was tired after her Saturday night shift.

Enez looked around to see Redd walking into the restaurant. She walked behind the counter as he sat down. “Good morning, Redd. I like your suit you’re wearing,” she told him as she eyed the burgundy, double breasted pinstriped suit. “Would you like some coffee?” she asked.

“Yeah, I think I will have a cup of coffee before going to Church.” Redd stirred cream and sugar in his coffee. “I’ve been watching you since you bought that car. You're different. Let me tell you something, Baby Girl. Do you remember when the devil tried to tempt Jesus with the world? Let me quote it to you." Redd opened his pocket Bible and began reading, "***Again, the devil taketh him up into an exceeding high mountain, and sheweth him all the kingdom of the world, and the glory of them…Therefore when thou doest thine alms, do not sound a trumpet before thee…***"

Redd finished his coffee and looked at his watch, "Enez, I'm going to pray for you. Here is the money for the coffee. Keep the change. I gotta get out of here. I don't want to be late." He quickly placed his brim hat on his head and exited the restaurant.

* * *

The Prodigal Daughter

She Walked through the Valley

"***Yea, though I walk through the valley of the shadow of death.***" Enez turned from God. "***But the fool walketh in darkness***"...it happened again..."***that this also is vanity.***" She remembered Redd telling her foolish pride is very dangerous to mankind. As long as she was in the house of the Lord, the gates of hell could not prevail.

Enez made a choice to step outside the house and enter the gates of hell. It was one of the worst choices she had made in her life. The hell forming in her life was like a mad dog on the loose.

"***When the unclean spirit is gone out of man, he walketh through dry places, seeking rest; and finding none, he saith, I will return unto my house whence I came out. And when he cometh, he findeth it swept and garnished. Then goeth he, and taketh to him seven other spirits more wicked than himself; and they enter in, and dwell there: and the last state of that man is worse than the first***" (Luke 11:24-26).

The smell of rain was fresh in the air as Enez stared at the gray clouds on her way to her car. She was thinking of Nicko. She wanted him to see her in the new car, but she was afraid. Finally she thought, "I can drive by his house. Maybe someone will see me and tell him I was driving a car with the drive out tags on the rear window." She applied fresh lipstick and then left the parking lot to see Nicko. She saw Nicko as she turned the corner of Leatherwood and Sillet. She stopped as he approached the car. Raindrops began to fall as Enez rolled her window down.

Nicko's baseball cap covered his tangled hair. He was unshaven and very slim. Enez searched his light brown eyes for answers, but all she could see was that he was high on crack cocaine.

"Hi baby, you got any money?" he asked, smiling.

Enez looked away, "No, I don't have any money."

Nicko stepped away from the car. A man across the street waved at Nicko and called out his name. Enez looked into Nicko's eyes once more as he walked away. Then, she put the car in drive.

Enez heard from the car dealership two weeks later when they told her to return the car. Debra followed Enez to the dealership, where Mr. Raye met them at the door. "Ms. Brown, I'm sorry, but you do not qualify for this car. Like I told you over the phone, I have another one you do qualify for. It's a Toyota Corolla ,5 speed, with a cassette player. The notes will be cheaper on it. Let me show it to you."

Enez thought she would not like this deal. Her heart was set on the car she had to return. They walked onto the lot, where Mr. Raye stopped at a candy apple red car trimmed in black and gave the keys to Enez. She opened the door and saw plastic covering the seats and paper mats on the floorboard.

The mileage only read three miles. She turned to Mr. Raye, and her heart leapt with joy.

"This is a brand new car, Ms. Brown. I thought you might like this one better than a used one. I have your paperwork already typed. All you need to do is read and sign. Your payments will be $142.00 for three and half years," Mr. Raye said. Enez drove away from the car dealership with a brand new car and a new attitude. Her first stop was to see her sister and daughter.

Nicko started stopping by her job at the end of her shift soon after she purchased the car, and it was evident to Enez that Nicko was not planning to leave her alone.

Spring was breaking in Memphis. The mornings were cool and fresh, the afternoons were warm and sticky. It was April, 1988 and a very tired Enez got in her car after along night in the restaurant. She was looking forward to going home and relaxing. Looking through her rear view mirror, she saw Nicko pulling in behind her in a blue Mustang convertible as she pulled into the apartment parking lot. Her heart began to beat faster as she parked and opened her door.

"Enez, Enez," Nicko called out.

She thought to herself as she walked to her apartment, "He's driving an impressive car. I wonder which fool woman gave him the keys."

Nicko was a pimp, a card shark, a pool hustler, a drug dealer, and now a drug addict. He lived to hustle women, so Enez knew he was not visiting on a love call, but a hustle. Still, she lusted after him and invited him inside. They walked into the apartment, laughing and talking happily. She turned on the television and walked back to her bedroom to undress. "Nicko, I'm going to take a bath. Are you in a hurry?" she asked, walking into the bathroom not hearing his response. She took a quick bath and then put on comfortable clothes. As she looked through the French doors, she saw Nicko lying on the couch.

As she sat in an adjacent chair, Nicko looked at her, "You know that's not where I want you to sit. Come over here with me, baby." Enez quickly responded to his request.

The next morning, they moved closer to each other as they woke up. Nicko said drowsily, "Hey baby, it feels good to wake up near you." The sound of his soft voice seemed to spark love inside her. She was lonely for his touch, and she would do anything he asked of her if only she could see the day when they would never part again, when there would be no more drugs or other women. How sweet that day would be, she thought.

A car horn blew, and Nicko jumped up. He drew the curtain back from the bedroom window to see a canary yellow Cadillac parked at the back door.

"Oh man, girl, I got so into you last night that I forgot to take Mitch his car. That's him outside. Look, go and open the door and tell him I'll be out in just a minute."

Not want to spoil the moment, Enez did not ask any questions. She threw her robe on as she opened the door to let Mitch in. "Hey, I'm Enez. Nicko's in the bathroom. He said he'll be out in a minute. Would you like to come in and have a seat?"

He extended his hand to introduce himself. "My name is Mitch," he said as he followed her into the living room.

Enez knew how Nicko felt about conversations with other men who were not giving her money, so she returned to the kitchen until Nicko finished in the bathroom. Suddenly, Nicko walked into the kitchen, startling Enez. "Baby, I'm going to follow Mitch back to the hood with his car. I may need you to come by later to pick me up. So, you stay by the phone today and wait on my call." Nicko stepped in front of her, held her hand, and kissed her lips to assure her of his return. "I know you like it, Enez. Big Daddy com'in home to take care of you. You ain't gotta try to put a scheme on with me." He patted her on her buttocks and smiled at Mitch as they walked out the back door.

Enez was mesmerized by his parting words to her. She wanted more of him, and she waited by the phone all day for a call that never came. At work, Enez tried to dismiss her night with Nicko from her thoughts. She found comfort in her new friend, Black, who came to the diner during the early morning hours, alone. He stood at the counter as though he had not planned to stay. She walked over to him smiling, "Hi, Black."

He answered back in a bashful voice, "Hey, baby." She pointed to a vacancy where there were two stools together. Black said, "Naw baby, I didn't come here to sit. I came to give you something. I know waitresses don't make a whole lot of money, especially in this place." He reached out his cupped hand and placed something in hers then turned to walk out as he smiled at her.

Enez walked inside the kitchen and unfolded her hand to see four, crisp one-hundred dollar bills, neatly folded. Moments later, Nicko entered the restaurant.

Ms. Roberta took her by the arm and said, "Baby, when are you going to ever learn that he is no good and nothing but trouble?"

Enez returned to Nicko's lifestyle of stealing and doing drugs. She stole money from the cash register at work and started calling in sick when the drug addiction became too intense. She decided to move to a more expensive apartment, hoping to get away from Nicko's clutches and control her drug habit. She gave a two-week notice at her job before they suspended her because of the lost inventory and money shortage on her shift. One sunny Thursday morning, Black drove his pick-up truck to Enez's apartment to help her move into a two-bedroom apartment with wall-to-wall carpeting and central heat and air. But moving to another apartment would not stop her addiction to Nicko or change her lifestyle.

Enez found a job, working at an adult book store: sex, sex, and sex. She was the only employee on her shift, so she had control of the cash register. She stole from her employer once again. Almost every night, Enez failed to ring up expensive purchases. Some nights, Nicko came to her job, asking for money, and she gave it to him from the cashier's drawer. Before the night was over, she would replace it. When he would pick her up from work, she would have more money for drugs.

The warm morning was almost over as Enez stood at the window of her apartment. She had no money and was very hungry after a night of getting high on crack cocaine. Nicko had left in her car hours ago. She searched the dresser drawers and under the couch cushions, looking for change but not finding any. Suddenly, she heard a knock on the door, and the loud noise brought her search to an abrupt halt. "Who is it?" she called out. There was another knock at the door as she looked through the peep hole and was delighted to see Black. "Come on in, Black," she said excitedly. She motioned him to sit on the couch as she quickly replaced the cushions.

"What are you doing, Enez?" he asked, standing tall.

"Oh, I'm just cleaning the couch, Black," she said, grinning up at him.

"Can I sit down now?" he teased Enez. She did not answer him as they sat down.

"So, to what do I owe this pleasant visit?" She looked away from him, hoping he had not noticed her physical anxiousness.

"Enez, I've not seen you in weeks, and I was concerned about you."

She now allowed herself to look at him. "I'm not doing too good, Black. I'm working at an adult bookstore and barely making ends meet."

He took her small warm hand and held it. "What can I do to help you?" She hesitated to answer him because she did not want to run him off. She knew she needed groceries and to pay her rent, utility bill, and car note. Finally, she told Black about the bills and groceries. He stood and pulled his wallet from his back pocket. As he sat back down, he counted out several hundred dollars from his wallet and gave them to Enez.

Enez's eyes filled with emotional tears, and her hands trembled as she wrapped her arms around his neck. He grabbed her waist and kissed her on her lips, but she moved away from his face. She asked, "Do you have time to take me to the grocery store?"

"I have time," he said as he looked at his watch. "Where is your car, Enez?"

She could not hurt him by telling him the truth. A quick lie came to her, "My neighbor downstairs needed it to take care of some business." Enez hurried to the bathroom to freshen up before Nicko showed up. She looked in her closet for a pair of comfortable shoes and quickly escorted Black out the front door.

Later that day, Enez prepared fried chicken, mashed potatoes, and green beans. She was glad that it was her night off at the bookstore. Nicko had still not returned before she fell into a deep sleep. Nicko would not arrive until the next morning. She woke to the sound of keys tinkling in the living room, where she found a young man sitting on the couch with her key ring in his hand.

Nicko stood in the bedroom doorway and motioned for her to come. He closed the door behind them. "Look baby, I pawned the car yesterday, and I owe this man some money. I can give him a few more hours with the car or pay him."

"How much do you owe him?"

"Thirty dollars."

She thought quickly. She did not want Nicko to know that she had money, and she did not want this man to drive off with her car. "Let me see if I can borrow some money from my neighbor until after work tonight."

Nicko agreed and returned to the living room as Enez quickly turned to her hiding place and counted out $30 dollars. She slipped on a pair of pants and a wrinkled shirt and flip flops before she went to the living room.

"I'll be right back, okay?" She quickly closed the door behind her and ran to her neighbor's apartment, two doors down. She was surprised by how fast her neighbor answered Enez's knock on her door. She stepped across the threshold just enough so that if Nicko were watching, he would think she had gone inside. Enez looked at her neighbor and said, "I'll talk to you later." Enez returned to her apartment. The man was walking towards the door as if he was leaving, followed by. Nicko. "Nicko, I got it."

Nicko held out his hand, and Enez gave him the money as he motioned for the man to follow him into the kitchen. Enez sat on the couch, waiting on the return of her car keys. She heard the two men laughing as they walked from the kitchen, and the man said, "Hey man, Lewis is out here waiting on me, and I don't want him to think I got trouble, so I'll holler at you later." Nicko escorted him out and locked the door behind him.

Nicko brushed Enez's arm as he passed her, and she followed him into the bedroom to find him laying on the bed. A crack rock was on the night stand, and he pulled out his crack pipe and cigarette lighter from his pocket. "Baby, go get the razor blade from the kitchen drawer." Enez did as he said and returned with the razor. Her stomach was nauseated, her heart raced, and anxiety ran through her veins. She rushed to the bathroom, determined not to spend her money on crack. Then, she went to the living room, turned on the air conditioner, and sat on the couch. She heard Nicko calling her.

"Enez, Enez! Come here." She pretended not to hear him. He came into the living room with the crack and the pipe in his hand. He placed the crack on the pipe and told her to hit it. Enez saw fire in his eyes and was afraid, so she did as she was told. Finally, he sat next to her. "I saw Black's truck over here yesterday. What was he doing over here? I know he better been over here to give you some money. You must think I am a fool. Now get me the rest of my money."

Her lips began to move, but no sound came from her mouth. He placed another piece of crack on the pipe and hit it before putting the hot pipe in an ash tray on the end table beside the couch. He bent over to the carpeted floor and began sweeping it with his hands. Sweat dripped from his forehead, and Enez watched him calm down from the crack high. She thought of an excuse for Black's visit if he asked again. Finally, Nicko stopped sweeping the carpet and picked up the pipe. He pushed the crack to the other end of the pipe with a straight wire. She knew at this point that he had no more crack. "You haven't answered me about Black, Enez."

"Oh he didn't want anything Nicko."

"Well, where did you get the money to buy some groceries?"

"Nicko, I asked him to buy me some groceries."

"And you didn't get any money from him?" he asked as he prepared to heat the crack pipe.

"No, I don't have any money."

Nicko hit the pipe and was not satisfied with his hit. He looked at her, picked up the keys from the table and began walking towards the door.

"Nicko, I have to work tonight."

"I'll be back to take you to work," he said before closing the door behind him.

Enez showered and dressed before she walked to a nearby store to buy money orders for her bills. She walked to the apartment's office and paid her rent. Then she walked to a mailbox that was not far from the apartment complex to mail off her utility bill payment. She did not have enough money for her car payment. She thought to herself, "I'll earn enough on my next paycheck to pay it."

Instead, Enez's drug addiction became more intense over the next few days and so did Nicko's controlling abusive behavior. One afternoon after a long night of smoking crack, Enez received a phone call.

"Hi Enez, this is Glenda. I need to talk to you."

Enez sat up in bed, "Yeah, I'm here."

Glenda cleared her throat, "Enez, the apartment manager is going up on the rent. Would you be interested in a roommate?"

"Yes, Glenda I'd love to have you for a roommate. The first is next week." Enez liked the idea of having a roommate to help with the rent. Enez heard the front door open and saw Nicko come in. "What were you saying?" Enez asked.

"My lease is up next month, and I can move in with you next week. I'll have my half of the rent."

"Okay, we have a deal," Enez said.

After several weeks of working at the bookstore, Enez was asked to start working an early shift. The mangers were becoming suspicious because the inventory was coming up short. Enez arrived to work on her third day of the day shift to find both mangers standing behind the cashier's booth, looking at an inventory sheet and cash receipts.

"Enez, we're having a problem with the inventory and the cash drawer. We aren't accusing you of anything, but we don't have enough hours available at this time. We won't need you to come back to work," the pale faced, red headed man said, standing next to his dark skinned, stocky boyfriend. She walked home full of despair, afraid, lost, and alone. She thought about giving up on life.

When she opened the door, Enez found Glenda sitting at the dining room table, eating cereal. "Enez, I thought you were working today."

"I was laid off today. I believe it was because I was stealing, and they just didn't have proof that it was me, so they laid me off permanently. You know, I'm glad because I know what I was doing, and I could go to jail. So it was better that they let me go."

For the first time in many, many weeks, Enez began to pray. "God, help me. I need a job, Lord, one that will be pleasing to you, Lord. Amen." After praying, she laid across her bed and fell into a deep sleep.

Glenda worked the day shift at the same restaurant Enez had left months ago. One late afternoon, Glenda called to let Enez know the night shift waitress quit her job, and they needed someone to come in that night. Fortunately, Nicko was not using Enez's car, and it was available in the apartment parking lot. She quickly hung up the phone and got dressed.

She parked her car near the hotel desk clerk entrance. Inside, the owner stood behind the front desk. "Hello, Enez," she smiled, pushing her long blonde hair behind her small ears. "Can I help you with something?"

Enez looked at her humbly, "Mrs. B, I was wondering if you had any job openings."

Mrs. B motioned Enez to join her in her office. Enez walked quickly behind the front desk and entered her office. "Have a seat ,Enez. Yes, I have the same waitress position available. The young lady I hired last week quit this morning. Can you work tonight?"

Enez quickly assured Mrs. B, "Yes, I'm ready to start working tonight."

Later, Enez sat in a booth, looking from the tinted windows. The leaves were changing their colors, and the skies were gray, a sign for the season's change. As Enez looked up, Nicko stood next to her. "Come on, baby, let's go," he said motioning towards the door. In the car, Nicko turned the ignition and moved the car into reverse. "Enez, Stacy is back."

Enez's heart sank to her belly. "How did she get here?" Enez asked angrily.

"She said she hitchhiked a ride with a truck driver. She wanted to see me." Nicko looked Enez in her eyes as they waited for the traffic light to change. "Where is my money? I'm going to stop in on Lucy Street to get a package."

Enez handed him the money and stared out the window. Quickly, Nicko parked the car near the curb of a white house, trimmed in yellow. A woman stood behind a wrought iron door and opened it for Nicko to come inside. She quickly closed it behind him.

Nicko returned to the car, sweating and paranoid. He swiftly placed the car in drive and moved fast. He removed the crack rocks from his mouth and handed them to Enez. They rode in silence until they reached Nicko's house. He pulled into the long driveway and stopped. Stacy sat on the porch in a patio chair. Nicko blew the horn to get Stacy's attention as he spoke to Enez, "Enez, roll your window down." He told Stacy, "Hey, I'll be right back. You stay here." He put the car into reverse.

Stacy moved quickly from the porch, running to the driveway to stop Nicko. "Nicko, Nicko! Give me some money for food."

Nicko felt in his pocket and pulled out a five dollar bill, "Look, walk to the store on the corner and buy yourself some food. I'll be back," Nicko said, looking away from Enez. Stacy turned to walk towards the house. Nicko continued to move the car in reverse until they were in the street and proceeded to Enez's apartment. As they reached the corner of Leatherwood and Sillet, a tall, brown skinned man with a short afro flagged Nicko to stop.

Nicko stopped the car, and Slim walked over to the driver's side. "Hey Nicko, let me use your pipe. I let T-Baby go around the corner with mine, and he hasn't come back."

Nicko opened the door to let the man in the back seat. He reached in the ashtray to give Slim the pipe. Slim quickly placed a piece of crack on the pipe and hit it. Nicko watched him from the rear view mirror. "Slim, give me my pipe back. Me and my baby got business to take care of." Nicko opened the door to allow Slim from the back seat, and Slim slowly got out and returned the pipe to Nicko.

Enez thought they were on their way to her apartment until another man flagged Nicko. Nicko stopped the car once again. The man's hair appeared to not have been combed in days. His clothes were loose and dirty with paint stains on the shirt. "Nicko, take me to get something, man."

Nicko said, "What are you trying to get? I might have some right here."

The man held out a twenty dollar bill. "Man, I want a twenty for fifteen dollars. I wanna get me some beer and cigarettes with the change."

Nicko spit out two small pieces of crack and turned his hands towards Enez to chop up the two small pieces. "Here man, I'm going to give you all of this for your twenty," Nicko said, holding the crack in one hand and reaching for the twenty with the other.

"Man, you get me every time," the man said as he gave Nicko the twenty and scraped the crumbs from Nicko's hand.

Nicko looked at Enez and smiled, "Baby, I didn't pay but ten dollars for those pieces and got some left." He spit some more crack from his mouth and placed them in his hand as they finally reached the apartment.

The apartment was quiet except for the sound of the television coming from Glenda's bedroom. Enez heard a man's voice as well. She thought to knock on Glenda's door, but Nicko jerked her arm and pulled her inside the bedroom. She sat on the bed, watching Nicko. "Give me that hand mirror on your dresser," he said as he placed the crack pipe and lighter on the table.

Her mind was not on smoking cocaine. She wanted to know about Stacy. As she walked back from the dresser to lie on the bed, she asked, "Nicko what are you going to do with Stacy?"

"Enez, you know better than to ask me that. What you need to do is make sure she feels comfortable."

Enez sat on the edge of the bed, staring down at Nicko who was sitting on the floor. She looked at him with hate in her eyes as she remembered the last events with this woman and Nicko. Malice manifested in her heart as she left the bedroom. She stood at the living room window, looking at the magnolia trees in the front yard.

Nicko came to the living room with her keys in his hands, "I'll be back later. You know I gotta take care of my business."

Silently, she closed the door behind him and went back to the window. She followed him with her eyes as he left the apartment complex. A few days later, Nicko was ready to move to another state with Stacy. Enez heard him calling out her name. Enez knew he had a plan. As they walked through the living room, Nicko put his hand on her shoulder to draw her back to him, "Baby, I'm taking you and Stacy across country. We're leaving in two days, so get yourself together. You just make sure you steal enough money from your job."

Enez walked slowly away from Nicko. She walked to her bedroom, feeling confused. Nicko's words cut her deeply as they brought back past hurts and pains. She knew in her heart that she wanted to follow Nicko. She also knew he would leave without her in her car. She thought to herself, "Maybe I can earn enough money to pay my car note." She laughed out loud as she reminded herself that she was a prostitute junkie with a junkie pimp. Enez stared out her bedroom window. She watched the birds flying from one tree branch to another.

Some birds flew away to be unseen in the sky. She heard chirping near her window and turned to see a mother bird feeding her young. Enez sat on her bed, thinking how fun it would be to be free. She hoped to have that same freedom someday as the birds she saw from her bedroom window, flying high in the sky.

"Enez, Enez. I'm ready to go," Nicko said as he entered the apartment. She had not seen Nicko since he had informed her they were leaving town. She stared at the woman standing in her living room with Nicko. Nicko pulled Enez into the bedroom and said, "Look woman, I don't want any trouble out of you. Get you stuff and let's ride. And give me my money" Nicko said.

Enez walked to the dresser and gave Nicko the money. He stuffed it in his pocket and said, "I'll be outside in the car."

Glenda had already left for work, so Enez wrote her a note. "I am leaving with Nicko to Washington D.C. Back in a week." She turned the night light on for Glenda and walked to the door with her luggage. A car horn tooted, and she jumped in surprise. "Come on, Enez." She locked the door and quickly walked downstairs to the parking lot.

The passenger door opened, and Stacy got out of the car to let Enez in. "What's the matter, Stacy? Aren't you going?" Enez asked as she slid into the front seat.

Stacy looked at Nicko as he told her, "Get in the back seat."

Nicko moved through the traffic towards his neighborhood. "I'm picking up Twin to drive us to D.C. He's driven there before, so we shouldn't have any problems."

Twin stood at the corner as Nicko pulled up next to him. "Come on, man, I'm ready to roll. Enez, get in the back seat with Stacy. Twin, you sure you know how to drive a stick shift?" Nicko asked as he changed seats with Enez.

"Man, I used to drive a truck." Both men laughed as Twin pushed the front seat back for more room for his long, skinny legs. Nicko looked confused at Twin and asked, "Man, where is your luggage?"

Twin chuckled, "I got clothes in D.C."

An hour later, Twin was ready to rest. "Man, I've been awake all night. Let me get a few winks," he said as they pulled into a gas station.

Nicko asked, "Anybody want something from the store?"

Enez said with anger in her voice, "I'm going to the bathroom. I don't want anything."

Nicko looked in the backseat and asked Stacy, "Baby, do you want something?"

She grabbed his hand and said in a whisper, "Yeah, you Nicko." With fire in her eyes, Enez looked back at her and walked away.

The sun was behind them as they headed east on Highway 75 near Carolina when Enez woke up to

Nicko's voice. "Hey man, it's time for you to drive. I'm sleepy now," Nicko told Twin as he pulled into a gas station to fill up the tank. Twin went inside to pay for the gas. Stacy and Nicko got out of the car. Enez decided to stay in the car until one of them returned. Twin came back first to fill up the car. Enez went inside to purchase a Coke just as Nicko and Stacy came back from the bathroom area. They passed her without any expressions. When Enez returned to the car, she found Nicko in the back seat with Stacy. Her heart fell to the bottom of her belly. She was distraught. The back rest was flat, and they were lying down next to each other, with Stacy snuggled under Nicko's arm. Enez slid onto the front passenger seat with Twin as a tear drop fell from her face. She did not look in the back to see her pain. Finally, Enez fell into a deep sleep. They finally arrived in Washington D.C., an all too familiar place to Enez. She woke to see the night lights lining the hooker track.

Nicko sat upright with Stacy beside him. "Stop here, man. I see Earl standing over there in front of that store. Park the car," Nicko said as he put his shoes on his feet. Nicko and Twin got out of the car and walked to the store to visit their pimping friend, Earl. Earl was of average height and smooth brown skin. The men gave each other gentlemen's hand shakes.

Enez could hear Nicko from the open window, as he said, "Pimping is my livelihood, man. I don't need any instructions!" He began walking towards the car. "That's right, Earl," Nicko opened the door to allow Enez and Stacy out. Earl pulled out a bankroll and began counting one hundred dollar bills.

Nicko spoke to the women with a hard look on his face. "I want you two to hit the track and get my money." Enez turned away quickly and proceeded walking to the hooker spot she had left almost two years earlier.

She heard Earl say to Nicko, "I'll happily loan you some money, man, till your hookers come back with your trap." The sound of the men's voices faded as Enez walked across 14th Street. As she approached a hotel on 14th and L Street, a man stopped her by the entrance. He was staggering and had a strong whisky smell on his breath. "Hey baby, I'm looking for a good time," the drunken man said.

Quickly, she sized him up and asked him to buy her a drink. "I got something to drink in my room. Come on. I got a room in this hotel." He grabbed Enez's arm and escorted her to the elevators as he held on to her for balance. They entered the elevator, and Enez asked seductively, "Which floor you on, baby?"

He leaned on her and pushed the button for the eighteenth floor. When they got off the elevator, Enez helped him to his room. "Baby, where is your key card?"

The man pointed to his shirt pocket, and Enez reached inside for the keycard. She gave it to him, and he fumbled with it until he handed it back to Enez. Enez opened the door, and they entered. The drunken man staggered towards the bar in his room and poured himself a Scotch on the rocks.

"What are you drinking?" he asked Enez.

"I'm drinking white wine tonight," she said as she walked towards the bar.

After he finished pouring her drink, he sat down beside her. He put his hands on her clothed breast and stepped back to look at her. "You wanna make some money tonight?" She looked at him in surprise. "Oh, was I out of line?" he asked as he fell backwards on the bed. Enez sat quietly for a few seconds. The man was not talking anymore. He began snoring like a running train. Enez stepped over to him and shook his body. He did not move. Enez noticed his wallet on the night stand and tiptoed over to it and found several one hundred dollar bills inside. She quickly unzipped her pants and pushed the money inside her panties before quietly walking out of his room. In the elevator, she pushed the button to the hotel garage and quickly walked to the street.

She was a good three blocks from where she had last seen Nicko. As she turned the corner, she saw Nicko in her car. He unlocked the door. "What's up? You musta made a sting because I know you ain't back so quick without my money."

She unzipped her pants, pulled out the money, and gave it to Nicko as he counted it. "This is $500, Enez! We can get a room now. I just need to wait on Stacy."

Before he finished speaking, Stacy appeared. He opened the door for her, and once again Stacy and Enez were in the backseat together. Before Nicko asked, Stacy gave him her money. "Looks like you need to go back to work, Stacy. You stay here and get down some more I'll be back for you," he said, staring at the young, white girl. Stacy exited the car again and brushed against Nicko on her way out. He slapped her butt as Stacy looked back and smiled before she walked away.

"Nicko, I know where you can get a room," Twin said.

Nicko nodded his head, bouncing to the sound of Led Zeppelin on the radio. "Yeah, man. Find a nice hotel."

Twin drove by pedestrians and through green traffic lights until they reached a hotel in Prince George County, Maryland. Twin pulled into the parking lot.

"Enez, go inside and pay for one night and two rooms," Nicko said as he gave her two of the hundred dollar bills she had given him earlier. Twin opened the car door, got out, and flipped the button to allow the front seat to move forward. Enez went inside and paid for two rooms. She returned with the keys and change. Twin drove them to their room.

"Twin, help Enez with her luggage, man," Nicko stayed in the car. "Enez, I'll be back. I need to stay on top of my business with Stacy." He kissed her on her lips, and she turned to walk to her room.

She was too tired and did not want to react to Nicko. Twin brought her luggage to the room and placed it on the luggage rack, leaving the door open. Enez followed him to lock the door. Enez slumped down on the bed and looked in the mirror, "You really created a problem this time," she said to herself.

She walked to her suitcase and pulled out her baby doll pajamas and bath soap. In the bathroom, she found a bottle of bubble bath so she ran a hot bath. She slipped out of her clothes and sunk her tired body in the water. She laid her head back and fell into a deep sleep. She was startled awake when she heard a hard knock at the locked bathroom door. "Enez, Enez! Are you alright in there?" Nicko asked anxiously.

"Yeah, yeah. I'm alright." She began to splash soap and water on her body. Enez stood up to turn the shower on to rinse her body. Nicko knocked on the door again, "Enez, come out of there. I need you to ride with me."

She quickly grabbed a towel, wrapped it around her body, and opened the door. Nicko walked inside and stood beside her. "Are we here alone?" she asked quietly.

"Yeah, baby. We're here alone." Enez walked out into a dim lit room and began to dress.

As she and Nicko walked to the parking lot, she noticed Stacy standing in the window. Nicko looked up at her and motioned for her to close the curtains. When they drove from the parking lot, Stacy had disappeared. Nicko removed a small package from his pocket. He slid a pipe to Enez, then pushed the lighter to her.

"Well now," he said almost in a whisper, "Put those items in your purse. Twin, hip me to a crack house."

Enez stared from the car window, wishing she had never decided to come to Washington D.C. His voice drowned out her thoughts as they pulled into a driveway. "Come on, baby, these people are cool."

Enez was nervous as she walked behind Nicko to the doorway. Nicko knocked, and a slim, dark complexioned woman with short blonde hair answered the door. She looked at Nicko and smiled without any teeth. The wrinkled in her face drew back to her hair line as she invited them inside the smoke- filled room. They followed her across the hardwood floor to a bedroom near the rear. The woman pushed the flowery curtain to the side to gain entrance. She pointed to a chair, looking at Enez, "You can sit here."

Enez sat in the chair, feeling very uncomfortable. Nicko stood beside her. Quickly, Twin came in, smiling at the woman. Enez watched Nicko with keen interest for about five minutes before he asked for the items in her purse. He examined his package and removed a crack rock from it. "Here, Twin, I know you been waiting on your lick," Nicko said smiling.

"Man, you got that right. Here Faye, let Scotty beam you up," he told the wrinkled, toothless woman.

Enez watched Nicko intensely as he placed the crack rock on his pipe. He reached over to her, "Hit this pipe, baby." She sat up in the chair, glanced into his eyes, and did what he requested. Nicko and Enez smoked for fifteen minutes as Faye stared at them.

"Hey, Nicko, you wanna get another working fifty? My man is a phone call away," Faye said.

"Naw Faye, I'm straight," he said as he reached in his pocket and pulled out the car keys. Nicko began walking towards the door, and Enez followed him. Nicko and Enez got in the car, and Nicko sped off quickly. "Baby, you got that pipe put away?" he asked nervously."

"Yeah, it's put away, Nicko."

The morning sun peered through the clouds as they drove onto the hotel parking lot. Nicko smiled at her, and she briefly wondered if he was going to sleep with her or with Stacy. She quickly discarded the thought as Nicko came into the hotel room with her. Enez removed her clothes, as did Nicko. She blushed shyly from head to toe, as they stared into each other's eyes. They lay together on the bed, when Nicko suddenly went to the bathroom. Enez listened to the sound of the running water coming from the bathroom, and she became fully aroused with passion. She opened the shower curtain to join

Nicko and saw his caramel body lathered with soap. They made love for what seemed like hours.

Enez knew her peaceful time with Nicko was over. Stacy was in the next room, and he had to take care of his business. "Enez, get my socks and underwear out for me. Listen, take out those brown slacks and beige shirt. You might have to run the iron over them," he called out from the bathroom.

She slid lazily from the bed and came into the bathroom, where Nicko was shaving. "Did you hear what I said woman?" She nodded her head as she flushed the toilet. As she passed by him, he looked at her in the mirror. The look he gave her now was very different from earlier in the morning. No longer was he high on crack, now he was high on pimping.

She leaned against the headboard as she watched him dress in the bedroom. Voices from the television caught her attention. She noticed it was a horror movie, and she sat in amazement as the characters ran, screaming for help. Nicko bent over and kissed her on the forehead before he left her room. The smell of his cologne lingered in the room, reminding her of his recent presence. Her ears became her eyes as she heard him trying to use the key to the hotel room next door. He knocked and said, "Stacy, take the latch from the door." Soon, she heard the door open and close. She turned to the television, but her mind was blank as she fell into a deep sleep.

She woke up hungry. The sun's rays were no longer piercing through the closed curtains. She looked at the clock. Evening had appeared, but Nicko had not. She rose from the bed and walked to the window to see her car in the parking lot. She always kept a spare key and some change with her. Quickly, Enez showered and dressed before she looked out the window again. Her car was still there, parked next to a white Cadillac with Pretty Ricky on the front tags. She did not recognize the Cadillac, but she thought the owner might be an associate of Nicko's. Her heart raced with fear, but her belly ached with hunger. Enez knew if she left in her car without Nicko's permission, there would be trouble. She also knew she had better not call Stacy's room looking for him. As she scanned the view, she noticed a sign for a mom and pop restaurant that she had not seen before. The phone rang as she was putting on her shoes to walk over to the restaurant. She rushed to answer it. "Hello," she said, trying to catch her breath.

"Sounds like you are already up. Are you dressed, Enez?" Nicko asked.

"Yes, I'm dressed," she responded nonchalantly.

"Baby, come down to the end of the walkway to Room 295 and get you some money for food," he said before he hung up.

Enez knocked on the door of Room 295, and a man answered, "Who is it?"

She heard Nicko respond, "That's my woman. I told her to come to me." Nicko opened the door and invited Enez inside before he returned to the table where he had been sitting. His keys and a lit cigarette were on the table before him, and a dark complexioned man with curly permed hair and a firm look on his face sat across from Nicko.

"Come here, baby, and get this money," Nicko said as he counted out some bills. He looked into her eyes as he handed her the money. "Baby, I'll meet you back in the room."

She said softly, "Okay Nicko." Enez turned toward the door when she heard Nicko ask, "You got the spare key to the car?" She turned to look at him and nodded her head. As she reached the door to open it, a tall woman with wide hips stood at the door. She wore high heeled shoes and had shoulder length red hair. The freckles on her face were covered with makeup, and she wore ruby red lipstick. She entered the room, swiftly passing by Enez without speaking. Enez left the room and closed the door behind her.

With her keys in hand, Enez walked to the car. She looked up and saw Stacy looking out the window as she pulled into the traffic. She finally reached the mom and pop restaurant that she had seen from her hotel window. She ordered food to go and reentered the busy traffic to go back to the hotel. As she reached the parking lot, she saw Nicko entering Stacy's room. She said to herself, "Just relax, baby, you are bigger than that." She smiled and said out loud, "Don't you know it." She hummed to the song playing on the car's cassette player. It was called "Rose" by Willie Hutch. In the hotel, she entered the elevator to go to the second floor. With a hot meal in her hand and a Willie Hutch tune in her head, Enez smiled. Inside her room, she placed the food on the table and turned on the television. She still had not heard from Nicko by the time she finished her dinner. She knew he would not be pleased if she was not ready for work when he arrived, so she began laying out her work clothes when the phone rang. She let it ring several times before answering, "Hello."

"I know you're getting ready for work."

She was silent for a few seconds, not daring to remind him of their conversation before she left Room 295. She pulled the phone away from her ear and stuck her tongue out to the receiver as she heard him ask, "You hear me talking to you?"

"Yes, Nicko, I hear you." Next, she heard a dial tone.

Nicko came to her room almost an hour later. She glanced at her reflection in the mirror and approved of her image. She wore a shoulder length dark brown wig, very little make up, and ruby red lipstick. She wore sheer nylon black stockings over her shapely legs, black pumps, and a tight red and black dress with spaghetti straps. Nicko sat on the bed and watched Enez as she bent over to get her purse. He stroked her leg under her dress, and she quickly moved away to tease him. Suddenly, he stopped and said, "Come on. Stacy is waiting in the car."

The white Cadillac was no longer in the parking lot. Stacy was already in the backseat of the car, and Nicko slid in the driver's seat as he looked in the rearview mirror. "Stacy, give me my keys." Stacy reached between the front seats and gave Nicko his keys. Nicko drove expertly through Maryland as if he knew the city. Finally, they reached downtown D.C., and Nicko stopped the car near an alley, away from potential customers and the police before Stacy and Enez went their separate ways.

The tension disappeared from Enez as she walked to her favorite night spots, going from one hotel lounge to another. Finally, she broke luck for one hundred dollars. Just as she returned to the hooker strip, a man in a brown Ford pulled up next to her and rolled his window down. "Hey baby, I've been watching you all night. You look good to me," he said in a drunken southern drawl. Enez did not feel sure about this man. He looked too young to want a hooker, but he followed her. "Hey, how much you want?" he asked. Finally, she walked over to the passenger side window to talk to him, and he pulled out a twenty dollar bill. "I got more where that came from." Desperate to get Nicko's money, Enez got in the car with the man.

"Look, we can take care of our business on Cincinnati Avenue," Enez gave him directions to a secluded ally, and their business was finished within five minutes. She quickly opened the car door and raced to the main street, where she flagged a cab. The cab driver rolled his window down and asked in a Jamaican accent, "Where are you going, lady?"

She answered as she reached to open the back door. "I'm going near Peggy's Place." She slid in the cab quickly and looked back towards the alley where she had come from. She had taken the man's wallet, and she hoped he had not noticed it missing yet. The cab driver drove her around the pimp spots, and she looked for Nicko before returning to the hotel. She saw her car parked on12th Street, but she did not see Nicko in it. Enez asked the cab driver to stop. She paid her fare and used her spare key to wait for Nicko in the car. A grey convertible Cadillac passed slowly by. Enez looked in the rearview mirror to see the car's brake lights and Nicko climbing from the back seat, walking sluggishly. She waited as he fumbled to unlock the door with his key. Finally, Enez reached over and unlocked the door, and Nicko staggered into the front seat. Enez knew he did not drink liquor, but he appeared to be drunk.

"Baby, I've been drinking dog medicine."

Enez looked at him dumfounded, "Dog medicine?"

"Yeah, syrup." Nicko took his time driving. He stopped at 17th and Rhode Island and parked in front of a hamburger place. His asked her in a cold voice, "So, where is my money?"

She was hurt by his tone, "What, baby?"

He looked at her with his cold brown eyes, "You heard me." She reached inside her panties and gave him the money. "So did you rip someone off?" he asked while he counted the money.

"Nicko, I robbed a man when I was standing on the street corner. He may come back to look for me."

For a brief moment, Nicko stared at Enez. "It's still early, and this is the first of the month. I'm going to take you back to the room to change your clothes and hair." He put the money in his pocket as he put the car in drive. As the car pulled away from the parking lot, Enez was lost in thought. She sat quietly while Nicko drove through the streets of downtown D.C. to Maryland. When they reached the hotel room, Enez removed her wig and clothing quickly. As she slipped on a blouse and skirt, she mumbled to herself, "I don't feel like making anymore money." Nevertheless, she followed Nicko out the door.

In the darkness of the night, women walked the streets to and fro, looking for men who wanted sexual favors. The light of day shined upon her tired body when Nicko drove up beside her with Stacy in the front seat. Enez had not seen Stacy working the streets all night long. Enez was exhausted as she slid onto the backseat and fell asleep before they reached the hotel.

"Enez, Enez, wake up," Nicko said loudly. "Pack your clothes. We're moving to a hotel in D.C." She sat up to see they had arrived at the hotel. As they walked through the parking lot, Stacy whispered in Nicko's ear, and he looked at her with a half smile.

The elevator was empty, when it arrived to the main floor. Nicko stood between the women as they all got on the elevator. "Enez, go on to your room. I'll be there in a minute," Nicko instructed her as the elevator stopped on her floor. Enez went to her room and sat in a chair next to the bed before turning the radio on. Gladys Knight was crooning "Midnight Train to Georgia," and Enez sang along softly as she thought about her daughter and her life. Tears began to flow from her eyes. She heard the key turn the lock on the door as Nicko entered. She quickly wiped away her tears and continued to pack her suitcases.

Nicko lay back on the bed, watching television. "Make sure you have all of my things packed also, Enez." He rolled over and promptly fell asleep. The phone rang, and Enez rushed to answer it.

"Enez, I need to speak to Nicko." She called Nicko's name, but he did not move. "Nicko is asleep." Enez did not wait for an answer as she placed the receiver on the cradle. When she finished packing, Enez slid under Nicko's arm and slept with him the rest of the night. Much later, the phone rang again. Nicko grabbed the receiver and clutched it firmly. Enez could hear a man's voice with a foreign accent, "This is the front desk. It is noon and check out time. Do you plan to stay another night, Sir?"

Nicko sat on the edge of the bed, "No, no. I'm checking out. I'll be down in a minute to give you the key." Nicko grabbed his shoes quickly and said, "Enez, get up. Let's go. I'm going to the other room to get Stacy. We need to leave now."

Nicko and Stacy caught up with Enez at the car. Nicko said, "Enez, turn the keys in to the front desk clerk. I'll swing around and pick you up."

The office clerk was very nice. Enez returned the keys and returned to the car. Nicko said, "We'll stop at Shoney's for breakfast before we check in to the other hotel." He looked at Stacy in the rearview mirror. "Are you hungry, Stacy?" Stacy did not answer, so Nicko and Enez walked into the Shoney's restaurant without her. As the hostess appeared, Stacy finally joined them. They sat quietly as they ate breakfast. Enez was getting sleepy. "Nicko, I'm tired. Can we leave now and check in to the hotel?"

Nicko waved toward the waitress, who responded with a beautiful smile. "We're ready for our ticket now."

The waitress slipped her hand inside her pocket and placed the ticket on the table. "Can I get anything else for you all?"

Nicko picked up the ticket and looked at it carefully. "No, I believe we are finished." As they got up from the table, Nicko placed a five dollar bill on the table. "Come on, let's ride," he called out to Enez and Stacy.

He drove through the heart of D.C. As the sun brightened the scene, it looked different from the night scene. People were busy walking hurriedly to and from the tall buildings. They wore dress pants and skirt suits, ties and shirts, and carried briefcases. Taxis pulled up to the curb as quickly as pedestrians waved for them on the busy street corners.

They checked into a motel on the east side of D.C. for one night. "Grab those suitcases, Enez and Stacy. I'll meet you back in the room in a minute," Nicko said as he lit a Kool cigarette.

Enez was not too happy with the motel room arrangements. She had made enough money to have her own room, she thought to herself. Holding the key in one hand and the suitcases in another, Enez opened the door to the room, followed by Stacy. Enez dropped the suitcases and fell on the nearest bed as Stacy walked to the closet and placed her suitcases on the floor. She turned to see Enez staring at her. She picked up the remote control and turned the television on. She was not happy to be sharing a room with the woman who wanted her man.

Enez went to the bathroom and looked in the mirror. She thought, "A bath would make me feel a hundred percent better."

Stacy asked, "Where is the key? I'm going downstairs to get some ice and a Coke. Would you like something?"

Enez reached inside her pocket for the motel key, "No, I'm okay. I'm going to take a hot bath." Enez slid into the hot bath water and rested her naked body in the bubbles. She fantasized about being home in her apartment with her daughter. Suddenly, there was a knock on the door. She called out Stacy's name but did not receive an answer.

Quickly, Enez wrapped a towel around her body and peeked out the window to see Nicko. She opened the door and returned to the bathroom as Nicko asked, "Where is Stacy?"

"She said she was going for ice and a Coke several minutes ago." In the bathroom, Enez decided to lather, rinse and dry off her body instead of continuing with the bubble bath. When she returned to the room, she saw the television was off and crack smoke filled the air. She looked at Nicko, bent over the table as he sat rubbing his hands across the carpeted floor. He quickly moved to the window as Enez was changed into her lounging clothes.

"You say Stacy's been gone how long?" Nicko asked. Before Enez could respond, Stacy walked in. That put a smile on Nicko's face as he sat at the table. He pulled out an eight ball of rock cocaine and three pipes with a package of ten lighters.

Enez was furious. Her expectations of coming to D.C. were gone up in crack smoke. She lay on the bed while Stacy and Nicko smoked the crack. Enez's weakness for the drug disease that had haunted her for several years wanted to be fed. She joined them in a night of getting high on crack cocaine. Several times during the night, Nicko and Enez left the room to ride the dope track for drugs. Finally, the morning sun entered their dark path. All the drugs and money were gone as checkout time arrived. They were all tired and ready for some rest, but Nicko looked at the women and said, "You know what you gotta do. We don't have money to pay for another stay. Pack your bags and let's hit it."

Enez looked at him. "Nicko, we've been up all night, smoking. Baby, I'm sweaty, and I need to freshen up before I hit the streets."

With his flaming brown eyes staring at her with malice, he said, "I need a bath too, but we don't have time."

She threw on a green mini dress with no panties or a bra before she brushed her wig and placed it on her head. Her face was flushed with perspiration, and her throat was as dry as the Phoenix desert. They left the motel keys on the dresser as they left the room. Enez felt sick from dehydration as she carried her suitcases to the car and passed out as she bent over to put her suitcases in the car. Nicko snatched her wig off and poured water over her head. Slowly, she regained consciousness and got in the car. Her head was soaking wet as she leaned back on the headrest.

"Enez, we're going to Atlantic City after you and Stacy make this money," Nicko said, looking at her in the rearview mirror. She nodded her head in response. Before long, they were near downtown D.C. Stacy and Enez walked their separate ways. Enez felt uncomfortable working the streets in the noon day, and she was particularly uncomfortable about her hygiene. She walked the block for nearly an hour before a man finally approached her. He gave her fifty dollars for a quickie in his car. As the man dropped Enez off, Nicko walked toward her.

When they reached the car, she saw Stacy sitting inside. Nicko handed his key to Enez, "You drive, Enez, but first I want to take a little detour after we get gas." Nicko used the seat lift to slide into the backseat.

Enez got in the driver's side and adjusted the mirror and seat after she fastened her seatbelt. Stacy sat next to her in the front seat. "Stacy, give me that money you got. You can reach me yours too, Enez." Nicko said as he held out his hand between the front seats. "I should have made both of you work the street a little bit longer," he said, counting the money. "Here, Enez. This twenty should fill the tank up. Stop here at the gas station to the right." Nicko pulled out his crack pipe and began to smoke the residue as soon as they left the gas station. He was frustrated that he could not get high from the residue and gave Enez directions to drive in an unfamiliar area.

Old and stately homes with manicured yards lined the neighborhood streets. "Pull in this driveway to the left, with the brick house trimmed in yellow and let me out," Nicko instructed. After he knocked, he disappeared inside and quickly returned to the car. Before Enez could clear the driveway, Nicko placed a crack rock on the pipe and began smoking it. He smoked crack for almost an hour before they reached the Harbor Tunnel.

"Hey baby, we gotta pay a toll fee. I need two dollars," Enez said as she drove up to the cashier. Nicko sat forward sluggishly to reach inside his pocket and give Enez two crumpled up bills.

Everyone was quiet inside the car as Enez drove. She looked in the rearview mirror and saw that Nicko was fast asleep and Stacy's head bobbed back and forth. Ten minutes later, Enez slowed down for another toll fee as they crossed into Delaware.

"Nicko, Nicko, we have reached another toll fee. I need two dollars." Once again, he reached inside his pocket and gave her two bills. She continued to drive on towards Atlantic City, New Jersey. Rain spattered against the window as Enez turned on the windshield wipers. Nicko sat up in the backseat in disgust. He shook his head to clear his thoughts as Stacy stared at the wipers. Her words had the same effect as the lightening and thunder above their heads rumbling from the clouds, "This is going to be one hell of a night without an umbrella."

Enez looked ahead and thought to herself, "It's been a hell of a week." She continued to drive through the rain. Finally, they reached Black Horse Pike in Atlantic City.

"Enez, pull over to that store on the right near the White Castle burger place," Nicko moved towards the front seat as Enez parked the car. "Ya'll got any condoms?" he asked, looking serious.

Enez looked in her purse. "Yeah, I got one, Nicko," she replied, waving the unopened package in her hand.

"Stacy, what about you?"

"No, I used my last one in D.C." Nicko reached inside his pocket and gave Stacy five dollars. "Go in the store and get a box." Stacy slipped her shoes on to go into the store.

Enez listened to Nicko while they waited for Stacy "We need money for a room, Enez. You and Stacy are going to get out here and get some money." She took a long sniff of herself and became nauseated. Stacy returned to the car without a bag. She reached down in her pants and pulled out a box of condoms.

"Stacy, that was stupid. I didn't send you in there to steal a box of condoms. Crazy woman, what if you would have gotten caught? Then what!" Nicko asked in an agitated tone. Stacy held her head down as Nicko continued to give instructions. "Stacy, you and Enez get out here and get some money for a hotel room. Okay, so what are you waiting on? Get out."

Enez opened the door, and Nicko slid from the backseat. Stacy opened her door and walked away from the car. Nicko called her name. "Stacy, come here to me." She slowly walked to the other side of the car, and Nicko lifted her chin in his hand. Their eyes connected as he said, "Don't disappointment me, baby." She nodded and turned to walk away again as he patted her on her butt.

Enez stood near the curb, waiting on a car to pass. She jumped back quickly as the tires pushed a puddle of water on the sidewalk, almost splashing her. She walked across the street, racing from the rain drops. As she walked the street, Nicko drove by several times, staring angrily at her. Several hours later, Enez felt even more uncomfortable with her hygiene and appearance. A young man slowed down and rolled down his window.

"You looking for some fun, baby?" she asked desperately.

"Yeah, I got twenty dollars."

Enez walked away, feeling like a twenty dollar hooker, but she knew better.

It was three o'clock in the morning, when Nicko and Stacy finally picked Enez up from the corner. As Enez slid in the backseat, Nicko asked, "You got my money?"

She looked at him through the rearview mirror. "No, Nicko. I can't make any money like this." She sniffed herself and turned up her nose.

Nicko kept driving until they reached a secluded beach shore. He parked the car and got out. "Enez, sit in the driver's seat. I'm going to get me some sleep in the back." He walked a few feet away to urinate.

A knock on the window awakened them. Enez was startled to see two police officers facing her. She rolled the window down quickly. "Madam, you are parked on private property."

She looked around and noticed the torn down sign, facing the ground. "Sir, I'm sorry. We'll leave now," she said as she started the car.

"Madam you can't just park your car and sleep anywhere."

"Yes Sir," Enez said as she put the car in reverse.

Nicko and Stacy remained silent until they were out of the officer's sight.

"I'm glad the lock is down, Nicko," Stacy turned to Nicko.

Enez asked, "Where are we going, Nicko?"

"Just keep riding. I know I saw a hotel on this street last night." Suddenly he saw the hotel. "There it is! That's the hotel I saw last night. Stacy, give me that money." Stacy pulled out a small bankroll and gave it to Nicko. "Enez, go inside and pay for one room. Remember, you didn't make any money last night."

Enez stared at him with hate in her heart. She returned to the car and gave Nicko the key then drove them to their room near the front of the hotel. She parked to let Nicko and Stacy out of the car. Enez watched them as they closed the door to their room.

A few moments later, Enez entered the room to see Nicko removing the bath towel from his showered body. He stepped into his underwear. Enez looked to the bathroom door as Stacy came out. Nicko lay down on the bed and covered himself with the sheets as he stared at Enez. She stared back at him. There was only one bed in the room, so Stacy pulled out extra blankets from the closet to make a pallet.

Nicko noticed Stacy making up the pallet. "What are you doing? Get up here in bed with me. Enez, you didn't make any money for a room, so you sleep on the floor." The room was quiet except for the sounds coming from the television.

"I'm going out to get a Coke," Enez said. She walked calmly to the ice machine and vending area then returned to the room with a Coke. Her eyes connected with Nicko's as she opened the door. Stacy was lying in the bed next to him. Her heart fell to the pits of her belly, and she ached to scream. Instead, she said, "I'm going to get the luggage from the car." She turned and closed the door quietly.

Enez started the ignition and put the car in reverse. She did not look back as tears ran down her cheeks. She trembled as she held the steering wheel tightly, wishing this was all a bad dream. As she looked down at the gas gauge, she noticed she had a full tank of gas. Eventually, she reached a toll headed back to D.C., so she pulled over to the emergency lane searching the car and her purse for change. She panicked when she could not find any coins. "I can't go back to Nicko. I wanna go home," she said to herself. Moments later, she pulled into the traffic and blew her horn at a truck driver.

He rolled his window down. "Can I help you?"

"Yes, yes! I'm trying to get back home. Will you help me, please? I need money for the toll fee."

The man pulled over to the emergency lane, followed by Enez. He walked to her car and gave her five dollars. She once again pulled out into the interstate traffic, and the truck driver pulled out behind her. As she neared D.C., Enez began to feel freedom.

Enez was familiar with D.C., so she drove to Rhode Island Avenue to seek aid at a traveler's missionary house. She parked her car behind a white framed, two-story house. Enez tiredly climbed the back stairs and rang the door bell.

"May I help you?" a voice came from the intercom next to the doorbell.

"I'm from out of state, and I've run out of money for a place to rest. Can you help me?"

After a brief moment, an older woman with a small waist and wide hips opened the door. She looked at Enez, "You look tired. Come on in and get a bath and some food."

Enez followed the woman as they passed through a living room full of mismatched furniture, a coffee table, and two end tables with dingy shades on the dimly lit lamps.

"I am Carmicheal. I am the program director for the center," the woman said as she looked in the kitchen. She asked the cook, "Are you almost finished with lunch, Mary?"

"Yes, Ms. Carmicheal. Lunch will be on time."

Enez's stomach began to growl from the aroma of fresh bread baking in the oven. Finally, they reached a small office next to the kitchen. Ms.

Carmicheal pointed to a wooden chair with a flowery cushion, "Have a seat, Miss. What is your name?"

Enez cleared her throat, "Enez."

The woman reached for papers from a file, "Enez, where are you from?"

"Memphis, Tennessee."

Without looking up from her shuffled papers, Ms. Carmicheal asked, "Do you have any identification?"

Enez searched in her purse for her driver's license. "Yes, I have a Tennessee driver's license."

Finally, Ms. Carmicheal's eyes connected with Enez's. "So, what happened?"

"I came here with my boyfriend. He found another woman and left me. I want to go back home, but I don't have any money or family to help me out."

Ms. Carmicheal continued writing as she asked, "Where is your boyfriend now?"

"I left him in Atlantic City with his new girlfriend."

Ms. Carmicheal moved from behind her desk, "Wait right here, Enez."

Enez looked around the office as she waited. On one wall, there were several certificates and awards with Ms. Carmichael's name on them. She saw pictures of smiling men, women, and children. They appeared to be happy as they stood at a cookout in the back of this house.

Ms. Carmicheal returned and startled Enez as she was admiring the wall. Holding the papers in her hand, Ms. Carmicheal said, “Enez, we have a room for you, and I can get you help with gas to return home. This will take a few days.”

Enez was escorted to her room by another counselor. “Hi, my name is Vickie. I used to live here several years ago, until one day Ms. Carmichael suggested I go back to college and receive my degree in social work. This is your room. The bed next to the window is yours. Your roommate is Anita. She’s in school today, working on her GED. Here are your sheets, towels, and some shower shoes. The shower is to your left. Lunch will be ready in twenty minutes, so you’ll have to shower quickly.” Vickie turned to walk down the stairs, “Do you have any clothes?”

Enez nodded her head in response, “Yes, I have clothes in my car.”

“Okay, good. We have a clothes closet for those in need.” Vickie disappeared downstairs as quickly as she had appeared.

Enez ran downstairs to get her luggage and then returned to her room. She chose fresh underwear and a jogging suit from her suitcase before quickly getting in the shower. She slipped her small feet into the clear shower shoes and turned the shower on. The hot water and lathered soap covered her body. Thoughts of her coming to D.C. with Nicko ran down the drain as did the dirty water from her body. Enez had a shower, a good lunch, and needed rest before dinner time.

The next morning came with new hope and a new attitude. Enez jumped up to a sitting position in her bed when she heard a knock at the unlocked door. She was afraid Nicko had found her as she asked, "Who is it?"

A voice came from behind the door, "Good morning. A bus will be here in an hour for anyone who would like to attend Church services." Enez heard the woman's footsteps as she moved on to another closed door.

Enez slid to the edge of the bed. She noticed her roommate lying in the next bed, opposite her. The woman's eyes were open as she turned toward Enez, "Hi. I'm Anita, and you're Enez from Memphis."

"Yes, my name is Enez, and I am from Memphis." Enez moved towards her luggage and began looking through it.

Anita asked, "Are you going to Church?"

Enez slumped on the edge of the bed, her eyes filling with tears. She could not hold her composure as her body jerked with sobs. Enez felt the comforting arms of her roommate as she pressed her head against Anita's shoulders and sobbed with relief. "How can I go to Church after I have let God down? I am too ashamed to ask Him to forgive me.

I am a continual mess up. He fixes me up, and I tear it down." Enez looked down at her hands.

"Well, Enez, I'm going to Church this morning. I have a lot to be grateful for, and so do you. You know, you can come as you are." Anita gave Enez a warm hug and walked towards the closet in their room.

"Yes, Anita. I do have a lot to be grateful for today."

Anita spun around on her heels, "Well, we'd better hurry up and get dressed before the van leaves us."

Enez left Church, feeling encouraged and full of hope. She was quiet throughout the day. After dinner, she lay in bed with her eyes closed and thought back over her past mistakes. A smile spread across her face as Anita came in, and the hallway light splashed over her.

"Enez, you're smiling! You must have had a happy thought," Anita said, smiling back.

"Yes, I was thinking about home and how much I miss being there. I have a daughter who lives with my mother. I'd love to see her again." Her smile lit the dim room.

Monday morning, Enez was anxious to return home. The sun's rays shone through the windows and passed the light blue curtains. She slid from under the fresh sheets, sat on the edge of the bed, and placed her feet inside her slippers. Enez faced the window to face another day.

Anita burst through the door. "Good morning, sleepy head. Girl, you must have been short on rest. I have never seen anyone sleep like you."

Enez shook her head as she put on her robe and gathered her toiletries. "Anita, I believe today is my day. If I'm not here when you return, that means I'm on my way back to Memphis."

"I know that's right, girlfriend."

Enez hugged Anita in case she left before Anita returned from school, "Thank you so much for your encouraging words in my time of need."

The afternoon went by quickly, and Ms. Carmicheal called Enez to her office. "Enez, you've been approved for one hundred and fifty dollars from traveler's aid to help you get back to Memphis. I just received the check. The bank is on 14th and L Street, and you'll need your ID to cash the check. Enez, I hope you'll do the right thing. I understand what you've been through, and it's been my pleasure helping you. Remember, there will not always be someone to help you, but God is willing and able if you just trust Him and not some man. Now go and pack your things so you can begin your travel home. You have enough for one night's lodging on your journey."

Enez jumped up and ran around the desk to give Ms. Carmicheal a big hug. "Thank you so much," she said as tears rolled down her face.

Ms. Carmicheal handed her a tissue, "Girl, you'd better get out of here. It's getting late."

Enez turned towards the door and ran to her room. She packed her clothes quickly. Her steps were long as she peeked inside the office to wave good bye. "Enez, you know we must pray for your travels before you leave," Vickie said, coming from her office.

Vickie held Enez's hand and began to pray, "Lord, we know that we make choices in our lives that are not of your will. We are asking you right now, Lord, to forgive us of our sins and help us to forgive those who have hurt us. Lord Jesus, give Enez traveling Grace, Lord. We pray that you protect her from any hurt, harm, or danger as she travels back to Memphis. Be with her, oh Lord our Savior, in Jesus' name. Amen."

Enez pulled Vickie towards her and hugged her for dear life. Finally, she said, "Thank you, Vickie, for that prayer." Vickie walked Enez to the back door, and Enez climbed down the stairs that led her to hope. She put her suitcase in the car and drove to the bank on her way to Memphis.

It was late, and she drove through the interstate traffic. She was well rested, and she wanted to make the drive straight home. Seven hours later, her eyes were becoming tired, and the stars and moon lit her way. Finally, she pulled over to a rest stop, locked her doors, and fell into a deep sleep. The sound of a truck driver blowing his horn awakened her. She at up in her seat, startled, as she looked around at her surroundings. She got out of the car to walk to the restroom. In the restroom, she noticed a clock mounted on the wall. "Wow, I slept longer than I meant to." An older woman stood at the sink, washing her hands as Enez used the facilities and exited. The thought of going home brought a smile to her face as she started the car. Her stomach growled, "I can't believe I haven't eaten since this morning. I need to stop at the first place I see," she thought. After thirty minutes on the interstate, she noticed Exxon and Waffle House signs. Enez felt free for the first time in many weeks as she stopped to fill the tank with gas and get a bite to eat. The sun shone through the tinted windows as she drove for hours on the interstate.

She turned the key to unlock her apartment door. As she stood in the doorway, Enez took a deep breath. Everything was as she had left it. She was happy to be home. She went to her bedroom and lay across the bed as darkness descended. She heard her roommate's voice, "Enez, Enez, you're home!"

"Yes, Glenda. I'm back here in the bedroom," Enez announced happily. She opened her bedroom door and was surprised to find a man with Glenda. "Oh! I didn't know you had company. I'd better slip on my robe." Glenda and her company went to Glenda's bedroom and closed the door behind them.

The next morning, Enez sat at the breakfast table as Glenda's company rushed through the hall on his way to the bathroom. A few minutes later, Glenda came in and sat at the table with Enez.

"Glenda, how long have you known your friend?" Enez asked her.

Glenda played with the button on her robe. "Oh, I met him at work. He busses the tables at the restaurant." Glenda smiled at Enez, "His name is David. He graduated from a school in north Memphis. His mother died several months ago." They heard David call out Glenda's name. "He is leaving in a few minutes."

Enez finished her breakfast, washed the dishes, and returned to her room. David appeared to feel right at home, and he finally left, hours later. Enez decided to talk to Glenda about the living arrangements. "Glenda, does David have a place to stay besides my apartment? He appears to make himself very much at home here."

Glenda said defensively, "No, he's been staying here with me while you were gone."

"But Glenda, you never asked me if he could move in with you. You're *my* roommate, I'm not *your* roommate. If he's going to stay here, I'm going to have to go up on your rent a few dollars."

Glenda turned on her heels and disappeared into her bedroom, slamming the door closed. David did not sleep over, but he frequently had lengthy visits with Glenda over the next few days.

Thursday morning, Enez woke to find David in the bathroom, and an untidy mess in the living room and kitchen. She knocked on Glenda's bedroom door before entering. "Glenda, I need to talk to you," Enez said furiously. "I can't continue to clean up that nasty bathroom, kitchen, and living room after you. You need to find a place. I can't take it anymore!" She turned from Glenda's bedroom as David brushed past her in the hallway. He closed the bedroom door behind him. Enez poured cereal into a bowl as she heard noises coming from Glenda's bedroom. She turned to see David carrying Glenda's mattress out of the apartment. Enez continued preparing her breakfast and sat down to eat before Glenda appeared.

Glenda walked past Enez, "I'm moving out today," she told her angrily.

Enez knew Glenda owed her rent, but she was more satisfied to have Glenda and David gone from her apartment. "Okay Glenda, but I'll need my keys back. Glenda, I didn't want you to move like this, but you gave me no other choice."

After the last piece of her belongings were packed in David's truck, Glenda gave Enez her house keys and said goodbye. Enez walked to the window to see her ex-roommate drive away.

It was trying not to be noticed but failing in its attempts to be restrained. The off-white envelope had been tossed neutrally on the kitchen table with the rest of the week's mail, but even in the midst of the many envelopes, it was determined to be noticed. It would not take no for an answer. It commanded her to devote her full and urgent attention to it. As she sat down at the dining room table, Enez moved the other letters aside and slowly picked up the off-white envelope. She opened it after she read the return address. Another car payment was due immediately, and she knew she had bigger problems than an untidy roommate.

The next day, she was watching television, when a commercial to apply for financial aid and attend business school caught her attention. She quickly jotted the telephone number down before the commercial ended and immediately dialed the number.

A woman answered, “School of Business. This is Staci. May I help you?”

Enez cleared her throat, “When will your next class begin?”

“The next class starts next Monday. Are you interested in starting next week?”

“Yes, I’d like to start next week.” Enez replied.

“I’m sorry, I didn’t get your name.”

“My name is Enez Brown.”

“Ms. Brown, can I put you on hold? Let me see if one of our advisors is available to meet with you today.” Shortly, the woman returned to the phone. “Ms. Brown, are you available today at 1:00?”

Enez answered quickly, “Yes, I’ll be there.” Enez thought this would be a quick way to get money to pay her car notes, rent, telephone, and utility bills. She arrived on time for her appointment as she walked into the small building, ten miles away from her apartment. A balding man sat behind a wood framed desk and pointed towards the couch against the wall as he looked up from his phone conversation. Enez sat and waited.

A brunette, middle-aged woman approached Enez. She said, "Good afternoon, I am Mrs. Locke, and you are...?"

Enez rose from her seat. "My name is Enez Brown, and I have a 1:00 appointment."

The woman quickly turned on her heels and walked towards the front desk. She picked up sheets of paper, flipping them back and forth. "Oh, I see we had a reschedule. Follow me to my office." Enez followed her to an office at the end of a long corridor where Mrs. Locke gestured for Enez to enter first. "Have a seat, Ms. Brown." Mrs. Locke sat in a leather swivel chair on the other side of her oak finished desk. "You'll need to fill out these financial aid papers and admittance forms."

Quickly, Enez completed all the necessary papers. She did not want to appear to be more interested in the money than in attending school. "Ms. Locke, when will the school receive money for my tuition?"

Ms. Locke escorted Enez from her office as she replied, "You'll need to attend classes for sixty days before any money is applied to tuition or refunds."

Too anxious to wait, Enez clutched her suitcase tightly and decided to return to Washington D.C. She knew she needed to satisfy Nicko with money. Enez stopped in downtown D.C. to do just that when she arrived. She studied the pedestrians on the sidewalks and noticed a man staring at her. He winked his eye, and she looked back at him in response. He laughed as he lit his cigarette, and Enez approached him with an unlit cigarette to ask him for a light.

"You want some money, baby?" the man asked bluntly.

Enez looked closely at him to see if he was as serious as she was. She moved closer to him as he said, "I have one hundred dollars to spend right now. You want it?"

Enez smiled, put one hand on her hip and said, "Yes I want it."

Night had fallen upon her. She desperately wanted to see Nicko. Enez knew of one of the hot hotel spots where the pimps, prostitutes, and drug dealers lived. She drove through downtown D.C. into George County, Maryland. Enez puffed on her cigarette, hoping to catch a glimpse of Nicko. No luck, she stopped at a nearby phone booth to call the hotel. Perhaps the front desk would ring his room. As she dropped the coins in the telephone coin accepter, she looked up to see Nicko walking towards her across a store parking lot. Her heart beat faster, and she wanted to call out for help, not sure why.

He looked at her and grinned. As he walked past her, his voice echoed, "Girl, I'm not going to hurt you. Go on about your business."

She waited until he was no longer in sight before she ran to her car. Nervously, Enez opened the door and slid onto the seat. She cranked the car as fast as she breathed. Quickly, Enez moved into the flowing traffic. She slipped in an O'Jay's cassette and began singing the tune "Family Reunion." She drove to a hotel parking lot in downtown D.C. Fresh air from the Potomac River soothed her aching spirit. She parked her car to check in to the hotel. As she approached the entrance, she heard an unfamiliar voice in the dimly lit parking lot, "Aren't you Nicko's woman?"

She nodded her head and asked, "Who's asking?"

The man fell in step with Enez as she walked to the door. As he came closer, Enez recognized him. He was a pimp from Memphis. "Hey baby, I need a ride to take care of some business Are you trying to get a room here? I'm staying across the street. The rooms are much better there."

Enez agreed to take him to take care of his business, and she agreed to get a room at the hotel across the street. At his hotel, he led Enez to his room. He opened the door, and a woman lay on the bed. She appeared to be asleep under the bedspread. He waved his arm at Enez, motioning her to follow him to the bathroom, where he opened several capsules of crack cocaine and placed them on the counter. He burned the crack rocks until they were liquefied. After the liquefied crack dried, he scraped it off the mirror with the edge of a razor. Enez stood in the bathroom doorway, watching the process. Her stomach was nervous, her hands were sweaty, and her knees were weak as he placed crack on a pipe and gave it to her. She reached for the pipe to satisfy her hunger.

They smoked crack cocaine until the sun broke in the morning. As she looked for that last hit, there was a knock at the door. A woman with long legs and brunette hair came in and sat at the table as she crossed her legs and pulled out a small tin container. The man looked inside the container and grinned before he walked to Enez and whispered, "You need to go. I gotta take care of my business."

She knew what time it was for her. She had spent all her money and had nowhere to stay, but Enez left without a problem. Enez got in her car and stared at herself in the mirror. She burst into tears as she drove into the flow of traffic. "You fool!" she said aloud.

Up ahead, she recognized a woman she had met years ago at the shelter. She quickly pulled into a store parking lot and called out her name, "Tara, Tara." The woman turned around in response and walked slowly towards the car. "Girl, it's Enez," Enez reminded her as she jumped out of the car to hug Tara.

"What's going on, Enez? I thought you moved back to Memphis. How long have you been here?"

Enez swallowed her pride and told Tara about her recent fall. "Girl, I smoked all the money I made yesterday and need a place to bathe and lay my head."

Tara took a deep breath. "I know a few small time dope boys that you can pawn your car to for a hotel room and some dope."

Still looking for a quick fix, a place to sleep, and more crack cocaine, Enez did not hesitate to take Tara's offer. "Where are they, girl? Can you contact them now?" Enez asked anxiously.

"Yes, I can. Let's ride to 14th and L Street," Tara said as she jumped in the front seat. They pulled up to a set of row houses, and Enez waited in the car for Tara to return. When Tara returned, two young men were with her, and they all piled into the car.

"Hi, baby. My name is Ronnie. Tara told me you'll let us use your car for a few hours for a place to rest while you smoke crack?"

Enez looked at Ronnie through her rearview mirror. "Yes, I need a hotel room to rest, and some crack is okay too." She added in a serious tone, "Look, I don't want any trouble about this car."

Ronnie responded, "Okay, let's go."

Enez drove Tara and the two men away from the D.C. area. They gave Enez money for a room and three twenty-dollar crack rocks. She grabbed one of her suitcases to take inside the room. The men returned with Enez's car later that evening. Enez drove them back to 14th and L Street and then decided to drive to the hotel where Nicko lived. As she arrived, she noticed several men and women standing outside their hotel rooms. Enez drove slowly, looking for Nicko. Suddenly, she heard him calling out her name. She became frightened and began to speed away when she heard a thump on the back side of her car. Nicko had thrown a brick at her and was chasing the car. She quickly moved into the traffic and sped back to her hotel room.

The next night, Enez and Tara decided to make money at the Hotel Hilton downtown. Enez parked the car in a time limit parking zone. When they returned to the parking area later that night, the car was gone. They had stayed too long in the hotel lounge, and the car had been towed. Enez had very little money, and all her luggage was inside the car. They flagged a taxi and went to their hotel room.

Enez called the impound lot to make sure her car had not been stolen. She was informed her car was on the lot, and it would cost two hundred dollars to retrieve it. She thought her sister in Memphis would be able to help her. She called Dusty and announced her problems. Her sister immediately comforted her.

"Enez, are you able to get to a Western Union?"

"Yes, I can get there."

"Okay, then I'll send you the money Western Union in two hours."

A tear fell from Enez's eye as she whispered, "Thank you, Dusty."

The sun was shining as she arrived at the impound lot to retrieve her car. Tara came with her to retrieve her personal items from the car. The teller at the cashier's counter announced the payment amount, "That'll be sixty five dollars, please." Enez reached inside her wallet and gave the woman a one hundred dollar bill and got a receipt.

As Enez and Tara walked towards her car, Enez's mind was on getting rid of Tara. They found the car, and Enez presented her receipt at the gate and entered the flow of traffic on Rhode Island Avenue. "Tara, I'm going back to Memphis. Where do you need me to drop you off?" Tara sat motionless. "Tara, the party is over for me," Enez said as she pulled to the left lane to enter onto a one way street.

"Okay, you can drop me off on 18th Street." Enez dropped Tara off and waved goodbye. On Rhode Island Avenue, Enez decided to go to the house where she had once lived with Deena. Her heart beat faster as she approached Camilla Street. As she pulled up to the house, she noticed the paint was peeling from the wood frame house, and the yard was not manicured. She parked in the driveway and rang the doorbell.

A young woman with acne on her face answered the door. She wore an orange scarf over her head, a pair of brown shorts, a beige tank top, and white socks on her feet. "Yes, can I help you?" she asked as she stood inside the screen door.

Enez asked, "Do you know Deena?"

The woman looked suspiciously at her and asked, "Who are you?"

"Oh, my name is Enez. I lived here with Deena several years ago. I'm from Memphis, and I was in town so I decided to drop by to see if anyone may know where I could find her. When I lived here, she was planning to move."

The woman unlocked the screen door. "Hi, my name is DeDe. Come on inside and have a seat." Enez stepped inside and saw the house looked the same, but the furniture was in worse condition. "My husband and I rent upstairs. Deena moved in with an ex-dope man, Harry."

Enez was surprised when Harry's name was mentioned. She asked, "Is he a light skinned brother, about 6 feet tall, slightly overweight?"

DeDe wrinkled her forehead, "Yeah. Harry got on that dope real bad after he and Deena hooked up. Come on upstairs, Enez. I'll try to find her number." DeDe said as she walked towards the stairs.

The room was exactly as Enez remembered. Recalling the nights getting high in that room haunted her, and her stomach became nauseated while DeDe flipped through her personal phone book. Enez thought about getting high as she saw a crack pipe in an ash tray on the dresser .She asked, "DeDe, do you know where we can get a crack rock?"

DeDe looked up from the phone book, "Sure, what do want?"

"I just want one rock. I need to get on the highway."

As was the case many other times, one crack rock led to another, and one hour became twelve, then 24 hours. Before the sun came up, Enez had met DeDe's husband, her back window was broken out from a drug run, and she barely had enough gas money to return home. She left D.C. broken, and anxious. She drove for almost three hours on the highway before pulling over to rest before continuing home.

Several hours later, Enez once again returned home from Washington D.C. without Nicko. Sadness and fear filled her heart as she looked at the table by her bed. A Bible lay on the table, and she opened the pages and read. "***When your fear cometh as desolation, and your destruction cometh as a whirlwind; when distress and anguish cometh upon you***" (Proverbs 1:27).

She laid her head on her pillow as she thought about her life. "I have feared success. I have feared being alone. The fear of life itself has terrorized me. I've never given myself a real chance to experience self-worth, only ignorant pride, to cover up what I really feel about myself," she whispered to herself. She continued to read the next verse. "***Then they shall call upon me, but I will not answer; they shall seek me early, but they shall not find me***" (Proverbs 1:28). Enez prayed to God, asking for forgiveness. Her tears fell to the pages as she continued to read more of His Word. "***For that they hated knowledge, and did not choose the fear of the Lord: they would none of my counsel: they despised all my reproof. Therefore shall they eat of the fruit of their own way, and be filled with their own devices. For the turning away of the simple***

shall slay them, and the prosperity of fools shall destroy them" (Proverbs1:28-32).

Enez threw herself to the floor and kneeled beside her bed in prayer. "God Almighty, I know I am a sinner. Lord, forgive me of all my sins. I know it is because of You that the enemy has not killed me. I know it is by Your Grace and Mercy that I am here this morning, praying to you, Lord. Before my father's sperm connected with my mother's egg, God I know You had a plan for me." She allowed the Light to shine in her life once again. Although she had not returned to assembly services at Church of Christ, God blessed her with His Infinite Wisdom.

Enez filed for bankruptcy and succeeded in her efforts. Enez's car was repossessed by the finance company while she waited for the final bankruptcy papers. The telephone rang as Enez and her daughter lay in bed, watching a movie. "Hello," she said in a whisper.

"Hi, Enez. This is Betty. Tony went to jail last night, and they set his bond today. Can you take me to bail him out of jail?"

Enez took a deep breath as she looked at her daughter, "Yeah, I'll pick you up. Where are you?"

Quickly, Betty responded, "I'm on Leatherwood." The women hung up without saying goodbye.

Enez looked at her sweet daughter and said, "We'll finish the movie when we come back. I need to run an errand." They quickly slipped on their shoes and walked to the door. Enez opened it to find her car was not in the parking space where she had left it. Her heart began to race as she phoned Betty to inform her that she would not be able to accommodate her.

The following morning, she called her lawyer. His office reassured her that her car had been illegally repossessed under the bankruptcy law. She allowed her lawyer to handle the process.

"***But fools despise wisdom and instruction.***"

Her downstairs neighbor knocked on the door. Enez opened it, and her neighbor gave her a slip of paper. "Hey girl, Nicko gave me a number for you to call at a phone booth near his hotel room." The woman turned and walked away. Enez closed the door, walking slowly to the couch with the small paper clutched tightly in the palm of her hand. She looked down and unfolded the wrinkle paper. Her heart sank as she saw the area code, and she felt compassion for him. She wanted to phone him but did not want to make a long distance call on her neighbor's phone. For now Enez's phone was temporary disconnected. The rain drops danced on her umbrella as she walked to the nearest phone booth. She dialed the number and waited for the operator to indicate how much money to drop into the coin collector. After she dropped several quarters, the phone began to ring. On the third ring, Nicko answered.

"Yeah," he said. Her breath became short as she wanted to hang up the phone. "Impatiently, he said a second time, "Yeah."

Finally Enez said, "Hi, Nicko."

Quickly, he responded, "I almost hung up the phone. Enez, I need you to send me a bus ticket home. That Stacy broad left me after I whopped her the other night. She ran off with the dope and spent all my money, so I whopped her. She might call the police on me, baby, I whopped her pretty bad. I need to get out of this town fast."

For a brief moment, Enez thought of how terribly he had treated her a few weeks ago, but she still had compassion for him. "Nicko, I don't have any money for a bus ticket. Maybe your mother's sister will send you a ticket. Would you like me to call her and give her your number?"

He hesitated, "Yeah, talk to her and give her my number."

Before Enez could say goodbye, the operator asked for more money for the call. The phone lines disconnected, and she used the rest of the change in her pocket to call his aunt.

"Hello," a soft voice answered.

"Hi, Ms. Lorrine. This is Enez, Nicko's friend."

"Yes, I know who you are. How are you doing?"

Enez quickly replied, "I am okay, but Nicko asked me to call you for help. He is in Washington

D.C. and wants to come home. He needs a bus ticket, and I can't help him. He told me to give you a number to a phone booth that is near his hotel room."

Enez heard Ms. Lorrine talking to someone, "Ernie, give me that pen and paper on my desk, please." Returning to her conversation with Enez, she said, "Okay, now what is that number?"

Enez gave her the phone number and said goodbye.

In the next few days, Enez's attorney finished filing all the bankruptcy papers, and the bank was ordered to replace the repossessed car. This was another blessing and a lesson. She soon found a job, telemarketing for a long distance telephone company.

A week later, Nicko arrived. Even though Enez was getting her life in order, her behavior had not changed, so her situation did not change. She was seeing Nicko and using drugs again. She went to work tired or high from crack every day, and she missed a day of work each week. She would fall asleep on the phone in the middle of talking to customers, or she would hang up on them, feeling paranoid, if she was high on crack. Enez received a bi-weekly paycheck, and before the night was over she did not even have enough to buy a sandwich. Nicko started beating her severely again. He always waited on her to come home from work to take her car. Finally, she became tired of it once again.

Everyday, she came home from work to a nasty house and a lazy man.

It had been a long day at work, and Enez was very tired. Nicko walked down the stairs towards her as she arrived at the apartment and parked her car .Before she could close the car door, Nicko said, "Give me the car keys."

Enez refused to give him the keys and shouted, "I am not giving you my car keys. This is my car." Nicko pushed her to the ground. She lost her balance and tried to straighten her legs before falling on her ankle. Nicko got in the car and placed it in reverse as Enez lay on the ground. She saw the tail lights of her car as he sped off. Dusting herself off, she hobbled up the stairs to her apartment. Her ankle was swollen, and she was unable to walk on it for two days. Nicko still had not returned her car by the third day.

She hopped to her neighbor's apartment and asked if someone would take her to Nicko's neighborhood to look for her car. Within seconds of arriving to the neighborhood, Enez spotted her car as Nicko and his addict friends rode around, looking for crack. Enez promptly joined him. On Monday morning, she called in sick because of her swollen ankle and her night of getting high.

The following weekend was just as bad as the one before. It was pay day! She thought she would have a quiet evening at home, but Nicko brought his niece and daughter to spend the night. He simply dropped them off and told her to take care of them.

She agreed even though she did not want to. Nicko had not returned late into the night, and anger erupted inside her as she thought how badly he disrespected the little girls. She finally decided to take the girls back to Nicko's house in Haleview. "Girls, come with me." She knocked on her neighbor's door.

"Hi Enez, come on inside. Who do we have here with us?" her neighbor asked with a gentle smile on her face.

Enez pointed to the little girl with long pony tails, "This is Nicko's daughter, Maria, and this is his niece, Jay. I need a favor. I need a ride to take the girls home and to find my car. Will you take me?" Enez asked.

"Of course," her neighbor said as she put her shoes on and picked up her car keys and purse.

Enez's heart beat faster as they approached Haleview. The girls were tired and sleepy in the backseat. They drove up the steep driveway and blew the horn. Betty came to the door. As she opened it, Enez helped the girls from the car and said goodbye.

Enez found her car around the corner as they drove by an apartment complex. She walked to her car and saw Nicko's son, Lil'M, sitting in the front seat asleep. She unlocked the car door with her key and sat in the driver's seat to awaken the boy and then drove him to the house where the girls were and returned to her apartment.

When she got home, she searched the car for Nicko's cocaine pipe. She reached inside the fabric of the passenger seat and found it, loaded with hard melted cocaine. Her stomach was nervous, and her hands trembled as she tried to open the door to her apartment. Inside, she searched for a cigarette lighter to heat up the cocaine that was now hard inside the pipe. After several hits, paranoia reached its height as she stood at the balcony, looking down the drive convinced that Nicko was coming after her. Enez knew it would not be long before he would find out she had taken the children home and gotten her car.

As she stood on the balcony, she saw a set of headlights turn into the parking lot. She recognized the gray Lincoln Continental and the driver as he looked up towards the stairs. Nicko sat in the passenger seat. Enez ran inside and locked the door quickly. She ran to her bedroom where she sought safety. She could see Nicko and the man enter the apartment. They sat down to smoke cocaine. Enez lay across the bed, staring at Nicko. She looked into his eyes and witnessed the madness from his soul. Seconds, later he walked into the bedroom and began beating her.

Enez ran to the kitchen, screaming, with Nicko running after her, hitting, kicking and pushing her. As she ran to the bedroom, he pushed her into the doorway. She cowered on the bed and covered her head as he continued to beat her. He finally stopped when he noticed her bleeding profusely from her forehead. He led her to the bathroom to clean her up, "You're going to need stitches. I'm going to take you to the emergency room and leave you there, but first I'm going to get my daughter." He grabbed a towel and applied it to her forehead. "Where is my crack pipe?" Enez pointed under the bedroom dresser. Nicko bent over, using his hands to feel for it. He retrieved it and then escorted Enez and the driver out the door.

He held the small child in his arms as he carried her from the house. Her eyes were open, but her body appeared to be limp. She looked at Enez in the back seat and clung closer to her daddy. There was silence in the car except for the sound of the radio playing.

When they arrived at the emergency room, Enez walked through the automated doors with the bloody towel in her hand. She sat at a booth, giving information to the emergency receptionist and then was quickly whisked through the ER doors by a nurse. When it was all over, she had 20 stitches from her hairline to her eyebrows and six stitches in her upper lip.

As she lay in a hospital bed, a police office came in. "Ms. Brown, what happened to you last night?" he asked as he peered at her over his eye glasses, pen and pad in hand.

"My boyfriend and I were arguing last night and..." Enez began to cry silently.

The officer tried to comfort her. "Ms. Brown, if you want to press charges, I'm here to help you with that, but it is up to you."

Enez was silent, looking towards the hospital door. Finally, she said, “No, I don’t want to press charges, officer. I just want to go home.”

The officer put his pen and pad away and pulled out a business card. “Ms. Brown, don’t wait until he almost kills you before you make up your mind to press charges against this man. We are here to help you. Here is my card, put it in a safe place.” The officer walked out of the room and closed the door.

Moments later, a nurse and doctor arrived to give Enez her discharge papers and a prescription for pain medication. As Enez dressed, she noticed a telephone in her room. She phoned Nicko.

“Yeah,” he answered the phone, boastfully.

“Nicko, I’m ready to leave the hospital.”

There was a moment of silence. “So, what do you want me to do about it?” he asked sarcastically. “I’m not going to drive to the hospital and have you get me arrested.”

“Okay Nicko, I’ll find another way home,” Enez hung up and finished dressing. She started the long walk home. Her head was wrapped in white bandages, and her clothes were spotted with blood stains. A red pick up truck stopped minutes after she began walking.

The driver leaned over, “Lady, you look like you need a ride.”

Enez did not refuse him. She slowly got in the truck and gave him her address.

The Prodigal Daughter

"***For wickedness burneth as the fire...***" (Isaiah 9:18).

As they pulled into the apartment parking lot, Enez saw her car where she had left it the night before. The drive home had been silent until the driver parked, "Young lady, do you need any help?" The middle aged man went around to her side and opened the door to help her out.

"No, thank you so much for helping me get home." He helped her climb from the tall seat and closed the door behind her. She took a deep breath as she walked toward the stairs, looked back once again and said, "Thank you."

Her head pounded with each step she took, and she held the railing with a tight grip. At last, Enez reached the door and knocked and knocked. She saw Nicko's daughter peep through the front window before she opened the door. Maria ran to the bedroom and climbed into bed with her father. Enez made it to the bedroom and tried to lie down, but Nicko stopped her, "You can't lie down. Go cook me and Maria something to eat."

Enez obediently turned around and trudged to the kitchen to prepare the food. After they ate, Nicko and Maria left in Enez's car. She was in a lot of pain, but without insurance or money for medication, she suffered with the pain all night. She sat alone in her bedroom and wrote and reminisced about the events in her life. "Maybe the tears and howling cries from my soul will be cleansed someday. I have pushed down deep into the depths of my soul the shame, pain, and hurt of mental and physical abuse. I'm waiting for the day that I will say I am free!"

Nicko did not return with her car until the next day. "Enez, Enez come here," Nicko yelled from the living room.

She climbed from the bed, feeling dizzy as she stumbled into the living room. "Yes, Nicko," she said slowly.

"What are you doing in there? Didn't you hear me come in?"

Enez held on to the wall, "Yes I heard you, Nicko." She turned to walk back to the bedroom as he followed her. "Nicko, I'm in some pain. Do you have any money?"

He picked up the prescription and placed it in his pocket. "I'll be back later." Enez heard the door close and once again, she did not hear from him until the next day.

She called her job to say she had been in an accident. The following day, her manager told her to finish the week and not return the following week.

The following week, Enez received money from an old male friend. Immediately afterwards, she and Nicko went on a drug mission in Haleview. It was not long before they had smoked all the money on crack. Nicko searched for other crack users in Haleview. All of their associates were drugs users, and they used them to support their habit when they were out of money. Thursday morning ran into Friday morning and then Friday afternoon. Nicko caught up with one of his drug buddies. It was pay day for him. The man suggested a big package and then pick up his girlfriend, who was waiting for him. Nicko drove through the neighborhood and picked up the girlfriend after they purchased a large amount of powder cocaine.

"Let's go to your apartment, Nicko, to cook up the powder and smoke." Nicko agreed. Enez saw boxes and paper whirling in the wind as they approached the apartment complex. It looked like the items belonged to her. She ran upstairs and saw that her apartment was empty as she looked in the window. She tried to use her key, but it would not unlock the door. Her heart sank as she looked around and saw that there was nothing left of her stuff but paper and a box with trash. Her televisions, tables, radio, clothes, kitchen utensils, and all the furniture from her bedroom, living room, kitchen, dining room, and den were all gone forever. She had nothing left: no self worth, no pride, and no dignity. Enez sunk lower than a snake's belly.

Nicko, Enez, the man, and his girlfriend got high for hours in a motel. The woman made gestures to her man to ask Nicko and Enez to leave. Nicko talked the man into giving him two twenty dollar crack rocks before Nicko and Enez left the motel.

Nightfall came and they rode the streets of Haleview. They came to a stop sign, and Enez came face-to-face with her family. Enez's mother hollered, "Enez, come with me." Enez saw her daughter in the back seat, looking at her with tears in her eyes. Her gentle face pressed against the car window, and she whispered, "Momma, come home."

Enez looked at her. The shame and shackles of sin paralyzed her. Satan bound her and would not allow her to move from the car. Nicko drove off, and her sister followed them to the drug houses until finally, Dusty gave up and left. "***And the children shall rise up against their parents***" (Matthew10:21).

Getting higher was her way of coping with her problems and all problems that were yet to come. Enez stayed high on cocaine for seven days without sleep. She was afraid to sleep, afraid to face the reality that she had been evicted from her apartment and lost everything. When she finally fell asleep, she cried for her momma. Medicating her problem did not fix the problem, so she buried it within her soul. "***He that hath no rule over his own spirit is like a city that is broken down, and without walls.***" She lived like a vagabond on the street for many months, sometimes sleeping in her car, other times in a hotel room. The house on Leatherwood did not have electricity, water, or gas.

It was winter again, and Enez went to bed nights hungry, cold, and smelly. This was her way of living until the next season.

* * *

The Prodigal Daughter

God Sent His Angel

It was now the spring of 1990. The air was warm, and life was forming in the nature God created. Leaves were growing on the trees, flowers were blooming, and a newness of fresh air covered the land. A child was conceived on a spring day that year, their child. Enez was pregnant with Nicko's baby. She did not know that God had sent a blessing, an angel from Heaven.

She did not stop using drugs, even with the baby growing in her womb. The addiction to drugs and Nicko were more intense than the life of her baby. She wrote in her journal, "Crack cocaine is a very powerful drug. I must say this because no other power is greater except God. There isn't any way a drug addict can overcome this powerful drug or any mind altering substance without God. For many years, I blamed Nicko for my addiction to crack cocaine. It wasn't him; it was me."

Nicko was arrested for selling dummy crack cocaine to an undercover officer during the first trimester of her pregnancy,. Her drug addiction continued. She lived alone in the house on Leatherwood. Nicko's youngest brother was in jail also, and his wife moved into her sister's house. His oldest brother did not want to share the responsibility of the utility bill and moved elsewhere. Enez satisfied her addiction for crack almost everyday. This went on through a hot summer season.

Soon, a new season began. The leaves on the trees changed their colors, and the air became cooler. "***And let them be for signs, and seasons and for days and years.***" Nicko served his time in jail and was now on his way back home.

Enez wrote in her journal again. "My nightmare was not over yet. The days of my pregnancy were very crucial. I saw my doctor on an irregular basis, and my eating habits were almost none. The emotions of my mind were tortured. There were many times Nicko would bring other women into our home and have sex with them. I awakened from my sleep and caught him in the next room, having unusual or regular sex with other women. There were times he made me watch him. He offered women crack to comply with his sexual needs. I have often cried myself to sleep at night."

* * *

There was Joy in the Morning

Enez wrote frequently in her journal as her baby's birth neared. Nicko did not allow her to leave the house, and she was completely isolated from her family.

One journal entry in January was tinged with happiness and excitement. "We have become very excited about our baby, our baby boy. Nicko and I bought a crib, baby bottles, diapers, all the necessities for our new born. Nicko is a hustler, and for a moment, he has stepped up to the plate."

Enez rested most of the day of January 20, 1991. It was a cool winter night. The stars were shining bright, and a full moon lit the sky. Two associates of theirs visited their home. Enez was not interested in smoking crack, and Nicko was asleep. The two roamed around the house as if it was theirs. Later, the female, Doris, went to the kitchen to prepare something to eat. Enez joined her. The man, Robert, sat at the stained glass kitchen table, watching them.

Enez stood at the kitchen sink when suddenly fluid started traveling down her legs. She ran to the bathroom to see what was happening to her. She yelled, "Doris, Doris! Come here."

Doris walked swiftly to the bathroom and laughed, "Girl, your water has broken. It's time for you to have your baby." Doris walked in the bedroom to awaken Nicko, but he did not move.

Enez was nervous. The clothes she had packed in a suitcase a week ago were now in the dirty clothes hamper. There was no gas in the car. She walked to the bedroom to try to wake Nicko up again.

He looked at her, "Girl, why are you peeing on yourself?" He rolled over and went back to sleep.

Enez knew at that moment that he was useless. She walked to her neighbor's house next door. Mrs. Henry answered, "Come on in, Enez."

"Mrs. Henry, I'm ready to have my baby, and I need a ride to the hospital." Fluid began to fill her shoes.

"Baby, I'm too nervous to drive. I can phone you a cab."

"Yes, that'd be good, Mrs. Henry." Enez returned to her house to wait for the cab to arrive. After a long wait, Enez returned to Mrs. Henry's house to borrow five dollars for gas to put in the car that sat in the their driveway. Mrs. Henry gave Enez a five dollar bill, and Enez returned home. Nicko had still not moved from his previous sleeping position.

Later she wrote, "God covered all my pains from child birth to keep me calm. Robert and Doris drove me to the hospital in a two seat 280 Z."

Doris sat in the hatchback. When they reached the hospital, she walked Enez to the door and helped her into a wheel chair. She promised to contact Enez's sister. Dusty arrived shortly and watched over Enez throughout her labor that night. Enez could not deny her drug use when blood was drawn from her arm and tested positive for cocaine. She was scheduled to have a c-section the next day at 1:00 p.m. She did not have any pain, and Nicko never came to the hospital. Her angel, a dark brown skinned, curly headed boy weighing almost eight pounds was born on January 21, 1991, at 2:04 p. m. at Methodist Central Hospital.

Hours later, she wrote in her journal, "God sent me a perfect Angel, and I am so grateful. He has all his mental and physical abilities. His growth will be like any normal child, but what is not normal are his parents. I brought my child home from the hospital in a cab, to a world of mental, physical, and drug abuse addictions. An associate visiting our home paid my cab fare. Nicko was sitting at the kitchen table, getting high. Nicko looked at his son for the first time, hours after we came home."

Early one winter morning, Enez's neighbor, Tina, delivered a message from the Department of Human Services to her. Enez had just finished feeding the baby his formula and was burping him when she heard a knock at the door. She assumed Nicko was in the kitchen, so she did not respond to the knock. Soon, she heard Tina calling her from the kitchen.

"Hi Tina," Enez was surprised to see her neighbor.

"Can I hold the baby?" Tina asked as she reached her arms out to cradle the child.

"Yes, you can hold my baby."

"Enez, a woman just called our home. She said she was from the Department of Human Services. She left a number for you to return her call." Tina gave Enez her baby back and reached inside her coat pocket to give Enez the number. "She said she'll be in her office all day today and that you need to call soon." Tina pulled her coat closer to her body as she walked to the back door. "Enez, you can use our phone."

Enez looked down at the multi-colored carpet and answered, "Thanks for taking the message for me." After Tina left, Enez went to her bedroom, holding the baby closely in her arms. As she dressed the baby in warm clothes, she thought to herself, "It never dawned on me that the Department of Human Services would have any interest in the welfare of my child. I guess they would, after finding us positive for cocaine. Thank God I gave the social worker my neighbor's phone number for reference."

Nicko walked into the bedroom just as Enez was getting ready to leave. He asked, "Where are you going with my baby?"

She replied sadly, "Nicko, I got a message the welfare office called. I need to return the phone call, so I'm going next door to use the phone."

Nicko took the baby and removed his outer clothing, "You go on and take care of your business. I got the baby."

Enez went to make her phone call. She dialed the number nervously, and a woman answered the phone, "Hello, Department of Human Services."

Enez took a deep breath, "Hello, may I speak to Mrs. Shannon Wire?"

"This is Mrs. Wire."

"Mrs. Wire, I'm returning your call. My name is Enez Brown." Enez heard papers rattling in the background.

"Yes, Ms. Brown. I need to schedule an appointment for a house visit. You know we found cocaine in the baby's blood, and it is in the best interest of the child that we make a house visit. I will not make a surprise visit, so you tell me a convenient date." Enez scheduled a visit for one week later.

The baby was asleep in his crib when Ms. Wire knocked on the front iron door. Enez quietly opened the door to allow Mrs. Wire in. "Come on in, Mrs. Wire. May I get you something to drink?" Enez asked politely. She hoped Mrs. Wire would say no. Enez knew Nicko was at the corner, keeping his drug associates away from the house. Still, she was afraid someone would show up while Mrs. Wire was making her house visit.

"No thank you, Enez. I'd like to see where the baby sleeps."

Enez walked her to the bedroom, and Mrs. Wire saw the sleeping baby in his crib. She looked around and noticed a supply of diapers and baby wipes on a dresser. She nodded and quietly followed Enez out of the room, whispering, "Enez, where do you keep the baby's milk formula?"

Enez escorted Mrs. Wire to the kitchen and pointed at several cans of Similac under the sink. She opened the refrigerator and showed her the prepared baby bottles on a shelf. There was also cooked and uncooked food stocked in the refrigerator. Next, Enez opened the cabinets and pointed out the canned goods. Enez led Mrs. Wire through the breakfast nook and the dining room, opening the French doors. They ended up at the living room where they started the initial visit.

"Mrs. Wire, would you like to have a seat?" Enez asked.

"Yes Enez. I'd like to say I've arrived to a very clean house. Baby bottles were prepared in the refrigerator, and there was a crib for the baby to sleep in. I am very satisfied with my visit today. I will give you an A plus," she said as she wrote on her legal pad. Enez sat quietly. Suddenly she stopped writing. Mrs. Wire placed her papers inside her briefcase and stood. "Enez, considering the cocaine found in your system, your home is the best kept home I've seen in a long time. I find no reason to come back for a second visit."

Enez looked into her blue eyes, "Thank you, Mrs. Wire." The baby was still asleep when Enez entered the bedroom. Peacefully, she picked up her journal and wrote, "I am very grateful to God for this day. On any other day, before or after, I could have lost my child to Social Services." She heard Nicko opening the back door and met him in the kitchen. She told him about the visit as they sat at the kitchen table. He was happy to hear that Social Services did not take his son away.

That still did not stop them from using crack again and again. As always, their drug use was very intense. Every dime that came through their hands went towards getting high on cocaine. Eventually, the electricity was cut off. Their son was two months old, winter was upon them, and they lived in a house with no heat. Nights were covered with thick blankets and cries from her son.

The Prodigal Daughter

Enez knew it was time to escape the evilness that lurked within her. Enez and her son slept from place to place to find rest and food. It was an afternoon that she would never forget. Her friend had to give the room she had been staying in to his cousin, who needed a room. She walked to the bus stop, looking for hope. She held her baby as she sat on a bench at the bus stop on a cold winter's day.

An old lady walking with a cane sat on the bench next to her. She had a twinkle in her dark brown eyes that reminded Enez of her grandmother. The woman smiled with compassion as she held her wool coat close to her body to keep the wind from entering. Her black wool hat did not cover her gray bangs. Enez smiled back. She sat quietly, holding her baby wrapped in a blanket, coat, and hat. Finally, the woman broke their silence as their eyes met, "You got a girl or a boy?"

Enez replied, "I have a baby boy." She looked at the woman with a trembling heart.

"What's wrong, baby?" the woman asked with concern.

"My baby and I are homeless," Enez whispered.

"Have you heard of the Salvation Army? It's a place where you can receive refuge for you and your son. The Salvation Army provides emergency housing for women with children." As the woman's bus arrived; she looked at Enez, "God Bless you, child."

Enez walked to a gas station to use a phone. She asked the cashier for a phone book, where she found the number to the Salvation Army. She called for help, and the receptionist gave her the address to their downtown Memphis shelter. She then phoned a good friend, Mr. Nelson, to give them a ride to the shelter. As she placed the phone on the cradle, she thought back to the day she first met Mr. Nelson. She was seven months pregnant with her son. It was a warm day in November, and she was walking the street, looking for someone to feed her. She had no energy, and her spirit was low. As she turned the corner a few blocks from her house, she saw a short, bald headed guy climbing into his truck. She hurried to his truck and asked him for a ride. He obliged, and she knew once she got in the truck that she could make her move to ask for more than a ride. During their casual conversation, she mentioned that she was hungry. Being a gentleman, he offered to take her to a restaurant called the Four Way Grill in south Memphis. After lunch, he gave her $20, and she was touched by his kindness.

She wrote in her journal later that night, “Mr. Nelson picked us up today, my son and me, as so many other times in my life. He bought us to our place of refuge, and for that I am so glad. We are to live here for two weeks until God prepares a home for us.”

The next day, a middle aged woman sat across from her during breakfast. The woman held her head as she ate her Frosted Flakes cereal. When she looked up, Enez saw that both her eyes were blackened and swollen, her lip was cut, and her long red hair nearly covered the bruising around her neck. Enez stared.

The woman said, "I was trying to leave him, but he came home early. He caught me packing a few things. I thought he was at work. He grabbed me by my hair and dragged me all over the apartment hitting, kicking, and cussing me. I passed out when he hit me over the head with an lamp. When I woke up, I was in the hospital. The neighbors heard me screaming and called the police. He must have heard the police coming because he left. I'm afraid because he's still out there. The Salvation Army is helping me move to another state, and I have a warrant out for his arrest if they ever find him." She wept into her bowl.

Another woman sitting next to her said, "Believe me when I say, the enemy peeps into God's plan for you. He does not want you to enjoy life. He plays on your emotions, your weaknesses, and fears."

Enez nodded her head in agreement. The group was silent when a staff person entered the room. "We have bus passes for the women who would like to ride to Adams to apply for emergency housing with Memphis Housing Authority today. They're taking applications from 10 am to 4 pm." The woman walked away through the sliding doors.

With her baby in her arms, Enez walked swiftly to the office and picked up her bus passes before she went to get dressed. Enez and other women from the shelter rode the bus to seek a home. The application process went smoothly. The women were told they would have housing in two weeks. She left feeling very hopeful. Enez received a letter two weeks later with an appointment to talk to the resident manger in Foote Homes.

Enez and Mr. Nelson visited the apartment complex a few days later. They saw a one bedroom apartment that was available, and they toured a two-story apartment with a garbage dumpster near the window. Enez's attitude was not in the right place. "I don't want to live in an apartment with the garbage dumpster behind it," she said ungratefully. Next, she toured a single, flat corner apartment and gladly accepted it. Enez moved into her new apartment a few days later with the assistance of Mr. Nelson. He helped her with used furniture for the bedroom, living room, and kitchen.

After Enez had settled in, she sat in her living room, playing with her son when she suddenly recalled what the woman at the shelter had said, "The enemy knows when God has a plan for you. And the test will surely come forward. The test is for you, not Him. God knows all about you."

One rainy day, bored to no end, Enez overheard a conversation next door about drugs. The young man made several trips to her neighbor's house for a drug buy. She heard them talking again on the front porch. Enez pulled her curtain back slightly and peeked through the window. There, she saw a short, dark complexioned man reach into a plastic bag. He gave the woman something in return for money. Enez opened her front door and asked him to come inside. He followed her inside, and she closed the door behind him.

"Yeah what's up?" the man asked with slight irritation in his voice.

Enez asked quickly, "You got a twenty?"

He reached inside his bag and gave Enez a crack rock, and she gave him the money. As he pocketed the money, he said, "You need some more, give me a holler."

She closed the door behind him and quickly got high. Hours later, she pulled out her journal and wrote how disappointed she was in herself for giving in to her addiction. "Mr. Nelson gave me $60 for my beauty shop appointment. The drug demon, which lay dormant for three weeks, awakened. My stomach began to get nervous, and my heart was beating fast. The demon of drugs will tell you to buy just one, you can handle it. But one is too many for any junkie. I spent every dime in my pocket and began looking for credit. These guys didn't know me, and credit was not an option. When the sun began to shine outside, my ray of hope was lost. If only I had been patient on this day with God's plan."

The next day, Enez opened her Bible and read Proverbs 32-33: "***...for blessed are they that keep my ways. Hear instruction, and be wise, and refuse it not.***" Enez was afraid and ashamed to leave the apartment for several days. It was a bright and shining day. Enez stood at the clothesline, hanging out her washed laundry to dry. She pinned the baby's bib on the line when an unfamiliar car parked at the curb. Suddenly, she heard Nicko call her name. Enez quickly turned to see him walking towards her. She wanted to run, but her feet would not move as fast as her heart.

"Hi Nicko," she said in a pleasant voice. He stepped to the back door and allowed himself in the apartment. Enez turned to see the car had pulled off, leaving Nicko. She quickly stepped inside the apartment, where Nicko stood in the living room.

"Where is my son?" Before Enez could reply, Nicko went to the bedroom. Enez watched him as he leaned over the baby's crib and held their son in his arms. They walked to the living room, and he sat on the couch with their baby.

"Nicko, I see you came to visit your son. Is there another reason why you are here?"

He was silent, and Enez went to the kitchen to warm the baby's bottle. Nicko followed her with the baby. "Enez, you know Tony put our house up on a jail bond for a close associate. The guy jumped bond and now the time has come for the bonding company to take what was rightfully theirs. I need a place to live."

Enez reached for the baby and went back to the living room to feed the baby. She never said a word. How could she refuse her son's daddy a place to live?

* * *

The Valley Was Quite Low

Enez wrote in her journal again many nights later, "The mountains were quite high, and the valleys were often quite low, especially emotionally, spiritually, physically and definitely financially. Here I am in a dark place, a place that was all too familiar. The disease of addiction grew faster than ever. Satan had me bound. Drugs were plentiful, whether or not I had money. Nicko easily became friends with the dope boys. They were new in the game, and Nicko was a veteran. He knew how to talk his way into anybody's dope bag. Nicko cooked powder cocaine into a rock form for drug dealers, and they gave him a small amount of drugs for the service, just enough to make us chase the demon."

"I prostitute myself on the street for money. My home is a house for drug users, sellers, and gamblers. Satan has me bound. I can't wait until the first of the month to receive my welfare and food stamp issuance to buy drugs. I try to do the right thing before getting high, like buy pampers and home items, but sometimes I take the items back to the store for cash back. I redeem most of the food stamps for cash."

Six months later, Enez became pregnant with their second child, and still there were no changes in her life during this pregnancy. This was her third c-section.

She wrote, "He was another angel from the bosom of our Heavenly Father. Our baby is a healthy little boy, weighing a perfect weight, but he also tested positive for cocaine. When we arrived at my one-bedroom apartment, once again there were people lying all over the place, asleep or high. I laid my new baby down on my bed and asked for a hit of crack."

The following week, Enez's grandmother arrived to drive her to the food stamps office and grocery store. Her grandmother tried to help Enez and her sons, but Enez's addiction was more powerful than being responsible for her children. She returned home with just a few groceries and spent what was left of her stamps on crack.

Enez was in a dark place, and she did what junkies do. She smoked crack cocaine everyday that God gave her life. All hope was gone, and she lived each day to get high. To see the dope man coming was like seeing a man walk to her door and hand her a million dollars. The disease of addiction kept them all in constant danger for their lives.

Enez sat at home with her son, watching television when she heard a knock at the back door. She saw a familiar face when she peeped through the opened curtain. "Yeah, what do you want?" she asked.

The man walked to the window, "Is Nicko here?"

Enez knew the man was harmless, so she replied honestly, "No, but he'll be back soon."

He waved a few dollars at her, "I just wanna get some dope."

Enez opened the door, "You can have a seat here in the kitchen until he comes back." She sat across from him while he waited.

"Yeah, yeah, I won a big law suit from an auto accident. My lawyer gave me some of my money today."

Another knock on the door revealed Nicko's voice, "Open the door baby, it's me."

Enez rushed to the door, and Nicko came in and sat at the table. "What's up, man?" he asked the man.

"Here, man, I got fifty dollars. Can you get something good for that?"

Nicko took the man's money and left the house. The minutes passed slowly, and then there was another knock at the door. This time, it was a young woman who came to tell Enez that Nicko had been beaten pretty badly, and he needed her help.

Enez ran to Nicko and found him laying on the ground, severely wounded from all the blows a gang of thugs had inflicted upon him. She helped him up, and they walked back to the apartment. Nicko sat at the table while Enez went to the medicine cabinet for witch hazel and cotton balls. As she tended to his wounds, she asked him, "Nicko, what happened?"

"Baby, I was in the dope house and got into a confrontation with a guy about his woman." Enez stepped back to look in his face. "The young man did not like it. I thought it was over with. I bought my dope and was on my way back to the apartment. They followed me down the complex walkway. Before I noticed anything, one of them cornered me. Baby, I know it was at least five of them young fools."

Enez finished pampering Nicko. He said, "You know what, baby? I dropped those rocks."

The man was still sitting in the kitchen. He said, "Man, come morning I'm going to go look for those rocks."

After a horrifying night, Enez calmed her nerves by writing in her journal as the baby slept next to her. "Nicko was in our house gambling with a cowardly young man. He had several brothers in the drug gang who like to carry guns. Nicko won the man's money, and he became angry. The man came back to our house with a gun. Nicko would not allow him in the house, so he pushed the air conditioner from the window and came inside. I ran to the bedroom with my baby and so did Nicko closing the door. Someone in the front room talked to the young man, he calmed down and left our home."

Sometimes, Nicko made deals with the dope boys to sell their drugs for them. He chipped dope from the edges to get high as he was selling it.

When the money or drugs came up short, Enez walked the streets for money to recover the error.

She was home alone with their sons asleep next to her as she read scriptures from the Bible. "***Woe to her that is filthy and polluted, to the oppressing city! She obeyed not the voice; she received not correction; she trusted not in the Lord; she drew not near to her God. Her princes within her are roaring lions; her judges are evening wolves; they gnaw not the bones till morrow. Her prophets are light and treacherous persons…The just Lord is in the midst thereof; he will not do iniquity: every morning doth he bring his judgment to light he faileth not; but the unjust knoweth no shame***" (Zep. 3:1-5).

Their second son was several weeks old when she met Ronnie. Walking from the W. I. C. office one hot day in the middle of July, she crossed a busy street when she noticed an older man driving an old white pick up truck watching her from a Rally's Burger fast food store. Enez walked to his truck, and he invited her to sit down. During their casual conversation, Enez commented that she needed to pick up her sons' commodities, and Ronnie immediately drove her to the place of issuance.

Enez continued to write in her journal to express her deepest thoughts. On this night, she wrote about her relationship with Ronnie. "His wife of many years is sick with cancer, and Ronnie knows that she is dying. He is always so nice to me. He comes to my apartment with pampers and food every week. He gives me whatever I ask for or whatever he thinks I need. I told him Nicko is my cousin." Finally, Enez fell asleep until the next day.

Ronnie told her that he was once a gambling man, shooting craps. His dark past surfaced one night, and it was almost fatal.

Nicko and Enez were high on crack most of the day. Nicko was running his crap games, and darkness had not yet set upon the city of Memphis. Enez looked from the kitchen window to see Ronnie parking his white pick up truck. She rushed to open the back door to meet him outside.

Her hair was tidy and her clothes fresh. She said, "Hello, Ronnie. What brings you around today?"

He looked at her and smiled, "Let's go inside. I have something I want to give you."

He followed her inside the house. Nicko and some men were on the floor, shooting dice. Ronnie spoke to everyone and followed Enez to the bedroom as she closed the door behind them. Her sons lay on the bed sleeping as Ronnie and Enez talked. He gave her a one hundred dollar bill just as Nicko burst into the room.

"Hey man, do you think those fellows would mind if I get in the game?" Ronnie asked excitedly.

Nicko replied, "Sure man, come on."

Enez stayed in the bedroom with the children and the money Nicko had given her earlier and money Ronnie gave her. Ronnie returned to the bedroom and gave her another one hundred dollars. "Hey baby, I gotta go."

Enez followed him to the door through the kitchen, but Nicko stopped him, "Man, in honor to the loser give the man some of his money back."

Ronnie pulled out a couple of twenties before opening the door. Seven men stood nearby, waiting. Ronnie gave the head gambler the money and started walking to his truck when a young, black man came from behind and hit him with his gun. Ronnie stumbled, almost falling, and the man hit him again.

"Give me all your money," the gunman demanded. Ronnie reached into his pocket and gave him the money.

Nicko said, "Close the door, girl," as they went into the living room. "Give me that money you got."

Enez reached in her panties and gave Nicko all the money she had, and she heard the men kicking and banging at the door. Nicko ran out the front door as the men finally kicked the back door down and ran passed Enez as they chased Nicko. Enez reached the front porch just as she heard gunshots. The children slept through it all, even when the young men returned to her house.

"Why do you want to hurt us?" she cried out, running into the street.

One of the men turned and waved his pistol at her, "I will kill you."

Enez cowered behind an innocent bystander for protection. Alarmed, the bystander said, “Lady, you better get away from me.”

Afraid, Enez ran to a store across the street. As she stood in front of the store, she saw her children being escorted across the street by her neighbor. Suddenly, she heard an ambulance. Enez asked the woman if she would take the children as she ran down the drive, looking for Nicko. He was gone. Enez sat outside with her small children, not knowing what to do until a young man passed by and told her, “Nicko left the scene before the ambulance came. He ran to a neighbor’s house. He told me to come and get you and the children.”

Enez was afraid to go home, so she called for a police escort to gather some clothes for her family.

They lived in an apartment with a married couple and her grandchildren for a few days. On the third day, they heard rapid running up the stairs outside of the apartment. Nicko jumped up to his feet, and some men stood in the doorway. One man said “You can go home now.” They went home to a ransacked house and a fear of those men, but the situation cooled down for a while.

After a time, Nicko got reacquainted with the drug dealers, but this time he was not quite as trusting. Ronnie did not return for a long time. When he finally came back to visit Enez, he parked his truck on the street. Several weeks passed without any trouble occurring in the home, and they slowed down on their drug usage.

The clouds were gray, and the air smelled of fresh morning dew. Enez decided to take the boys for a stroll. Suddenly, she heard police sirens every where. Enez rushed home to find Nicko handcuffed on her kitchen floor with four young men she had never seen. As he was escorted to the police car, Nicko said, "Enez, don't allow anyone in the house."

She did not understand his reason for making that comment, but she did as she was told, as always. She locked the apartment doors after the police left and started to leave herself. A small framed woman walked across the driveway and approached her, "Open the door."

Enez did not know why the woman wanted to get inside her house, but remembering Nicko's instructions, she did not oblige her. Instead, Enez walked to the phone booth and called Nicko's son, Little M, to tell him what was happening. He told her to call the police back if there was any trouble. She walked back to her apartment to find her back door kicked in, and her apartment ransacked. She walked to the nearest phone booth to call the police. The police escorted her home and sat down in the apartment with her for a while to make sure she and the children were safe. Another good neighbor came to sit with her too.

Enez walked into the kitchen and noticed a mop bucket with dirty water in it. A big white ball bobbed in the water, winking at her. Calmly, she returned to the living room, "I am okay now," she told the police. She returned to the kitchen and fished out the white ball from the mop bucket. It was crack cocaine. "This must be why those people tore my house up and the reason Nicko did not want anyone in the house," she thought to herself. Being the junkie she was, Enez took a hit and gave some to her neighbor. Nicko was soon released from jail and immediately became paranoid when he got home and took a hit from the crack.

He peeped from the kitchen window and saw one of the four young men's uncle walking through the complex pathway. Nicko opened the kitchen door and shouted his name. Enez watched Nicko give the man the crack rock. The next weekend, she faced death at the end of a pistol.

Desperate for a fix of crack cocaine, Enez walked down Danny Thomas Boulevard, where a man stopped and asked if she needed a ride. She immediately jumped into his car and began telling him her well-rehearsed story, "I'm going to my uncle's place at the Jefferson Court Apartments to get some money, so I can feed my baby and buy some Pampers."

When they arrived at the Jefferson Court Apartments, Enez pretended to look for the uncle's car. "I don't see his car, and I really need some food and Pampers," she said casually, waiting to see if the man would offer her money or ask her for a date. The stranger did both and asked if she knew of a place to go. She replied, no. That was the wrong answer, but she took her chances, strung out on drugs. The man mentioned a place where they could go, and Enez agreed.

They drove up a deserted alley, where he parked his car and turned off the ignition. He pulled out a gun. "This is what it is going to be," he said as he forced Enez into the back seat. "Don't look at me, or I'll kill you."

Enez closed her eyes while he brutally raped her in every part of her body. She prayed that he would not kill her and that it would all be over soon. When he finished, he pushed her out of his car and drove off fast. Enez wandered around, lost, until she came to a main street that looked familiar. When she finally arrived home, she felt terrified and ashamed, feeling more worthless than ever before. Enez wrote in her journal, "As I look at my sons, tears fall from my eyes. I feel so dirty, so afraid, so lonely, and so hopeless." She closed her journal and returned it to her safe place. In the bathroom, she hoped a bath would wash away her feelings. Enez was not aware that her hope to leave Foote Home was coming very near.

A neighbor mentioned to her one day, "If a tenant receives death threats living in the projects, it is possible to receive a transfer."

Enez immediately began to work on her transfer. Her resident manger knew about the problems she had encountered in her apartment, and the police had records of her calls. She began looking around the city for better locations and apartments, and she found a nice place in the southwest area of Memphis, Cypresswood Town Homes on Horn Lake Road.

She wrote in her journal, "God has once again begun to set His stage for my life. The secretary at the Cypresswood office is a Christian woman who is a member of the Church of Christ at Horn Lake Road and Levi. She knows I am in trouble, and God has already fixed the move."

On a sunny clear day, Enez woke up, feeling very happy. She took her sons with her to a nearby store to use the phone. As she stood, dropping her coins into the slot, she saw a police car rush by and turn into her driveway and park in front of her apartment. She watched as they knocked on the back door and later escorted Nicko to the police car and left.

Enez wrote in her journal, "I don't know how, why, or where the police got information on Nicko's whereabouts because he always gave the police his Leatherwood address."

A few weeks passed before her life headed for another journey. Enez continued to write in her journal. She wrote, "I was not yet tired of using drugs. Again, crack was plentiful for me. I was smoking alone."

The madness did not last very long. Finally, her apartment in Cypresswood became available, and it was time to leave the neighborhood: the Day's, Cookie Man, Lil' Slick, and The Smoother. She had grown quite fond of many folks in the neighborhood, like Ba Ba and Sonia. They always had a spare chicken in their freezer or a pack of cigarettes. The older neighbor who lived across the street always took care of her children when she needed to run errands. Her days at Foote Homes ended one Friday morning.

The van was loaded with all her furniture, and Mr. Nelson took her and the boys to their new home, a home only God could bless them with. It was a two-story, two bedroom townhouse, large living room and dinning area, nice size kitchen, and a front and back yard. She was very happy for a few weeks.

The boys were asleep, and Nicko was still in jail. The apartment was quiet, except for a conversation taking place near her bedroom window. Enez slightly pulled the curtain back and peeked from the window. She saw a young woman talking to a man. Enez witnessed the man open a plastic bag and place something in the woman's hand.

She quickly went to her journal, hoping to stop the thoughts of her addiction. She wrote, "The disease of addiction I have battled with for so long has opened its ugly eyes. I am trying to fight the desire, but the desire is stronger than my fight. Prayer is not on my mind, but it should be. Perhaps I think too much. I am an addict. Addicts think we can fight the battle on our own. But only God has the power to deliver us and take the desire away if I am to let Him help me." She placed her journal underneath her mattress.

Enez walked back and forth to her bedroom window, hoping the drug dealer would come back or the young woman would come out of her house, even as she hoped the event would not unfold. Satan had her bound. He knew her desire was to get high, and he made it all possible.

The young woman came out of her house, and the drug dealer stood nearby. Enez ran to her front door and motioned for the young woman to come to her to ask her to fetch the drug dealer. Enez paid for a $20 piece of crack and used the young woman's smoking tools. With that, she embarked on another day's journey through another valley of drug addiction. It lasted 24 hours before she surrendered to Him. Several months would pass before she would indulge to crack cocaine again.

There was a knock on the front door. Enez looked down from her bedroom window. She asked, "Who is it?"

The woman stepped back, looking up towards the window. "Enez, it's Janet."

Enez smiled and ran quickly down the stairs to give Janet a big hug.

"I came by to see how you are." Janet looked at Enez, "Your sons are growing up, and you are growing out too. Enez, your weight gain has been rapid. Do you have any plans for school, seeking employment, or going to church?"

Enez searched Janet's face. "No, I am home everyday with my children. I'm satisfied with the peace and the money I receive from government assistant. My rent is $32 a month, I have no utility bill, and the food stamps I get are more than enough. I also get milk for the baby through the W.I. C. program, and I am sober."

Janet put the baby in his high chair and then walked back to the couch. "Enez, you have shifted into a high gear of fear: fear of failure, fear to make a change, fear of rejection, fear of the unknown, and the ultimate fear of success. Do you feel safe as long as you are in the house?"

Enez quickly answered, "Yes, this is my comfort zone. I have two friends, Mr. Nelson and Ronnie."

Janet held Enez's hand. "Enez, because you are not doing anything to build up your self worth and make a better life for yourself, you're making it so easy for the enemy to send his loyal solider back to you." Janet encouraged Enez as she continued to hold her hand. "I know you're concerned about Nicko because he is the father of your children. Have you seen or talked to him lately?"

Enez got up from the couch and walked over to the baby. "Yes, the children and I are visiting Nicko in jail on visiting days, and I accept his collect calls. Janet, he is my children's father, and I can't just leave him like that in jail."

Janet looked at her watch. "I must get back to work, Enez. It was good seeing you and the children." They walked towards the door. "Enez, I hope the best for you, friend." Janet opened the door to allow herself out as Enez watched her leave.

A few days after Janet's visit, Enez sat in her bedroom, listening to the University of Memphis jazz channel. She picked up her pen and opened her journal. She wrote, "I woke up at 4:00 in the morning to get myself and the children ready for the long bus ride to Shelby County Correctional Center. We rode the bus to downtown Memphis to transfer to another bus to take us to the prison. The bus ride was longer than our visit. Nicko was happy to us. He is now in a program called STARS. It is a drug program for inmates. Since he is participating in the program, Nicko will receive two days for every day in the program. I really enjoyed seeing him playing with our sons. Our visit lasted for only an hour before it was time for the long bus ride home."

Months passed, and now Nicko got out of jail. Enez allowed him to come home to his family. He told her their life would be different this time. Enez had heard this line so many times that she stopped counting, but she believed him anyway.

A familiar knock on the door excited Enez. Nicko was home from jail. Their oldest son walked quickly down the stairs crying out excitedly, "Daddy, daddy!" Enez met him at the door with the baby boy in her arms. Their oldest son jumped on Nicko's leg, reaching his arms out. Nicko picked the boy up and gave Enez a long kiss on her mouth.

As the day became night, Nicko became restless. The children were asleep, and Nicko sat in a chair in Enez's bedroom. "Baby, you've moved into a nice apartment," he grinned at her. Her composure was calm as she sat quietly on the bed. They heard a knock on the door, and Nicko looked out the window. "Oh, it's G from the Haleview. I saw him earlier today, and he told me that his woman lives in these apartments. I told him he could stop by later. Enez, you got any money? I wanna buy some weed."

She quickly announced that she did not have any money, but she had food stamps.

"Okay, give me a book of stamps. I can change it for money."

Enez did not want him to get upset, so she gave him a book of stamps. Nicko ran downstairs to open the door, and she overheard the visitor tell Nicko that he knew where he could exchange the stamps for weed. She heard the door close, and hours later Nicko came home. He said he had been at the guy's house, smoking crack. She was not surprised by his actions.

Nicko's addiction grew. The disease that was asleep in jail was now awakened like a roaring lion, looking for whomever it could devour. The battle was over because Enez did not fight against the disease anymore. She gave in to it willingly. This step back into the disease cost her many months of more pain, destruction, and self worthlessness.

"***...but the unjust knoweth no shame. For we wrestle not against flesh and blood, but against principalities, against powers, against the rulers of the darkness of this world, against spiritual wickedness in high places***" (Ephesians 6:12).

After two days of chasing the demon within her, she finally found her sanity and arrived home with her children. She gave them their baths and she too relaxed in a hot bath after putting them to bed. She lay in bed alone, feeling depressed. Enez lifted her mattress and reached for her journal. "I am powerless therein. My life has taken several steps backwards into the life I am very familiar with. The Lord tells us the fight is already fixed, the war ended on the day of His resurrection. '***...and the gates of hell shall not prevail against it.***' Satan can only get to me if I allow him. As long as I stay in the House of the Lord, he can't touch me. Living a life without God has always come to a dead end street." Enez finally fell into a deep sleep.

Because cocaine was not as plentiful in Cypresswood as in Foote Home, the hustle for it was more intense. Nicko could not create many crap games. Drug friends from the previous neighborhood where they lived came by often to get high. Unlike the Foote Home area, this area was not a hooker track. Enez mostly depended on money from her friends, Ronnie or Mr. Nelson. Every now and then she would pick up an older man who wanted sexual favors and he would become very fond of Enez and the children. She still received money from the government. On several occasions, they would receive cocaine on credit.

Enez found a job as a door greeter and stock person in Girl's Apparel at a Zayre's Store, hoping to change her life. She had not worked an honest job in many years. It was a long distance from where they lived, but she was determined to get there every day for her work shift. She rode the bus every morning if she had the money. If not, Ronnie or Mr. Nelson gave her a ride.

One rainy morning, neither Ronnie nor Mr. Nelson were available. Enez did not want to lose her job, so she started to walk to work. She walked for several miles on the highway, when a woman stopped to give her a ride. As they talked, Enez discovered the woman happened to be the sister of her mother's male friend. She dropped Enez off at work, and Enez was grateful. Before she laid her head on her pillow later that evening, she wrote in her journal. "Christ's Sermon on the Mount to his disciple tells me in Matthew 5:45 '***That ye may be the children of your Father which is in heaven: for he maketh his sun to rise on the evil and on good, and sendeth rain on the just and on the unjust.***'" She whispered, "Amen!"

Every Friday was pay day. Nicko was waiting for her whenever she came home with her paycheck. Most of the time, the dope man was with him. He kept the house and the children clean to make sure that Enez would not have any reason to say no to him or to the disease. By morning time, there was never any money left. This behavior went on for a month. Once again, Enez begin missing too many days from work, and she quit before she was fired. Things did not change for her. Enez thought she was hopeless. She became content with being a drug addict. Everyday, God awakened her, and she fed a disease that she had no control over.

Enez's life soon took a twist of faith. Someone must have been praying for her very hard, and God answered the prayer. God heard their cries for Enez's salvation "***Howbeit this kind goeth not out but by prayer…***"

It was 1993, and she was pregnant again with another baby boy, but that did not stop her from using crack cocaine everyday. The disease she fed also fed the child growing within her. Throughout this pregnancy, things continued as usual. Nicko knew most of the small time hustlers in the neighborhood, and he hustled gambling games and received drugs on credit with them.

Enez decided to attend Shelby State Community College. She tried hard to change her life. She received refunds from her Pell Grant and Student Loan during the Spring Quarter. She knew she had not attended enough classes to receive money from the school, but Enez continued to take it. She received credit from the dope man until the school's refund distribution. One of the drug dealers drove her to the school to pick it up.

A clerk at the financial aid counter said, "Ms. Brown, we can not give you a refund check." Her heart fell to her belly. She thought about breaking into the office and taking the money, but she knew the consequence would be jail time. Enez walked out of the building, equally afraid of the consequence waiting for her at home. There would be hell to pay. She thought to herself, "My life will not change until I release the shackles that hold me so securely."

The driver made left and right turns on their way back to the apartment. Enez remembered what an old friend once told her, "The keys to release the shackles are with you all the time. Faith and Patience in our Heavenly Father endureth all. God's Grace and His Mercy are with us always." She closed her eyes, hoping this was a dream and she would awaken soon, but it was not a dream.

The drug dealers were waiting on her to come home with their money. She walked in the house and told Nicko what happened. The drug dealers did not want to hear it, and they argued with Nicko. A fight broke out between Nicko and the drug dealers. Once again, Nicko ran and left Enez and the children alone. Enez paid the drug dealers in the next few days with money she received from a male friend.

* * *

A Time for Everything

"***To every thing there is a season and a time to every purpose under the heaven.***" Enez wrote in her journal, "March of 1994, my baby boy was born. He was our third son and my fourth child. God has sent me another Angel. He is a perfectly normal child. He too, like my other children, has endured the weakness of his mother's flesh. I hope he continues to be healthy."

She took her children for pediatrician visits regularly. Her youngest son needed minor surgery before he was six months old because he had a hernia in both testicles. Something else was going on with her son that only God knew about.

She did not know that she sat in the waiting room with one of God's Angel's on the day of the baby's surgery. Enez held her baby boy, and a woman watched him as he tried to suck the milk from his bottle. She said to Enez, "Your baby is not getting his milk." Her son was losing weight drastically, and she was in denial. Her baby was almost skin and bones, struggling to suck the milk from a closed nipple. The woman removed the bottle from his mouth and showed Enez that the hole in the nipple was not big enough. Enez saw the woman's concern for her baby's health in the woman's eyes. She suggested creating a bigger hole in the nipple and adding baby cereal to his milk formula to help him gain weight. "***And there appeared an angel unto him from heaven, strengthening him***" (Luke22:43). The woman was a foster parent to the baby she cradled in her arms. God had sent one of His Angel's to the waiting room that day, and Enez was grateful.

Several months after the birth of her third son, God had not given up on her. The drug habit was not as intense as before. Nicko was hardly ever home, and this gave her a chance to peek into her future.

Around this time, Nicko sold a piece of land that had been an inheritance to him after his mother's death. His mother's oldest sister bought the land, and the amount of the sale was enough money for two junkies. Nicko bought a 1981 De Ville Cadillac Sedan, clothes for the children, and plenty of crack. He only came home to change clothes or to have sex with Enez.

Enez sometimes grabbed the children to ride on their crack missions. God opened her eyes, and she would close them. Enez did not want to see reality until one night when they were parked at a hotel on Bellevue Ave to buy drugs.

Her two oldest children were asleep on the back seat, and her baby was in his car seat between his parents. A police officer parked his car behind them and got out. He flashed his light on Nicko and then flashed it around inside the car. He asked Nicko, "What are you doing out so late with these children?" The officer warned Enez, "If I catch you out here again with these children, I'm going to take you, the children, the father, and the car to jail." Enez was afraid of losing her children, but not to the point of no return to a disease of addiction.

The next morning, Enez wrote in her journal, "I am a junkie, and the demon who called me wants a direct answer regardless. I am powerless over a disease that has consumed me most of my life thus far."

* * *

The Church

Enez found a book in her closet as she cleaned house. She opened it and began to read about the philosophy of a man: each individual has within himself the seeds of fear and faith, anger and love, anxiety and peace of mind, despair and hope. We are a strange mixture of good and evil, and as a result, we are a battle ground within ourselves. She whispered to herself, "Again in my life, I am longing for Him, and I know I can find Him only in His Church."

A few weeks passed, and God led her to a congregation, Horn Lake at Levi Church of Christ. She had even more luggage and garbage to lie at the foot of the Cross.

The minister preached on the topic of the sower this beautiful Sunday morning. He read from the Bible, "***A sower went forth to sow. Some seeds fell by the wayside, and wickedness devoured them up; some fell upon stony places.***"

Enez thought to herself, "Because the Word was not deep in my heart, they sprung up and died."

The minister continued, "***Some seeds fell among thorns, and they were choked and never grew. But the seed which fell into good ground stayed***."

Enez began to pray, "Lord, I have been on the path of all the wrong places and faces. Your Words were choked out of me, and I have never given them a chance to grow. Help me, Oh Lord. Give me strength to have good ground. My weary soul is tired of me. I want to live, live for Christ. My spirit can not endure the pain of self destruction anymore. God, I know you have a plan to save a sinner like me from me. Lord, I know you can do for me what I cannot do for myself. Amen"

That day was filled with hope of a new beginning. Enez and the boys attended Church services faithfully for many Sundays. Members of the Church became very familiar with her and the boys. One of the sisters picked them up each Sunday morning, and she also attended Wednesday night Bible class. The old Enez began to see a new creature. Enez had not fully given up some of her old behaviors, but she began to feel guilty whenever she committed them. Enez was in constant war with her flesh and spirit.

Nicko still lived in her home, and she had not totally given up crack.

One Wednesday evening, a depressed Enez did not attend Bible Study. She was ashamed that she had given in to her addiction earlier that day. As she sobbed on the pages of her journal, she wrote, "This morning, Jesus was standing there waiting on me and so were the demons who I have allowed to control my life for so long. I have begun to use the Church to support my crack habit. I asked for money from people who really thought they were helping me. '***What the devil meant for bad, God meant for good.***'"

Enez once again stopped attending Church services because she felt guilty about using the

Church for her drug habit. She was under the full force of a powerful, mind altering substance that only God Himself through His Grace and Mercy could remove. The days rolled into weeks of agonizing and wrestling with her body, spirit, and soul until one fall night in 1994. She was led in a personal walk with God to be redeemed. It was not easy after that night, but she allowed the Lord to take over her spirit.

The enemy came to her door on several late evenings. One night, Nicko brought Robert to her house, and he returned another night. He knocked and knocked on her door, but she and the children were asleep. Enez was determined to trust her Savior with her life. Prayer was her only answer. Enez called upon Jesus in the time of storm, and He heard her. The devil was at her door. Nicko was kicking the door as hard as he could kick. She felt the vibration of his force on her bedroom window. But her God, Who is much stronger than any wickedness, sealed the door shut.

The next day, Enez stepped outside on the front porch. She noticed Nicko's foot print on the door. Her neighbor stepped out. Enez said, "Mind you, this door was very weak, and only one hard kick should have slammed it inside the apartment." Both women praised God's name and returned to their apartments.

Nicko returned another weekend. Headlights beamed inside her bedroom window. She walked to the window to see Nicko and a man talking in the driveway. She sat on her bed, hoping he would go away. She saw the headlights move backwards. Suddenly, there was a knock on the door. Enez hesitated to answer. He knocked harder, and the children ran to the window. "Daddy, daddy! Mommy, it's daddy!" they shouted with excitement. Enez walked calmly down the stairs, opened the door, and allowed the men in the house.

Nicko and the man walked quickly to the kitchen table, where Nicko pulled out his crack pipe and the man placed crack upon it. Enez ran upstairs with the boys to put them to bed quickly and then ran to her bedroom to pray as Nicko sat in the living room getting high with his friend. The next morning, God set His plan in motion.

Nicko was in the kitchen cooking breakfast, and the man was asleep on her living room couch when she came downstairs. Enez returned upstairs with her children when Nicko came running to her bedroom and hid in the closet. Suddenly, she heard a hard knock on the door and saw a police car in the driveway as she peered from the bedroom window. When she got to the door, the man on her couch had already let the police officers in the apartment.

The police officers asked her, "Ma'am we are looking for a man named Carl. We were told he was last seen here at this location."

She answered, "The person you are looking for does not live here."

They looked around suspiciously, "Do you mind if we search your home?"

Enez agreed to allow them to search her place out of fear. The police officers walked upstairs, and Enez's heart beat rapidly. They searched the closets and found Nicko in her bedroom closet. The officer asked Nicko, "Hey man, why are you hiding in the closet?"

Nicko answered, "I have a warrant for probation violation." He was quickly handcuffed and taken to jail for a year for the probation violation.

* * *

A Closer Walk With Thee...

Several weeks later, Enez studied her Bible after putting the children to bed one night. Her youngest son lay in his baby crib as she wrote, "'***The Lord is my Shepherd; I shall not want.***' Jesus promised me I shall not want for anything, He got me covered, I just need to ask Him. '***He maketh me to lie down in green pastures.***' He tells me all that He has created is good. ***'He leadeth me besides the still waters.***' Even when the storms shall rise in my life, He is there to give me peace. '***He restoreth my soul.***' I am a new creature in goodness and Mercy. '***He leadeth me in the path of righteousness for his name sake.***' God will not lead me in the wrong ways. '***Yeah though I walk through the valley of the shadow of death, I will fear no evil.***' Death will follow me, and He has fought my battle. '***For thou art with me; thy rod and thy staff they comfort me. Though prepares a table before me in the presence of mine enemies.***' He is in Heaven at the right hand of His father, waiting on the Day of Judgment for all mankind. '***Thou anointest my head with oil.***' He has blessed me. '***My cup runneth over.***' God's blessings are overly sufficient from His Grace. '***Surely goodness and Mercy shall follow me all the days of my life. Trust Him. And I will dwell in the house of the Lord.***' My reward is to have everlasting life and rejoice with the Angles of Heaven. The Father, The Son, and The Holy Spirit forever."

The following Sunday, Enez phoned a member of Horn Lake at Levi to arrange for transportation for them to attend Bible class and morning worship.

Each day, she recited the serenity prayer: "God grant me the serenity to accept the things I can not change, the courage to change the things I can; and the wisdom to know the difference." Those words gave her strength each time she recited the prayer. After a month of sobriety, the shackles on her soul were falling apart.

One morning after a peaceful night's rest, Enez walked to the bathroom with her head down, looking at the floor, and she began to cry. Tears rolled down her cheeks as she realized she could never again get high. When she looked into the mirror, her reflection stared back at her, and she was happy to see the new creature who was becoming Enez.

She allowed God's purpose for her to enter her life. It was over. In the next few months, her cup runneth over. God directed her path toward all the people who loved her unconditionally through seventeen years of crack cocaine addiction. Now, she had become a hard fighting solider in Christ. Her mind was made up. She wanted this new way of life and was determined to do whatever it took to get there, in God's name.

Enez enrolled at Shelby State Community College and enrolled her children in day care. Because she received government assistance, Enez was eligible for a Pell grant, free day care, book vouchers, and free transportation. Shelby State offered an Associate's degree in Drug and Alcohol Counseling. The enemy tried his best to pull her down like a crawfish.

Before starting college level courses, Enez needed to take remedial classes. English was her last class for the day. She was concerned about the class schedule because it meant she would arrive home late. If she was not at home when the day care bus arrived, Enez would have to make arrangements to pick up the children from the day care.

A writing exam was required on the first day of class. Her instructor said, "Any student who passes the exam with at least a C is no longer required to take this course." Enez passed her writing exam with a C grade. Later, a job opportunity became available at the college library, and she scheduled her work hours in between classes. She learned more about the disease of addiction through her courses at Shelby State. This gave her a chance to analyze her behavior patterns and learn more about herself.

Before the children arrived home one week day, Enez wrote in her journal, "God is showing me that taking these classes will not only help me help others, but they're also helping me. I am still sick; I haven't turned over all of my old behaviors to God, but the plan will yet move forward."

She was in the Church, a single mother of three children, going to school under the work study program. She was too busy to think about crack. Her life was coming together for the good. "***Even though the rose is pretty, the thorns yet surround her.***" Her heart still belonged to Nicko.

Enez and the children continued to take the long bus ride to the Shelby County Correctional Center every Saturday to visit Nicko. As with every time he found himself in jail, Nicko talked big about making changes in his life. Enez believed him, as she did all the other times he had said the same thing over the many years they had been together.

In spite of all her mess, God continued to bless Enez and the children. Enez had the courage to move forward because of a true friend who loved her unconditionally, despite the mess she had made of her life. This friend and her mother gave her clothes to wear to church and school, and they bought clothing for her children. Her friend was there when no one else would answer her call. Madelyn H. was her friend's name. Madelyn trusted God when she made decisions concerning Enez.

Enez needed her own transportation because her life was too busy to count on public transportation. The school owed her refund money from her Pell grant, so Enez looked in the classifieds for a car. She found a little white Ford station wagon for sale. She telephoned Ronnie. "Ronnie, I found a car in the paper. Would you mind taking me to look at it?"

He answered quickly, "Yeah, yeah. I'll take you. When would like to go see it?"

"Can you pick me up after work? I've already talked with the owner's father, and he's available tomorrow." Ronnie agreed to pick her up the next evening.

The next day, the owner's father showed Enez the car. "Ms. Brown, there's a problem with the motor. My daughter bought her a new car, and she wants to sell this one for five hundred dollars."

Enez looked at Ronnie. He quickly said, "Let me start it up. It's knocking pretty badly. I work on cars." Ronnie lifted the hood. "Enez, I guess it will be okay. When the motor quits, I'll replace it for you."

Enez agreed to return the next day with money to purchase the car. She had not prayed about this car or asked God to guide her in buying one. She called Madelyn to borrow money to buy the car until her refund money came in. Madelyn agreed. Enez thought it was a good deal since she only had to replace the knocking motor.

Enez rode around the city in her new car for a month until the car stopped running one day while she was driving down the interstate. She and the children cruised to the nearest station just off the interstate. God was with them. The Exxon was in perfect range as the car came to its final stop in the parking lot. Enez called Ronnie to pick them up and tow the car with his truck.

Enez no longer used Ronnie to support her drug habit with his money. She had almost completely stopped seeing him. Ronnie knew Enez was unable to afford a licensed mechanic, so they went to junk yards for parts to replace the motor. Ronnie repaired her car in exchange for sex.

The first motor replacement leaked oil, and the second replacement did as well. After the second time, Enez visited her minister at Horn Lake at Levi, James Hudley. She sat in a brown leather chair and told him her situation and conviction. He advised, "Enez, get a refund for the motor and transmission. Sell the car to the junk yard and call it a lesson."

The next day she called Ronnie. They returned the car parts and sold the car to the junk yard. Enez went home and prayed to God for His Forgiveness. Suddenly, a burden was lifted. She no longer had to have a relationship with Ronnie.

In the next few days, God's plan shined down on her. Enez surrendered and allowed God to do what was best for her. She paid Madelyn her money back and still had some left from school.

One quiet afternoon, Madelyn called, "Hey girl, I want you to look in the classifieds under car dealership ads to look for a car." Enez was lost for words. "When you call around, tell them I earn $35,000 a year. I'll call you back on my next break."

Enez said okay and immediately hung up the phone. Her eyes fell on the classified for Airport Toyota, where they were having a used car sale.

When Madelyn called back, she asked "Did you find anything?"

Enez answered excitedly, "Yeah, I called Airport Toyota, and they're having a sale. I talked to a salesman named Mr. Henderson."

Madelyn suggested coming to her home that evening to go car shopping. It was still daylight when they arrived at the Airport Toyota showroom. A short man with a warm smile greeted them. Mr. Bill Henderson was imprinted on his name tag pinned to his white starched shirt.

"Mr. Henderson, it's nice to meet you. I'm Enez Brown. I telephoned you this afternoon."

He stepped back to look at Enez and her small children. "Yes, yes. I remember talking to you. It is nice to meet you too. I've already looked around the lot, and I've found the perfect car for you. Follow me, Ms. Brown."

Before long, Enez signed for her first car in six years, with Madelyn as her co-signer. The car deal was completed, and she drove off the parking lot in a 1992, two-door, four-speed, blue Toyota.

The seasons were changing. The tree branches were naked. The ground was cold and covered with death. It was November, and Enez wanted more in her life. She wanted to become independent from the welfare system. It was 1995, and Enez sat in the living room of an older friend. "Mrs. Becky, I need to earn more money to take care of my family. I don't want to do the things of my past. God is good to me, in spite of me. I know the program says to 'Keep It Simple.' I have submitted an application for a job at Federal Express."

The woman held Enez's hand and said, "Have faith in God. In Mark 11:24, Jesus teaches us about having faith in God. '***Therefore I say to you, what things soever ye desire, when ye pray, believe that ye receive them, and ye shall have them.***'" Mrs. Becky comforted Enez with a hug.

The year came to an end, and with a new year beginning, God placed a woman from Enez's past in her path now to help her gain employment at Federal Express. This woman should have been bitter and angry with her over the past, but she proved to have compassion and concern for Enez. The woman was Nicko's ex-wife, Shirley.

Enez applied for the job and then telephoned Shirley to ask for her help. Shirley advised Enez, "There was a freeze on hiring until after the New Year of 1996."

Enez wrote in her journal one winter's night. "***...and let us run with patience the race that is set before us.***"(Hebrews 12:1)

In February, she received a letter requesting an interview for a position as a freight handler. Enez immediately responded and scheduled a date for the interview. She called Shirley the next day, and Shirley found out who would be interviewing Enez and put in a good word for her. On the day of the interview, Enez was very confident. After filling out all the necessary papers, she was called inside a room. Her interviewer was a short, stocky African American man. He closed the door and began the interview, "Do you know Shirley?"

Enez replied, "Yes, I do."

He smiled and said, "I wanted to know if I have the right person." By the end of the interview, she had a hire date of March 11, 1996.

At home, Enez rushed to her journal and wrote, "God is good in spite of me. For the first time in many years, I have a job I can be proud of, a job with security. I am on my way to recovery from the struggles of my life. After many years of being addicted to Nicko, my heart is slowly breaking from the chains which held me in bondage for so many years. God says. '***Whosoever shall say unto this mountain, be thou removed, and be thou cast into the sea; and no doubt be in his heart…***' Thank You, Lord, for this day. Amen."

Her hours at Federal Express were part time weekend. She did not have time to visit Nicko. Enez and the children talked to him over the phone a few times a week, and Enez had no desire to have him in her life anymore. She was becoming a new creature.

One summer day in 1996, it was time for Nicko to be released from jail. Enez picked him up in her new car and the children in the back seat. She was afraid to bring him back to her home because of the past disappointments of life's changes with him. She dropped him off in a familiar place, Haleview community.

Days passed before she saw Nicko again, and it did not bother her. She heard a knock on the door and looked from the bedroom window. She saw a truck parked in her driveway and Nicko and a man standing at her door. He called up to their oldest boy, "It's your daddy, boy! Come open the door. It's your daddy!"

Enez and the children walked to the door and opened it. Nicko stepped across the threshold, followed by the man. Nicko said, "I'm hungry and need something to eat."

Enez allowed Nicko inside, "Nicko, your friend will have to wait for you outside. I'll give you something to eat, but then you have to leave. You cannot stay here."

The man walked back to the truck, and Nicko went into her kitchen to prepare food for himself and the man. He called the man to the door to give him the food before he sat at her table to eat. When he finished eating, he refused to leave. He lay on her living room couch. Enez told the children to go to bed as Nicko hugged and kissed them good night. She followed the children to bed and said their prayers with them.

The oldest boy asked, "Momma, will God make daddy alright so he can stay here with us?"

Enez kissed her son and said, "Baby, I hope he'll be alright."

She turned out the lights and walked calmly down the stairs to see Nicko lying on her couch, half asleep. She thought to herself, "Nicko is a total wreck, both physically and spiritually. I no longer want to be a part of his life." She asked him to leave several times, and he refused each time.

When he finally fell into a deep sleep, Enez walked to the kitchen and got a knife from the drawer. She sat across from him in a chair, praying to a God she knew could handle this situation. She put the knife under the chair cushion as she waited for Nicko to wake up. She was determined that this man would leave her house tonight. She called her neighbor, Carol, who was also in drug recovery.

Carol advised, "Call the police."

Enez had strong reservations about calling the police on Nicko. Even though they were not seeing each other anymore, her fear of him ran through her blood. Enez remembered a passage in the Bible, and she began repeating it while she was on the phone with Carol. "***Wait on the Lord: be of good courage, and he shall strengthen thine heart: wait, I say, on the Lord***" (Psalm 27:14).

"Carol, be of good courage. The courage that was trying to rage in me was not good courage, but evil courage. I want him out of my house, and he will not leave."

When she hung up, Enez looked at the knife in her hand and thought of all the years of fear, beatings, shame, and guilt. These thoughts engulfed her mind, and for a brief moment, she wanted to kill Nicko. She wanted to get rid of him for the rest of her life.

The phone rang, it was Carol calling back. The evil trance she entertained perished. Quietly, Enez walked to her car to pray with Carolyn on the phone. God blessed her with peace, and this peace started to change how she had been thinking and feeling. Enez finally called the police without malice, but wanting what God wanted for her. After several calls to have Nicko removed from her home, the police finally arrived two hours later.

Nicko was still asleep on her couch when the police arrived. The officers woke him up to tell him he had to leave. Nicko threatened to come back and beat Enez up for calling the police on him. One officer took him outside and asked for his driver's license. Nicko did not have a license, but Enez had a copy of his birth certificate. Nicko wanted to see his children before he left, and the officer and Enez allowed him to do so. The children were sleeping in their beds as Nicko bent down to kiss them good-bye. The officers removed the handcuffs and warned him not to return that night or any other night. He quickly got in his truck and left.

When she was finally alone, Enez cried and wrote in her journal, "This was a distressing time for me. I need to hear Paul's encouraging words to the church in Philippi: '***Don't worry about anything, but pray about everything.***' With a thankful heart my prayers were answered and I am yet on my way to continue enjoying the life God has planned for me.

* * *

Contentment

Enez's heart was filled with contentment. God delivered her from the bondage that held her so close. She decided to give her entire life to the Lord. She no longer used Mr. Nelson for financial support, and the desires of the flesh were gone. Her heart listened to a different beat, and Enez was full of joy.

She wrote in her journal, "1 Timothy 6:6 – '***Now godliness with contentment is great gain.***' For the first time in my life, I am very proud of who I have became. I give all praise and glory to God. My grades in school were the highest they have ever been. I have a new car, new job, and a new life. Romans 8:28 says, '***All things work together for good to them that love God, to them who are the called according to his purpose.***'

"After so many years of disappointing my family and all the feelings of rejection, shame, and guilt, contentment has finally filled my heart. Psalms 68:6, '***God setteth the solitary in families: he bringeth out those which are bound with chains…***' My grandmother is the only one who shows me unconditional love. Her patience and longsuffering have brought joy to my spirit. She has supported me in my journey for salvation. God strengthened her according to His glorious powers to help me break the chains of self-destruction and malice. I love her with all my heart.

"I love my children. Feelings of shame and guilt engulfed me the first months of my sobriety, threatening my confidence to believe that I could be a good parent. God has shown me differently. He said, '***I poured all the ingredients inside of you before your father's sperm and your mother's egg were joined together to create your human body…for I have created him for my glory, I have formed him yea, I have made him.***' One of the ingredients God poured into my character is parental care. Deuteronomy 6:7, '***And thou shalt teach them diligently unto thy children, and shalt talk of them when thou sittest in thine house, and when thou walkest by the way, and when thou liest down, and when thou risest up.***'"

Enez woke the next morning with her pen pressed to the spine of her journal, snuggled upon her pillow as if to wait on her to finish it. She closed her journal and tucked it away under her mattress.

* * *

The Lust of Her Flesh

When anxiety attacks, it channels the idea of being distracted or divided.

Two years had passed since Enez last used crack cocaine. She was still in school, work study, interning at Memphis Recovery Center, working at FedEx on the weekend, and raising her three small boys. She attended many C.A. meetings to listen and learn how to stay sober. Enez heard the phrase "keep it simple" many times, but her life was not simple anymore.

Emotionally, she was becoming a train wreck waiting to happen at full speed. Enez was in a D&A counselor's class when she had her first anxiety attack. She sat in a group of four students, discussing life. She talked about what was going on in her life, and before Enez knew it, she was crying on her girlfriend's shoulders. Crying relieved some of the tension, but it did not cure it. This was the beginning of another twist in her life.

Enez began to fall by the wayside in her Christian walk. Having to work from early morning until late afternoons on Sundays caused her to miss worship services. She took her children to a church member's house on Sunday mornings so they would not miss the Lord's Day of worship. Enez tried to get to evening worship, but her body would not permit it. She had excuses and more excuses, and now she was missing Wednesday night Bible classes, too! The doors were opening for the enemy to come right on into her house.

Jesus knows we need Him to fight our battles with anxiety, frustration, stress and depression. Instead of praying for His wisdom, courage, and power to help her, Enez tried to fix it.

On a Wednesday night, she opened her Bible and reads a passage in Acts 20:29, "***For I know this, that after my departing shall grievous wolves enter in among you, not sparing the flock.***" The enemy came unto her by the lust of her flesh. She did not feel worthy of any man, except for those who had crossed her path in the past. The stage was set.

Enez's internship for A&D counseling began at Memphis Recovery Center. Some afternoons, she conducted the group meetings for outpatients. These patients were not residents, but they were in treatment for drug and alcohol addiction.

One man caught her attention during the meeting. Enez recognized the look in his eyes and the way he carried himself. She knew he lived a lifestyle that she was familiar with. She lustfully desired to be with him, but she did not talk to him outside of the group meetings.

In the meantime, Enez's behavior slowly changed, including her language, dress, and the kind of music she listened to. The lyrics in the music of Willie Hutch, David Ruffin, all the pimps and players music she listened to began to put her in a trance. She wanted to reach back to the life she once knew, the person she once was before she started smoking crack cocaine. Her old behaviors were slowly coming back to life.

On Labor Day, she went with her friend, Carol, to a drug and alcohol meeting and an annual celebration for the group call Serene. They served dinner for anyone who wanted to come and who had the desire to stay sober. After dinner, there was a recovery meeting. Enez did not usually sit by the door, but this night she did. As her eyes glanced back forth between the filled chairs and the door, Harold walked into the room. He was wearing a red and white brim hat, a red and white silk short set, and red snake skinned sandals. He wore gold necklaces with pendants around his neck and diamond rings on his fingers. He sat in a chair next to her. He was the man from the outpatient treatment center. Their bodies touched, and she immediately became thrilled with his flesh. They talked and laughed throughout the meeting, neither one of them paying attention to what the other group members were saying. After the meeting, they walked outside and talked some more.

Enez could not wait for him to ask for her phone number. Aggressively, she said, "I know you have a home phone number?"

He looked at her through his light brown eyes, "Yeah, I have a phone, but you know how that goes."

Enez looked at him curiously as if to say, "No, I don't."

Quickly he said, "I have a beeper number you can call me on it, and I'll return your call when I'm available"

She reached inside her purse and pulled out a pen and paper, "I'll tell you what: here is my number." She wrote her number down and tore off the paper from the pad. "Now what is your beeper number?"

He slowly recited the number to her as she wrote it down and then put her pen and pad inside her purse. As she walked towards her car, she said, "I will talk to you later, Harold."

Before she fell asleep that night, Enez wrote an entry in her journal. "1Timothy 4:1 – '***Now the Spirit speaketh expressly, that in the latter times some shall depart from the faith, giving heed to seducing spirits, and doctrines of devils.***'"

Enez endured another unhealthy relationship for the next three years. The mother of Harold's daughter lived with him. She was on crack and prostituting. Enez was a game to Harold. She offered him money, and he accepted it.

As her feelings for Harold grew stronger, she no longer wanted to be his secret. She wanted to be a true part of his life. Harold's life started to unfolded in a positive direction when the woman found out about Enez. They decided to break up, and Harold started school at Shelby State Community College to become an A&D counselor. Enez and Harold had fun together and with their children, and they enjoyed each other's company. Although Harold had not begun worshiping the Lord, he tried to live a clean life.

Near the end of their relationship, Enez grew tired of the financial burden and with their sex life.

She constantly helped him with his rent and paid for all their outings. The relationship was falling apart each day, until she finally called it quits and asked for her space.

* * *

Hold Onto God's Unchanging Hands

As Enez and Harold were about to go their separate ways, God gave her another blessing from His Goodness, Grace, and Power. She and the children still lived in low income housing, and Enez wanted to provide her family with a house to live. She looked for a house that she could afford for several months, but none were available.

Even though she had lived a non-Christian life for months now, her faith was still in her spirit. She prayed for a new home, "God, show me where to look and who to ask for help." She wrote in her journal after a good night's rest. "As I slept, a dream came to me. It was so real. In my dream, I was a grown woman, living in my childhood home. The house was painted black and white. My neighbor, Ms. Lillie, and I were standing outside working in our front yards. A calm voice spoke to me in my sleep, telling me to ask my mom if she would sell me her house."

Over the next few days, Enez searched for words to ask her mother about selling her house to her. She was afraid her mother would say no. Enez spoke to her minister, Brother Hudley, about the dream. He advised Enez about dreams, but she did not agree.

Two days later, Enez found the courage to talk to her mother about buying her house. It was November of 1996, and she sat nervously in her bedroom chair as she dialed her mother's phone number. After several rings, she finally answered.

Enez sat upright in her chair, "Hi momma. How are you doing?

She cleared her throat, "I am doing fine."

Enez knew her mother was very busy, and she did not want to take much of her time. "I wanted to know if you would sell me your house, since your house is empty." Enez paused, hoping her feelings would not be crushed.

"I don't know, Enez. I will have to get back to you in a few days. What is your phone number?"

With the cordless phone still in her hand, Enez relaxed her in chair. She thought, "Perhaps my mother does not trust this new person I have become, and maybe she never will." Enez waited for her mother to call. One night after dinner, the phone rang and Enez answered peacefully. The voice on the other end surprised her.

"Enez, I'm going to rent you the house until you can purchase it. You can live there for the first two months rent-free. The first note due on the house is in January for $260.00."

Enez quickly thanked her mother as a beeping sound interrupted their conversation, "I need to take this call. I'll talk to you later."

After Enez put the children to bed, she opened her Bible and read Psalms 35:13, "***…and my prayer returned to my own bosom.***" She rejoiced, praying to the Lord and thanked Him. "The God I serve never changes, He is the same as yesterday and tomorrow." She then turned her Bible to Joshua 24:24, "***The Lord our God will we serve, and his voice will we obey.***"

Many weeks after the boys and Enez moved into their new home, Enez wrote in her journal, "The boys and I are so happy to live in a house, our new home. With God's Grace and Miraculous Powers, He has given me comfort and peace in all of Satan's tactics to discourage me from being happy with my new home and life."

The first ordeal was a past due electric bill in the amount of $450 from the house on Leatherwood. She needed to pay a deposit of $150. God sent several people to help her take care of the past due bill. The congregation at Horn Lake & Levi Church of Christ loaned her $250, her grandmother gave her $200, and her aunt loaned her $150.

The second ordeal came before moving day. There was a busted water line under the house because her mother had not kept up with the maintenance for the house. God sent her to the maintenance man, who worked for the Memphis

Housing Authority. He replaced the pipes for very little money.

Oh, but the enemy was not finished with her. Upon turning on the water and gas, Enez learned the hot water tank was busted. God sent Enez to her mother, who asked her to find out the cost for a new tank and labor. The same maintenance man found a new hot water tank and installed it for very little money. Her mother wanted to change the electricity fuse box to a circuit box, and the electrician finished two days ahead of schedule. She needed a refrigerator, and her grandmother took her to Circuit City to buy a huge refrigerator for her new home.

Now they were ready to move into their new home. Mr. Nelson came over early Friday morning with his truck and trailer to move all the furniture and boxes in one day. God's plan was working in her life. The enemy wanted to sabotage God's plan for her life by hitting her in her weak spots and prodding her. But Enez was happy with the new Enez. Finally, her life had meaning, hope, and truthfulness.

* * *

The Prodigal Daughter

Conclusion

Enez was filled with a joyful spirit as she wrote in her journal. As the pen touched the paper, a joyful tear drop fell from her eyes. She wrote, "We have to remember that God wants us to have a joyful and prosperous life while living here on earth. He wants us to bring all our concerns, broken spirits, and heart breaks to Him. He loves us so much. He gave His only begotten Son to us so our sins would be forgiven and thrown in the lake of fire. '***He that covereth his sins shall not prosper: but who so confesseth and forsaketh them shall have mercy***' Proverbs 28:13. There are so many gospel songs we sing in worship on Sunday to remind me of God's Grace and Mercy and His love for me. When I am happy or sad, I catch myself singing a gospel song to fit the circumstance.

"Finally knowing God has made my life plain and simple. **'Teach me Thy way, O Lord, and lead me in a plain path.'** David's prayer in Psalm 119:133 is of great wisdom: '***Direct my footsteps according to your word; let no sin rule over me.***' As my faith grows with more of His Word living inside of me, I have instant access to godly guidance. When I am faced with a situation, a Bible verse comes to mind to give me the direction I need to righteously solve it. The situations we face on a daily basis are easily encountered when we have more of God's Word in our hearts.

"Everyday of my life, I am living under God's Grace. Yes, I still make mistakes. The knot in my heart tells me when I have missed God's plan. But I don't beat myself up about it. Instead of allowing my mistake to sit in the driver’s seat and drive, I throw it out of the car and allow God to take control.”

* * *

The Prodigal Daughter

From the Author's Desk

I hope this book has stirred useful thinking within you. I hope you can easily identify who you are, the person God created. All of us have a place and a purpose, but for us to have great clarity, we must have a greater understanding of God's plan for us.

As a benediction of encouragement for life's journey together, I offer this prayer from Isaiah 40:4: "***Every valley shall be exalted, and every mountain and hill shall be made low: and the crooked shall be made straight, and the rough places plain.***" May the God of peace be with you. Do His will, and it will be well pleasing in His sight, through Jesus Christ, to whom be Glory forever and ever. Amen

* * *